CARRY

BALLANTINE BOOKS
NEW YORK

CARRY

A MEMOIR OF SURVIVAL ON STOLEN LAND

TONI JENSEN

Carry is a work of nonfiction.
Some names and identifying details have been changed.

Copyright © 2020 by Toni Jensen

All rights reserved.

Published in the United States by Ballantine Books, an imprint of
Random House, a division of Penguin Random House LLC, New York.

BALLANTINE and the HOUSE colophon are registered trademarks of
Penguin Random House LLC.

Portions of this work were originally published in different form in
Bat City Review, Catapult, Ecotone, and *Pleiades.*

LIBRARY OF CONGRESS CATALOGING-IN-PUBLICATION DATA
Names: Jensen, Toni, author.
Title: Carry : a memoir of survival on stolen land / Toni Jensen.
Other titles: Memoir of survival on stolen land
Description: New York : Ballantine Group, [2020]
Identifiers: LCCN 2020015793 (print) | LCCN 2020015794 (ebook) |
ISBN 9781984821188 (hardcover) | ISBN 9781984821195 (ebook)
Subjects: LCSH: Jensen, Toni. | Métis women—North Dakota—Biography. |
Indian women activists—North Dakota—Biography. | Indian women—
Crimes against—North Dakota.
Classification: LCC E98.W8 J46 2020 (print) | LCC E98.W8 (ebook) |
DDC 978.400497—dc23
LC record available at https://lccn.loc.gov/2020015793
LC ebook record available at https://lccn.loc.gov/2020015794

Printed in the United States of America on acid-free paper

randomhousebooks.com

2 4 6 8 9 7 5 3 1

First Edition

Book design by Susan Turner

For my family

Contents

CARRY

ONE

Women in the Fracklands

I.

On Magpie Road, the colors are in riot. Sharp blue sky over green and yellow tall grass that rises and falls like water in the North Dakota wind. Magpie Road holds no magpies, only robins and crows. A group of magpies is called a tiding, a gulp, a murder, a charm. When the men in the pickup make their first pass, there on the road, you are photographing the grass against sky, an ordinary bird blurring over a lone rock formation.

You do not photograph the men, but if you had, you might have titled it "Father and Son Go Hunting." They wear camouflage, and their mouths move in animation or argument. They have their windows down, as you have left those in your own car down the road. It is warm for fall. It is grouse season and maybe partridge but not yet waterfowl. Despite how partridge are in the lexicon vis-à-vis pear trees and holiday singing, the birds actually make their homes on the ground. You know which birds are in season because you are from Iowa, another rural place where guns and men and shooting seasons are part of the knowledge considered common.

Merriam-Webster's Collegiate Dictionary defines *in season* in relation to timing, levels of fitness, and whether a thing is "legally available to be hunted or caught." The first use of *off-season* comes in 1847. Definitions include:

1: a time of suspended or reduced activity, *especially:* the time during which an athlete is not training or competing
2: a period of time when travel to a particular place is less popular and prices are usually lower
3: *sports:* a period of time when official games, tournaments, etc., are not being played

Magpie Road lies in the middle of the 1,028,051 acres that make up the Little Missouri National Grassland in western North Dakota. Magpie Road lies about two hundred miles north and west of the Standing Rock Reservation, where thousands of Indigenous people and their allies have come together to protect the water, where sheriff's men and pipeline men and National Guardsmen have been donning their riot gear, where those men still wait, where they still hold tight to their riot gear.

If a man wears his riot gear during prayer, will the sacred forsake him? If a man wears his riot gear to the holiday meal, how will he eat? If a man enters the bedroom in his riot gear, how will he make love to his wife? If a man wears his riot gear to tuck in his children, what will they dream?

Magpie Road is part of the Bakken, a shale formation lying deep under the birds, the men in the truck, you, this road. The shale has been forming over millions of years through pressure, through layers of sediment becoming silt. The silt becomes clay, which becomes shale. All of this is because of water. The Bakken is known as a marine shale—meaning, once, here, instead of endless grass, there lay endless water.

Men drill down into the shale using water and chemicals to perform the act we call hydraulic fracturing or fracking. The water-chemical mix is called brine, and millions of gallons of it must be disposed of as wastewater. In the Bakken in 2001, more than a thousand accidental releases of oil or wastewater were reported, and many more go unreported. Grass won't grow after a brine spill, sometimes for decades. River fish die and are washed ashore to lie on the dead grass.

There, just off Magpie Road, robins sit on branches or peck the ground. A group of robins is called a riot. This seems wrong at every level except the taxonomic. Robins are ordinary, everyday, general-public sorts of birds. They seem the least likely of all birds to riot.

When the men in the truck make their second pass, there on the road, the partridge sit their nests, and the robins are not in formation. They are singular. No one riots but the colors. The truck revs and slows and revs and slows beside you. You have taken your last photograph of the grass, have moved yourself back to your car. The truck pulls itself close to your car, revving parallel.

You are keeping your face still, starting the car. You have mislabeled your imaginary photograph. These men, they are not father and son. At close range, you can see there is not enough distance in age. One does sport camouflage, but the other, a button-down shirt, complete with pipeline logo over the breast pocket. They are not bird hunters. This is not a sporting moment. The way time suspends indicates an off-season moment. The one in the button-down motions to you out the window with his handgun, and he smiles and says things that are incongruous with his smiling face.

II.

The night before, in a nearby fracklands town, you stand, with your camera, in your hotel room doorway. You left Standing Rock for the Bakken, and the woodsmoke from the water protector camps still clings to your hair. You perform your fracklands travel protocol, photographing the room—the bedspread and desk, the bathroom. In your year and a half of research for your novel, of driving and talking to women in the fracklands, you have performed this ritual, this protocol, dozens of times. Women are bought and sold in those rooms. Women are last seen there. You upload the photos onto a website that helps find women who are trafficked, who have gone missing.

The influx of men, of workers' bodies, into frackland towns brings an overflow of crime. In the Bakken at the height of the oil and gas boom, violent crime, for example, increased by 125 percent. North Dakota attorney general Wayne Stenehjem called this increase in violent crime "disturbing," and cited aggravated assaults, rapes, and human trafficking as "chief concerns."

In each place, each frackland, off each road, you wait until checkout to upload the photos of the rooms. In the year and a half of driving and talking and driving and talking, if you've learned nothing else, you've learned to wait. Because it is very, very difficult to sleep in a hotel room once you learn a woman's gone missing from it.

III.

In the Marcellus Shale in Pennsylvania, a floorhand shuts the door to his hotel room, puts his body between the door and a woman holding fresh towels. A floorhand is responsible for the overall maintenance of a rig. The woman says to you that he says to her, "I just want some company." He says it over and over, into her ear, her hair, while he holds her down. She says it to you, your ear, your hair. She hates that word now, she says, *company*. A floorhand is responsible for the overall maintenance of a rig. A floorhand is responsible.

But who is responsible for and to this woman, her safety, her body, her memory? Who is responsible to and for the language, the words that will not take their leave?

In a hotel in Texas, in the Wolfcamp Shale, you wake to the music of the trucks arriving and departing. This hotel is shiny tile and chrome bathrooms. It is a parking lot overfilled with trucks, with men from the fields who have an arrangement with management. An arrangement can mean flowers in a vase. An arrangement can mean these men pay for nothing, not even a room. In the morning, the parking lot is all trash can. Beer bottles and used condoms and needles, the nighttime overflow.

In a hotel in Texas, in the Permian Basin, you report to the front desk re: the roughneck in the room above. You dial zero while he hits his wife/his girlfriend/the girl he has just bought. You dial zero while he throws her and picks her up and starts again. Or at least, one floor down, this is the soundtrack. Upon his departure, the man uses his fist on every door down your hall. The sound is loud but also is like knocking, like hello, like Anybody home? You wonder if he went first to the floor above but think not. Sound, like so many things, operates mostly through a downward trajectory.

At a hotel where South Dakota and Wyoming meet, you are sure you have driven out of the Bakken, past its edge, far enough. The highway that night belongs to the deer, though they are not yet in season. All forty or fifty of them stay roadside as you pass. You arrive at the hotel on caffeine and luck. The parking lot reveals the calculus of your mistake—truck after truck after truck, and a hotel clerk outside transacting with a young rough-neck. Their posture suggests a shared cigarette or kiss or grope—something safetied through vice or romance or lust. You'd take it. But here the posture is all commerce, is about the positioning of the body close so money can change hands. You are in a place that's all commerce, where bodies never go out of season, where bodies are commerce only.

When two more roughnecks stagger into your sight line, the hotel clerk and her partner are heading inside. She meets your eyes like a dare. The staggering man is drunk, the other holding him up while he zips his fly. This terminology, *fly*, comes from England, where it first referred to the flap on a tent—as in, Tie down your tent fly against the high winds. As in, Don't step on the partridge nest as you tie down your fly. As in, Stake down your tent fly against the winter snow, against the rubber bullets, against the sight of the riot gear.

The men sway across the lot, drunk-loud, and one says to the other, "Hey, look at that," and you are the only *that* there. When the other replies, "No, I like the one in my room just fine," you are sorry and grateful for *the one* in an unequal measure.

You cannot risk more roadside deer, and so despite all your wishes, you stay the night. A group of deer is called a herd; a group of roe deer, a bevy. There is a bevy of roe deer in the Red Forest near Chernobyl. The Bakken is not Chernobyl because this is America. The Bakken is not Chernobyl because the Bakken is not the site of an accident. The Bakken is not Chernobyl because the Bakken is no accident.

IV.

On Magpie Road, the ditch is shallow but full of tall grass. With one hand, the button-down man steers his truck closer to your car, and with the other, he waves the handgun. He continues talking, talking, talking. The waving gesture is casual, like the fist knocking down the hotel hallway—hello, anyone home, hello?

Once on a gravel road, your father taught you to drive your way out of a worse ditch. When the truck reverses, then swerves forward, as if to block you in, you take the ditch to the right, and when the truck slams to a stop and begins to reverse at a slant, taking the whole road, you cross the road to the far ditch, which is shallow, is like a small road made of grass, a road made for you, and you drive like that, on the green and yellow grass until the truck has made its turn, is behind you. By then you can see the highway, and the truck is beside you on the dirt road, and the truck turns right, sharp across your path. So you brake then veer left. You veer out, onto the highway, fast, in the opposite direction.

Left is the direction to Williston. So you drive to Williston, and no one follows.

At a big box store in Williston, a lot sign advertises overnight parking for RVs. You have heard about this, how girls are traded here. You had been heading here to see it, and now you're seeing it. Mostly, you're not seeing. You are in Williston for thirty-eight minutes, and you don't leave your car.

You spend those thirty-eight minutes driving around the question of violence, of proximity and approximation. How many close calls constitute a violence? How much brush can a body take before it becomes a violence, before it makes violence, or before the body is remade—before it leaves all seasons, becomes something other than the body it was once, before it becomes a past-tense body?

V.

Q&A

Why were you there on the road?
Because Indigenous women are almost three times more likely than other women to be harassed, to be raped, to be sexually assaulted, to be called a *that there*.

Because when the governor of North Dakota made an order to block entrance into the camps at Standing Rock and then rescinded it, he said the order was intended toward "public safety." Because in his letter to the Standing Rock tribal chairman, the commander of the Army Corps of Engineers said he was "genuinely concerned for the safety and well-being of both the members of your Tribe and the general public located at these encampments."

Because these statistics about trafficking, about assault, are knowledge considered common, but only if your body is not considered a general-public body.

Because you're a Métis woman.

Because you and they and we misunderstand the danger at Standing Rock, the danger of this pipeline going in there or elsewhere or everywhere. Because you and they and we misunderstand peaceful protestors as the ones bringing danger. Because you and they and we misunderstand the nature of danger altogether.

Because each person in Flint, Michigan, once rationed four cases of bottled water per week, now must buy their own bottled water or drink poisoned water or go without. Because you can see this future upriver or down. Because everywhere is upriver or down.

Because your first memory of water is of your father working to drown your mother.

Because you are four or five, and you need to use the bathroom, but instead, find yourself backing out the bathroom doorway and down the hall where you sit on the rust-colored shag. Because you wait for your father to quit trying to drown your mother. It seems crucial in the moment not to wet your pants. It seems crucial to hold the pieces of yourself together. If you make a mess on the carpet, if your father doesn't kill your mother, then she will have to clean the carpet. It seems crucial not to cause any trouble. So you sit. You wait. You hold yourself together.

Because all roads used to lead back to that house, and it is a measure of time and hard work that they no longer do. Because all roads lead to the body and through it. Because too many of us have these stories and these roads and these seasons. Because you carry theirs and they carry yours, and in this way, there is a measure of balance.

Because you are still very good at holding yourself together. Because these times make necessary the causing of trouble, the naming of it.

Because to the north and west of Magpie Road, in the Cypress Hills of southern Saskatchewan, in 1873, when traders and wolf hunters killed more than twenty Assiniboine, mostly women and children in their homes, the Métis hid in those hills and lived. Because they lived, they carried the news. Because they lived, you carry the news. Because the massacre took place along the banks of a creek that is a tributary that feeds into the greater Missouri River.

Because these times and those times and all times are connected through land and bodies and water.

What were you wearing, there on the road?

Not riot gear.

Why didn't you call the police?

See the water cannon on the bridge at Standing Rock. Listen to the Sheriff's Department men call it a "water hose" like this makes the act better. See also: Birmingham, Alabama. See also: Minneapolis, Minnesota. See the dog cages constructed outside the Morton County Sheriff's Department to hold "overflow." See the overflow—the water protectors, Dakota and Lakota women and men in cages. See it all overflow. See the journalists arrested for trespass and worse. See the confiscated notebooks, the cameras they will never get back. See the new statistics— how 8 to 10 percent of homicide victims in America are killed by police. See the woman struck by a tear gas canister. See how she will no longer be able to see through her right eye. See the children whose grandmothers and grandfathers are hospital- ized with hypothermia. See the elder who has a heart attack. See how science newly quantifies what some of us have long known—how historical and cultural trauma is lived in our bodies, is passed down, generation to generation, how it lives in the body. See the fires that elders light to keep warm. See the water extinguish those fires. See the children seeing it.

Why were you by yourself?

On a road like this, you are never alone. There is grass, there is sky, there is wind. See also: the answer on historical and cultural trauma. See also: Cypress Hills. See also: the everyday robins who are in formation now. See also: their ordinary, general-public bodies in riot.

What did you do, after?

You drove north and west and sat in rooms with friends, old and new. You hiked and ate good meals and talked about art. On a hike, one morning, you startled a rafter of turkeys. They flapped and squawked and strutted their necks. You laughed the laugh of one also startled. How they were in season did not come to mind till later. How your father hunted turkeys did not come to mind till later. You wrote things down. You began the work of stitching yourself back together. You did this on repeat until the parts hung together in some approximation of self. In Livingston, Montana, you made use of the car wash. You left the tall grass there.

Further questions should be directed toward: Proceed to the Route. Upon arrival, pick up loose roadside threads. Use them to stitch shut the asking mouths.

VI.

At Standing Rock, the days pass in rhythm. You sort box upon box of donation blankets and clothes. You walk a group of children from one camp to another so they can attend school.

The night before the first walk, it has rained hard and the

dirt of the road has shifted to mud. The dirt or mud road runs alongside a field, which sits alongside the Cannonball River, which sits alongside and empties itself into the Missouri.

Over the field, a hawk rides a thermal, practicing efficiency. There on the road, in the mud, three Herefords block progress. The cow snorts to her calves, which are large enough to be ambulatory, young enough for the cow still to proffer protection. She places her body between you, the threat, and her calves. She stamps her hooves into the mud, and they stick in a way you imagine unsatisfactory.

In that letter to the Standing Rock tribal chairman, the Army Corps commander wrote that the people must disperse from camp, "due to the concern for public safety" and because "this land is leased to private persons for grazing and/or haying purposes."

A cow holds public hooves whether stuck in mud or otherwise. A cow is not a concern to public safety, no matter the season. But what of these children? Are they considered public or private? If they don't graze or hay, if they cannot be leased, what is their value, here on this road, in this, our America?

That day, there on the road, once the mother cow allows safe passage, you walk on. After school but before the return walk, the children and you gather with hundreds to listen to the tribal chairman speak of peace, to sit with elders to pray, to talk of peace.

On this day, it is still fall. Winter will arrive with the Army Corps' words—no drilling under Lake Oahe, no pipeline under Lake Oahe. The oil company will counter, calling the pipeline "vital," saying they "fully expect to complete construction of the pipeline without any additional rerouting in and around Lake Oahe." The weather will counter with a blizzard. After the words and before the blizzard, there will be a celebration. A gathering of larks is called an exaltation. Even if it wasn't so, you like to think of larks there, like to think of their song, there with the people in the snow, there, alongside the river.

Back in the fall, you walk the children home from school, there on the road. You cross the highway, the bridge, upon your return. This bridge lies due south of the Backwater Bridge of the water cannons or hoses. But this bridge, this day, holds a better view. The canoes have arrived from the Northwest tribes, the Salish tribes. They gather below the bridge on the water and cars slow alongside you to honk and wave. Through their windows, people offer real smiles.

That night, under the stars, fire-lit, the women from the Salish tribes dance and sing. Though you've been to a hundred powwows, easily, you've never seen this dance, never heard this song. You stand with your own arms resting on the shoulders of the schoolchildren, and the dancers, these women, move their arms in motions that do more than mimic water, that conjure it. Their voices are calm and strong, and they move through the gathering like quiet, like water, like something that will hold, something you can keep, even if only for this moment.

TWO

Songs Without Words

I.

When I am four years old, we live in a tall, white house with a slanting foundation and brick petunia beds out front. We're three houses off Highway 71. I fall asleep summer nights, my window open to the whir and hiss of semis. There's a curve on the highway, a sharp one that requires slowing to pass through Brayton, our town of 150 people. Every few nights I wake to the sound of a Jake brake, the pop-boom similar to that made by gunfire.

I know, because my father has explained it to me, that the sound comes from the semis, from a valve releasing pressure so the big trucks can make the curve, can slow enough to stay on the road. My father doesn't often have the patience or inclination to answer my questions, my many, many questions. So I remember and hold dear his answer.

During daylight I ride my tricycle on the sidewalk and sometimes out into the street in front of our house. Over and over, I leave the cracked and bumpy sidewalk for the road. I ride around and around, preferring circles to straight lines, liking the feeling of cornering fast, of making the curve.

In a few more years, I'll have thick, oversized glasses to correct my almost uncorrectable myopia. In a few more years, my long, brown hair will be cut into a perfect round bowl. But at four, I'm still free to ride and squint and throw my long hair side to side as I pedal.

My sister is not interested in my games, and we're still a whole year away from when my best girlfriend moves to town. So I'm a solitary sidewalk rider.

The sidewalk is dirty, though, and sometimes I fall onto it if I'm not paying strict attention. Once, a flock of geese flies over during heavy fog and lands in the middle of this street before squawking and flapping toward the sidewalk. A grouping of smaller birds descends on the geese, pecking and tearing at their necks, diving and attacking until the geese are chased off, back beyond fog, into the sky.

According to Webster's, the small birds' behavior is called mobbing, with Webster's fifth definition for *mob* as "a flock, drove, or herd of animals," their first definition of the verb being "to crowd about and attack or annoy." The noun form of the word enters the lexicon in 1688, the verb form in 1696. Our town won't become a town till 1878, almost two hundred years later.

That day with the geese, I remember feeling wonder and awe, not annoyance, that these small birds could shift the larger ones. In the morning, when the fog had cleared, when I came out again to ride, I remember feeling a distinct revulsion for the leftover bird-shit mess.

I can't say for certain whether this is when I take to the street, but I can say with certainty that I know, even this young, mine is behavior my mother won't like. But my mother is busy, she works and cleans the house and works more, and also, my sister is sick a lot.

Growing up, I never want to be a mother because mothers have to work so hard—one job and then another job and then cooking, cleaning, bill paying, driving, yelling. Mothers are not treated well, either, by bosses or by people like fathers, and though they take care of everyone around them, nobody takes care of a mother.

On weekends during tax season and sometimes in the summer, our mother works a half or sometimes whole day at the law office where she's the legal secretary. One Saturday, she arrives home earlier than usual to find me making my circles on the street in front of the house.

Her hands pull me from my tricycle toward the sidewalk, back to what she thinks is safety. She doesn't know I do this all the time. She doesn't know how much I love it, the stories I tell myself as I pedal.

"What are you doing?" she says. She's wearing lipstick and her short brown hair is shiny, is perfect in its Dorothy Hamill–style cut. But her face is scrunched. She holds me by the shoulders, and I do my best to shrug out of her grip, to face her.

"You could have been killed," she says. "Don't you know that?"

It's true this time I'm closer to the highway than I've gone before. It's true I was curving closer and closer, liking the sound of the highway noise, making it a part of my game.

"You could have been killed," she says again.

"Well," I say slowly and with a shrug, "you'd still have Maggie."

"Don't say that," she says. She lets go of my shoulders then and looks across the street and all around like she's wondering if anyone's overheard, like maybe whatever's wrong with me might be contagious.

I'm correct, though, of course, at the level of the factual. She would still have my sister.

And also, I've not been raised to think of myself separately from my sister, from my family. At Christmas, from my grandparents, we get matching presents—pajamas, for example, mine blue and my sister's pink, but otherwise identical. On my sister's birthday, if she gets a green sweater, I get a purple one and so on.

These grandparents are my father's parents, Métis and a recent Danish immigrant. My grandmother had six boys, trying for a girl. My grandmother's mother moved her family back and forth from Alberta to the States, divorcing and remarrying and divorcing her husband. My grandmother's childhood featured these separations from her own sisters. My sister and I are her closest girl grandchildren.

My mother frets over the presents—it's too much, I hear her tell my father. They don't need presents on the other one's birthday. They'll get spoiled.

But we did need the presents. We needed to be reminded that we were not one over the other or one under the other. We needed to be reminded that we were together, that we were to take care of one another, that we were not easily made separate, that together, we were whole.

And, too, we needed the pajamas or socks or sweaters. They arrived at Christmas and at our birthdays, and though my sister could make a sweater last the year, I outgrew mine or made holes in it rolling down hills or snagging seams on stray tree branches. The extra one I received at her birthday helped me to have a spare. We were not the sort of children to receive presents throughout the year, and clothes were presents only.

Despite these repeated conversations with my father, neither my mother nor my father ever does shift my grandmother from her practice.

The look my mother gives me on my tricycle that day as I curve around the middle of the road, practicing my Jake brake, it clings to me in a different way than my favorite purple chenille sweater. It stays with me, this look, this shift toward shame, but it does not quite take root in the way my mother seemed to hope. It does not shift me toward valuing personal safety over the whole of our family. It does not shift me into thinking of myself that way, as a distinct, separate person.

Already, at four years old, I've learned the lessons from my grandmother and her family. They'd set for life my ideas about responsibility and belonging and what that means in the day-to-day. My mother's look may have laid the seed of a sort of discontent, a sort of contagion, perhaps, but I stay warm in my sweater. I stay warm in the knowledge that there will be others arriving on my sister's birthday, that if anything happens to me, my sister will wear my sweater and be warm and think of me.

II.

The small towns where I grew up, where my family settled, in the States, where my father still lives, are in Audubon County, Iowa. The hills there roll and roll, and the rivers cut through like snakes or ribbons, depending on the vantage point.

The county is named for John James Audubon of bird painting fame. His avian watercolors are legendary. It is less well known that he was born in what was then Saint-Domingue, what is now Haiti, on his father's sugarcane plantation. The son of French naval officer and businessman Jean Audubon and

Jeanne Rabin, a woman from the Congo who was Audubon's chambermaid, his slave.

Audubon's earlier biographies altogether skip his mother's heritage and his father's slave trading. More contemporary ones foreground both it and how he was born to parents who were unmarried—many times calling him Creole or a Creole bastard. The way the details are put forward, I suppose, is meant to titillate. But there's nothing particularly unusual about a white-passing son passing for white for the rest of his life, gaining advantage from this passing. It is the history of many of us. It is the most American of histories.

The first use of the word *Creole* as a noun dates to 1697, the year after *a mob of birds* joins the lexicon. According to Webster's, to be Creole is to be either "1: a person of European descent born especially in the West Indies or Spanish America, 2: a white person descended from early French or Spanish settlers of the U.S. Gulf states and preserving their speech and culture," or "3: a person of mixed French or Spanish and black descent speaking a dialect of French or Spanish."

As writer Georgina Dhillon notes, "In colonial societies in earlier times, definitions of 'Creole' seemed to be based more on what the word did not include rather than what it did." All contemporary sources, though, cite cultural commonalities through land, food, religion, and music as ways of belonging, of being Creole today.

Though the word *Métis* doesn't join the lexicon until 1816, at least according to Webster's, it too first defines the people by the European concept of "mixing," as "a person of mixed blood," and adds, "*especially, often capitalized:* the offspring of an American Indian and a person of European ancestry." Today Métis from different regions define the term distinctly, but all definitions include that a person's ancestry, self-identification, and some form of connection to and/or acceptance by the people and land are necessary to be Métis.

From within, then, being Métis is about land and people and belonging.

For young John Audubon, his beginning set a sad trajectory toward his eventual belonging. His mother, Jeanne Rabin, died when he was only a few months old. His father, instead of the usual abandoning, took both young John James and a half sister with him back to France, where Audubon, Sr., already had a wife. The children both were then adopted by Audubon and his wife, Anne Moynet Audubon. This is perhaps the even less usual part.

John James would become famous for his drawings and paintings of the birds of North America, for his study of those birds. But he also would be known for his cruelty both to birds and to animals. According to Warren Perry's profile of Audubon for the Smithsonian's National Portrait Gallery, "He killed thousands of birds and cruelly experimented on many animals, including catfish, a bald eagle, and his very own hunting dog. With friends, he buried a rat in a pot, its tail protruding from the dirt, and gave the complete ensemble to another friend, claiming it was a rare flower."

Though illustrators in this time often killed the birds they drew, Audubon was rejected for these other cruelties by many illustrators and naturalists in North America. He was rejected in larger society, too, for his poverty, his inability to pay his debts. Both earned him censure and isolation. But he and his work found a home in England, where he still enjoyed popularity. And, of course, he was popular enough to become the namesake of the county where I'm from—a place where many men hunt birds and eat them, where many men work also to save the birds' habitat and see no contradiction in these impulses.

John James Audubon died in 1851 of what some cite as "various illnesses" and others cite as dementia.

My father has spent his life walking the hills of Audubon County looking for birds—out of season, just to see them, and in season, hoping for a clear shot. My father was born in this place, and he's lived most of his life there. One day in the near or distant future, he'll die there, too, most likely also from complications related to dementia.

III.

The fall after I turn four years old, I wear my first leotard and pale pink shoes to dance class and then, after, to the bar to pick up my father. Our class includes six girls and one boy, and together we learn to point our toes, to round and elongate our arms, to tuck in our butts when we plié. I have long brown hair that is straight at the top and wavy at the bottom. I'm sturdy and round-faced. I forget often to tuck in what teacher Marianne calls my derrière.

The dance class building abuts the bar where my father has a favorite stool, where my father waits in the late afternoon for class to end. Exira, Iowa, is a no-stoplight town, holding fewer than a thousand people but more than one bar. My family lives a few miles down Highway 71, still in Brayton. My mother is working, so my father is assigned the task of fetching and driving me home.

To be clear, my father is at this bar most afternoons or early evenings whether it's dance class day or not. To be clear, at four years old, I know already my father is the sort of drinker who brings home either a jovial self or a monster. To be clear, there's no trauma story here, in this moment—my father's guns this day remain tucked away at home, way up on the high shelf.

The building housing the dance studio sits two stories tall with the studio on the second floor, tucked around back. The wide, almost square room holds big windows that frame the door. It holds music, mainly classical. It holds worn linoleum floors and teacher Marianne, who points her own toes with precision, who delivers her directions to us in a steady, strong voice. Teacher Marianne has the same sort of rare power and grace as my grandmother—no one shouts or shoves in a room either of them inhabits.

I think of the music Marianne plays in the same way I think of the songs my grandmother sings as we walk the hills around her farm—songs without words. My grandmother mostly hums melodies but sometimes breaks into what I recognize as words, but not words in English. She points out plants, telling me what they do, how they grow, how they're helpers, naming them and singing her songs and doing more naming. Both types of songs, in the hills and in dance class, provide comfort. Both anchor my childhood in a rare, peaceful way.

I know now this place, this dance class studio, to be a regular place, to be perhaps even somewhat shabby in its construction. I know now it's not a fancy place most likely by anyone's standards. But this fall I feel so fancy in my leotard and tights, and this place feels so fancy.

I imagine the cost of these lessons is made possible by the extra hours my mother works or through a grandparent's generosity or both. Part of why it feels fancy is because I know, even this young, my presence here to be precarious, anomalous, rare. I know already we don't have money for a good many things, so I know this is special.

Toward the end of each dance class, teacher Marianne turns us loose to chassé in circles around the room. According to Webster's, in French *chassé* simply means "to chase," and that's what our feet do, back feet chasing front feet, as we bend our knees and point our feet, moving at something close to a leap/run. We're together, our hair and cheeks flapping. We laugh and smile wide and breathe hard.

After class, I'm the only one to move by myself down the back steps of the two-story building and up the side steps of the building next door. My father the first day had shown me how. We practiced. By this day, I've almost mastered plié and chassé. I've well mastered the art of down one staircase and up another. I've mastered the art of keeping secret from my mother that my father doesn't pick me up, that I go over to pick up him.

I hold the secret close because I love both dance class and the bar. I love the songs without words, mirrors at the front, my soft shoes scuffing on the wide expanse of linoleum.

The bar holds low ceiling tiles, dim fluorescent lighting, and metal stools where I sit and am allowed to kick my feet against their rungs. My father drinks beer, and I drink orange soda and snack on barbecue potato chips.

Country music plays on the jukebox or radio, usually old-school country, what my father calls real country music. The other country music that sounds like pop or Top 40 is called horseshit or horseshit country.

Today it's old-school country, and I know my father hasn't been drinking too much because he only sings along for one stanza to see if I will, too, so I do though it's not my favorite thing to sing in front of people. I can sing. I know this already to be true, and it's a thing I love privately but not publicly, except for church and the bar with my father.

It's almost pheasant-hunting season, so my father wears camouflage pants, worn leather boots with tie-up laces. He's been out scouting a new place to hunt. He tells the bartender and other men about it while I crunch chips. They laugh and the bartender offers each of us a refill, and I say yes after my father does.

There's a danger in writing about my father's drinking— I know this. Native men, including Métis men, so often are depicted as drunk, hopeless, more drunk, more hopeless. My father is Métis and also he drinks. We're far from culture and homelands here in Iowa. We're not returning. My father's drinking is about many things, not the least of which is the pressure to fit in, to comply with the dictates of whiteness.

When I show him day drinking, then, please note there are other day drinkers lined up beside him on their stools. Please note all of them are this thing America calls white. They are all striving to be better at whiteness, at prosperity. They are all failing. They all go home each night to their families with beer on their breath, with pockets a few dollars short.

These are not stories of people embedded deeply in culture, but, rather, they are the stories of the people who left. These are American stories; these are stories of trying to move into the American space we call whiteness, about trying to live, instead, there.

This isn't a story, then, so much about being Indian in America or even being Métis in America. It's a story about being those things and striving toward whiteness; it's about the cost of that striving.

At four years old, I don't, of course, understand any of this. I love the bar. I fear and love my father.

Later in the fall, we'll ride home sometimes with birds in the back of the truck, and later in the winter, with pelts from the trapline. We ride home with a shotgun for the birds or a handgun for the trapline. We ride home hoping my mother does not yet have dinner on the table. We ride home with our secret.

IV.

In the summer that year, for the annual Fourth of July celebration, I perform at the bandstand in the park with a few of my dance compatriots, and my father and his band perform, too. They do covers of country songs and switch some of the words to include our town's name or to make them more patriotic for the occasion.

My father's face holds a sheen of sweat, and he swipes at it with a folded bandanna he pulls from his jeans pocket. It's a warm day, but I know also how long he's spent in the beer tent and, before that, in the bar. I'm not invited into the bar in the summer because there's no dance class.

There's no orange soda before or after my performance, but we do all have cotton candy and ride the Tilt-A-Whirl, round and round like a chassé until we're dizzy and satisfied.

Once when my father was about four years old, his father took him into town for the Fourth of July parade and carnival, and somewhere in the crush and mix of people in from out of town, my grandfather lost my father. He looked and looked for him, not wanting to have lost him, of course, but also not wanting to return home to my grandmother without him.

Upon my grandfather's return, my grandmother is reported by all to have said in a steady voice, "Go back to town and find him or don't come back at all."

Their farmhouse sat on top of a high hill, a mile or so

outside town. When my grandfather made his way down the sharp gravel drive and turned onto the highway to town, there, coming up the steep hill, was my father. He had known his way home. He told his father thank you, but he didn't need a ride up the driveway. I'm home, he said. I'm already home.

I love this story like I loved the dance studio, the bar, the hills surrounding the farmhouse. It's okay, I've learned, to love the things that make you, even if they also are the things that unmake you.

We don't know the year I'm four that we only have a decade left with my grandmother. We don't know how fast the time will go. My grandmother's presence could stop any meanness in a room. She held us together. She held together our better selves. She helped keep at bay the worst of my father, or more accurately she helped keep him from being all the time his worst self.

She'll pass on the winter I turn fourteen. By that spring, my father will be drinking and raging almost all the time.

If in a life, in the telling of it, you're going to give so much of the after, you must also give the before. The year I'm four years old, I'm stitched together tight by love and land and story, and if these things later become my unstitching, what I'm left is a life's work, learning how to chase a thread and move with it, learning how to make something from leftover ribbon and thread.

THREE

The Invented Histories of Domestic Birds

I.

My sister is calling from her house, a trailer outside Boulder where she has a perfect square of backyard, where the air is dry, the sky correct. Only people who've loved the West and lived elsewhere know about the incorrect sky. Webster's might define it as prominent in places such as Pennsylvania, Arkansas, Ohio. God save us from the Pennsylvania sky, says Webster's. See also: hazy. See also: the irritation of clouds that provide no rain or if rain, then no attendant relief from the heat. Under the incorrect sky, rain provides only mosquito infestation, sweaty foreheads, fat ticks, the suck and pull, the humid-thick.

My sister and I are thick with apology. We overflow our do-you-remembers. My sister is calling me at home in Arkansas, where I live under the incorrect sky. My sister is calling because it's 2016, and we're deep into the summer of guns. My sister is calling because a nice white woman has pulled a gun on my nephew and his brother, in a nice suburb, on a nice, white-hot June day.

Listen, this is not going to be the kind of story in which someone narrates from a distance the experience of a young man America has decided is Black, a young man with a gun pointed toward him, where his body is used to insert narrative tension into what is, essentially, another person's story. This is not that kind of story.

This young man is my family. America may have decided my nephew looks Black and I look white, but we're both Métis. This suburb may be the most American of all territories, but it was once the land of the Cheyenne and Arapaho people, many of whom still live in the area. More than one hundred thousand people who identify as tribal people live in Colorado today. Almost half live in urban areas. To call my nephew Black, to call me white, is semi-accurate at the level of phenotype. To call him Black, to call me white, is the most American form of erasure.

So this hot summer day, we're both Métis, in this, our America, but I know the difference in our lived worlds. I walk around each day, including this one, in my white-privilege raincoat. It doesn't matter much that the sleeves are too short, the shoulders tight; I know I'm wearing it. I know its uses and its limitations— I know, for example, the intricacies of how it fits most poorly at the cocktail party when white people want to talk to me about Black people, about Native people, about, about, about. It does not protect against the white people who get between a cocktail and me. But this coat—at a traffic stop—its efficacy rate is almost a hundred percent.

My nephew and his half brother this day in the suburb, the very American suburb, are wearing no such coats. And though what I am about to tell will reduce the thread of narrative tension, so it sags a little, maybe, like power lines after a minor storm, so that even the invented birds go elsewhere to roost, I'm telling you: this is a narrative in which all of us get to live.

II.

In our childhood, my sister's and mine, our father kept his guns locked on the high shelf. They came down for the trapline—in case some caught thing needed to be shot; they came down for shooting birds and sometimes deer and sometimes rabbit or squirrel. They came down to be cleaned sometimes after he hit our mother or one of us.

Here is the thing about rabbit or squirrel cooked without love, cooked out of necessity, cooked with embarrassment over the necessity: it is dry, stringy, horrible. Cooked with love, say, at a grandparent's house by someone other than a mother, it tastes like anything else—it is food like any other. It is not the mother's fault she wishes for grocery-store chicken, plucked and clean and bearing the marker of the middle class, the cellophane pulled tight by unseen hands.

Here is the thing about the sky over the trapline: always blue over white, always the sharp blue of winter, the coldest sky. Here is the thing about the myth of our mother and "one of us": there is no "one of us." I'm equivocating, choosing the plural over the singular, all the stall tactics, all the cover. Here is the thing about guns in a house like ours, locked away or otherwise: there is only one person who knows how to shoot.

III.

My sister is calling because she has a story but also because she wants mine. Something past or present that is funny, maybe, if possible, from someone who knows her, who will joke away the hurt. She does not often come to me this way. Childhood prohibits this closeness, maybe. I was the one who put my body in between. She was the one who shut herself in her room. But the narrative is never that simple, of course. No narrative is ever that simple.

My sister was born before I was, and she was born premature, less than four pounds. The story my father tells is one of going home from the hospital in Minneapolis to change his clothes and returning to find my sister gone from her spot in the ICU window. All the other tiny, sick babies lined up in their pastel blankets under the bright lights—all but her. "It stopped my heart," he says. "It stopped my heart." My father is not prone to such speech, and the look he gets on his face is an even rarer sighting—like love and fear in equal measure, given equal weight, like the wings of a crane, the push and pull before the flight into sky.

When my father and I talk in that 2016 summer of guns, he wants to know what my yard is doing, here in Arkansas, in the humid-thick. The yard that summer is always doing things, inexplicable things—making food and drawing in creatures and ticks, oh god, the ticks, a horror movie amount. He is especially interested in the birds who come to my feeder—what kinds and when and what do I feed them.

The truth of the bird feeder is that it's not mine, it's ours, or more particularly it is my then-husband's. I am an academic, yes, but not in the field of ornithology. Even by casual observer standards, I know less than I probably should about birds. In the end, in the near future, I will learn I also know less than I probably should about husbands, about marriage, about permanency.

As for these summer birds, they fly or they don't, are colorful or dull. To illustrate further, I give the example of the hummingbirds. I know them to be small and lovely creatures, and I overhear my then-husband one day talking about them with my daughter, and I say, "Where are they?" I say, "I've never seen them." I'm squinting through the patio double-doors at the large, black feeder where other, larger birds congregate.

"At their feeder," my then-husband says. He says this to me like he says a good many things—like this is a thing about which I would know if I'd bother.

"Where?" I say. I'm not at all sure now that I care very much about hummingbirds after all. This is getting a little boring, maybe, or he and our daughter are making things up just to tease me, or who knows. Birds, perhaps, remain unknowable.

He leaves his desk, puts down his elaborate sandwich, and stands behind me at the double doors. He turns my shoulders, so I am facing off at a right angle instead of straight ahead. "There," he says, "at their feeder."

A red, beautiful object hangs there, made of glass or ceramic, containing some dark liquid. As if by magic, there is, in fact, a minor swarm of hummingbirds.

"What did you think that was?" he says.

"A hummingbird feeder," I say. "Of course." Really, though, I had thought it was some sort of art.

Each time my father calls, I have the impulse to hand off the phone to my then-husband, who chafes at all chores categorized as housework, at picking up or dropping off from school our daughter, at anything resembling full-time employment. But he is a man who has bothered, who will continue to bother on behalf of these birds.

My father, though, calls to talk to me. So each time I do what I'm good at—I make things up. There are almost never any birds at the feeder when he calls, but I report them, these invented birds. I craft and deliver their lives, their histories: the yard features birds with flecks of orange on the undersides of their wings, and dark red birds who fight each other over the seed, and a nest of baby birds, one time, to which a large, blue-winged mother delivers seed and sometimes worms and some-times ticks. I have no idea if birds eat ticks, but if I am inventing, dear god or gods, dear Webster's, make it so.

My father posits various bird names, possibilities, based on my bullshit, and I say, "Yes, I'm sure that's the bird." It goes like this for a good half hour and then we hang up.

But I don't want to bullshit my sister. Not today, not right now. "Remember how I used to steal your candy?" I say.

She says, "Just candy?" and "Is that right?"

I did steal her candy and also her blank notebooks, her clothes—everything but her shoes, which were and are a full size too small. She was better at caring for things and so her things lasted longer. Only one of us could make an Easter basket's con-tents, its Peeps and odd, pastel M&M's, last till summer. My sis-ter's best practices for candy longevity included the following:

Step 1: Tear the M&M mini-pack across the top, making a straight, even line.

Step 2: Select no more than two M&M's, preferably of complementary colors.

Step 3: Eat said candy through nibbling, through bites so small they would shame any decent mouse.

Step 4: Seal shut the perfect cut with a straight, perfectly fitted and aligned piece of Scotch tape.

Repeat steps 1–4 each day until Fourth of July or, if possible, till Halloween.

A whole package of mini-M&M's is, of course, already so small. Impossibly small. My belief then and now is that her behavior was directed toward me—was a form of torture designed to antagonize me, to test my belief systems, which, then and now, include efficiency and consumption, which include the ripping of a corner jagged, the pouring of all contents into my waiting mouth—where all the little pastel pieces fit like perfect, colorful magic.

Once my sister had finished her taping, she bit the heads off one or maybe two marshmallow Peeps and returned their bodies to the package for other days. *Other days.*

By the time she'd decapitated her first row of Peeps, I had long since emptied my entire basket into myself, and, yes, I was side-eyeing hers, finding all the hiding places in the room we shared, the one with an actual piece of masking tape down its center. Which is to say, we are sisters, yes—we love each other—but we are not natural-friend sisters. We are not of similar natures. We are foreign to each other in essential ways that are equal parts colorful and jagged.

IV.

In the backyard of this summer, my nephew is with his half brother at an uncle's house in a wealthy suburb of Denver. These young men are many things. My nephew is a biology student, is Métis and Irish and French and African American, is seldom found in his natural habitat without his laptop and its intricate online world of fantasy games; his brother is a high school student, is of similar descent, minus the Métis, is interested in basketball and travel and the outdoors. But in the language of this, our America, in this, our summer of guns, they are Black. They are Black boys by a private lake. Never mind they are here to fish, are holding fishing poles. Never mind they've been invited.

The day passes into late afternoon when the baby monitor the uncle has been holding erupts with the sounds of the younger, inside children awaking from their naps. He goes to tend them, leaving my nephew and his brother alone to fish.

When the neighbor sees them there, at the edge of her manicured lawn, waterside, she goes into her house and brings down her gun. She crosses the space of the lawn with it in front of her body, in the position we refer to as *drawn*—as in how is the scene drawn? Is the light just right? How is the timbre of her voice when she demands to know who they are and what they think they are doing, these boys? Who the fuck are they, who the fuck, who the fuck?

David, the brother, keeps repeating his name. "I'm David," he says, "I'm David."

His voice, his voice. I don't know how to report this. I don't. My nephew stands next to him, silent.

Here is the thing about my sister's children, my nephew and my niece: if my sister's and my childhood is of the B-grade, family-saga variety, her children's includes moments that rival a horror movie. The children's father behaves as if he were a minor cult leader. Their childhood featured all the requisite trauma you can imagine and some you can't. The curtains in their house were drawn against daylight, against prying eyes, because the world was going to end and their enemies lurked, and don't tell anyone what goes on inside this house, or the bad men will come, and the bad men will take you away.

But the bad men, of course, were already inside. It is the truth of this violence we call domestic that the bad men already are inside.

In the backyard, near the woman and her gun, where the

uncle has abandoned it, the baby monitor comes alive. Webster's defines its crackle and hum as salvation. The uncle hears David repeating his name, hears the woman, her who-the-fucks. The uncle, though white and of privilege, he loves these boys. He shouts down his neighbor from inside the house, he leaves the house and crosses through the double doors, he crosses the lawn under the late afternoon sky at a run.

No one calls the police, after. Headline after headline delivers the stories of Black men and teens and boys falsely arrested by police, shot by police, killed by police. If quantifying helps makes this clearer, statistician Patrick Ball in his report in *Granta* found that police are responsible for almost a third of all homicides committed by strangers.

I am interested in the sociopolitical, familial, and geographic boundaries of this story, of our language, of our storytelling. If the lake is adjacent to but not located in the uncle's backyard, is this considered a domestic space? How close does a relative have to be in order for a crime to be domestic?

Does a domestic-violence bullet enter the body and exit differently than a regular bullet? What is an irregular bullet? If the move toward the language of domesticity is a lessening, a demoting of sorts, then what is the language of violence about race? An escalation? A shout to the whisper of the domestic?

Don't mistake me—I am not advocating here for more whispering. We have all of us been quiet too long and at such cost. I am asking for a shift in language that allows us to consider the intersections between these types of violence we hold separate—to consider them not so much as intersections, as places of sharp corners, but, rather, as places that exist most often in the actual, in the physical, in the soft bodies of our children, of ourselves.

Here is the thing about domestic abusers: they don't

quarantine themselves—they to and fro. They leave their domiciles at regular intervals. They go to the nightclub in Orlando; they go to the concert in Las Vegas; they go to the elementary school in Newtown; they go to all the places in between—they take down their guns and go.

V.

When I call my sister again nearly two years later, I am fact-checking. I'm asking how this day, this moment is or has been affecting my nephew and his brother. "You're writing about this?" she says. She says my nephew's name then, twice, with a long pause in between naming. "It was just David," she says. She says my nephew's name again like she'd like to kill me with it, like how dare you. "He was never there," she says. "Why did you think that?"

"Everyone's moved on," she says. "Everyone's fine."

I tell her I'm not naming the half brother by his given name, which is distinctive. I tell her I'm making him "David."

"Tell it to me, again," I say. "Tell the story to me again. I'm listening."

She is all of a sudden very busy. She has another call. She will talk with me soon. She will. She hangs up the phone as I say "okay," as I say "goodbye." It is an hour or more before it occurs to me she doesn't have a landline, only the one phone, the cellphone on which we were speaking.

Outside, in my backyard, I watch the lone hawk swoop and dive over the field. The clouds over him grow darker and darker, but I know if rain were imminent, he'd have gone back to his tree. I know only this little bit about the behavior of hawks. I know even less, perhaps, about the behavior of sisters.

VI.

In my childhood, the sky over the trapline is an early morning sky, still navy dark against the winter white below. Being a bad Métis involves not being able to follow tracks, to identify tracks. See also: dawdling waterside to look at the sky or the ice that forms on the pond. See also: falling into holes. For the uninitiated, traps are checked pre-dawn or at dawn and then again at dusk. For the uninitiated, girls aren't the usual companions of their fathers on traplines, but no son is old enough yet for the trapline. Before her brother is born, the girl is named for a great-grandfather, Anton, and is raised to do the outside work while the sister stays inside. A brother will be born when the girl is nine years old, so the day she falls into the hole, she must be no older than ten or eleven years old. Because as a grown person she has a daughter who's twelve, let's make this girl at the trapline nine or ten. She's not twelve years old. She's not.

They're at the trapline, the girl and her father, because it's trapping season. They're at the trapline because the bottom won't fall out of the fur market until later in the eighties. This day, a mink pelt still will fetch $24; a raccoon, $34; a coyote, $47; a river otter, nearly $80. They catch more muskrat, for $6 per pelt, than anything else, which seems unfair, given how the effort expended is equal. Beaver pelts sell for almost $35, but a beaver also is difficult—prone to thrashing and lunging with those sharp teeth, if the trap hasn't pulled it under, if it's not been drowned. So I imagine that day they're hoping both for and against catching a beaver.

The hole the girl steps in, it's deep and narrow, a post hole most likely, and, yes, she is looking up, not down. One minute she has both feet on land, the next, right leg on land, left leg under, caught. The girl is up past her knee in under, in stuck. Her father is ahead, moving toward the reeds at the pond's edge.

Here is the thing about checking traps with her father. It is the only time she's with him alone. It's the only time she's with him alone when he's taken one of his guns down from the high shelf. A pistol or a shotgun, depending on the traps they've set together, depending on what he's expecting to catch. And she knows better than to yell, but what else? The birds are bringing their morning songs, and the sky is shifting from navy to the pale blue it later will be.

When her father turns, the look on his face is one of deciding. He returns to her, crosses the ground, and she feels a measure of relief but also of dread. When he reaches her, instead of offering a hand, he uses one hand to steady the gun, a pistol this day, the gun at his side, and he uses the other to touch the girl's hair as he says, "Maybe you'll learn something once," then turns away.

It's not yet light, not all the way, when he rounds the pond's edge to check the other traps, all of them, one by one. He moves his body clockwise around the pond and checks and checks.

Here is the thing about waiting: it makes her patient, then impatient, then resourceful, even if she'd rather not be. There is a stick and she can reach it, just, and there is room for it in the hole, just, and she can wedge and shimmy. She can wedge and shimmy and free her leg. When she loses her boot down there, the stick works to retrieve it, though this takes some time, and now her hands are stiff, and the sun is up, and there is full light on the snow crust.

Here is the thing about ice-cold water—it is good for ankle sprains. She doesn't have to lean on anybody else to get to the pickup. She has that stick. She has her boot, which is back on her swelling foot.

When she reaches the truck, her father has been in it long enough for it to have grown warm. Before she enters, she uses her stiff hands to break the stick into three distinct pieces, to throw them out to the snow. She takes her time with this process. Though the pieces do not go far enough to make the act satisfying, it helps her quiet herself, and so the drive back to town is a quiet drive under an all-blue sky.

At the house, the domicile, the sister stands on the back porch with a plate of cookies she has made. The birds are in the trees, not offering much by way of color or song.

The cookies, chocolate chip, are already wrapped in cellophane the sister has crimped tidy at the edges. The sister has been waiting for the father to return, so he can take her to an aunt's house, to deliver the plate. Her face holds its impatience at a distance, almost.

When the girl reaches the bottom step, the sister moves the plate to shoulder level, to where it is out of the girl's reach. But, then, the girl takes the last steps, closes the distance, and the sister sees her face, and she reads the morning there—she reads it correctly. She brings down the plate and begins the slow and careful work of peeling back the plastic, of selecting. She offers to the girl the smallest of the possible cookies, and the girl takes it, and it is still warm, it is still soft.

FOUR

Give and Go

I.

The winter I turn ten, men come to my childhood home and lift it. One moment, the front door rests, hinged and ordinary. The next, it levitates, a portal for birds only. That cold, bright morning, I dribble the sidewalk out in front of our house in Brayton. It's early morning, the neighbors in their houses awaken one by one to hear the sparrows screech in rhythm with the metal cranes, the whir and grind, the shouts of the men, directing flight.

I have taken from my house the necessary things: my high-tops and teddy bear, my basketball. I imagine my mother has taken her cigarettes, my father, his guns. I dribble the sidewalk, shaking my bowl haircut side to side in disbelief until my mother threatens the ball and sends me to the street. My mother cut my pretty hair because I would not stop sneaking gum from her purse. I'd fall asleep with it tucked in the pouch of my cheek like a common squirrel. My mouth needed the gum, of course, the way hers needed her cigarettes, to work and worry, to keep the words in.

She'd been Catholic before my father. She might have had worry beads, a rosary like her sister. But the priest saw my father, my five dark uncles, and declared the whole lot unfit to attend the wedding unless they converted en masse. The point or points scored after a touchdown in a football game are Webster's fourth definition for the word *conversion*. But in our family this definition is primary.

We cheer for our high school team, the Vikings. We cheer for the college team, the Hawkeyes. We cheer for the regional NFL teams, the Vikings and sometimes the Chiefs, whose fans perform an act they call "the tomahawk chop," who wear red face, who perform limp imitation war whoops.

For a time, we cheer, out of region and place, for the San Diego Chargers because my mother's cousin Jack Pardee is their defensive coordinator. When cousin Jack is the head coach of the team from Washington, we cheer for them, this team whose fight song lyrics include "Braves on the Warpath!" The team from Washington has fans that tomahawk chop like the Chiefs. They put on red face and whoop. They wear dark wigs with single braids made from stiff synthetics that have more in common with plastic than with actual human hair.

Their team jackets, though, are shiny like silk, like the darkest red silk. On the back, each jacket features a profile of America's idea of a Native man. The team jackets are made of satin or sateen fabric, and I so very much want one—to hold and run my fingers over again and again and again, and then to hang in my closet. I don't imagine myself wearing it. I can't. The man on the back looks enough like my father to inspire mixed feelings. The tomahawk chop, the war whooping also make me feel strange. And everyone in my household, everyone in my town, worships at the altar of football.

My sister on her birthdays wishes for dolls and fabric for sewing, but already, at eight or nine, I have my own *Sports Illustrated* subscription, which was the only item on my birthday wish list. Already, I know which defense a team is running—what a left tackle does, if a center varies the snap count and why, the difference between a wide receiver and a tight end. I know the role of each part of the holy trinity—offense, defense, special teams. I get attention for knowing—high fives from my father, low chuckles from my uncles. When we sit in the bleachers or in front of the television on Sundays, everyone shouts, but no one shouts in anger.

My mixed feelings then are very mixed feelings. They also are personal, are feelings I know to keep to myself. There is no cultural currency for saying them out loud. I chew them away with the gum stolen from my mother's purse.

But this cold levitation morning, I have my basketball. I dribble the street, blow improbable bubbles, try to keep the popping mess off my glasses, my hands, my short hair, the ball.

Our house is mostly white, a foursquare made of two stories. Its foundation has begun a tilt back to earth my mother hopes these men can right. If all inside our house is going to fail and fall, the outside, at least, can be made level.

From the sidewalk before me, my mother shakes her pack, Virginia Slims Menthols, and together but apart, we watch the levitation of our house through her smoke. There rises the living room television, altar to Sunday football. There the brown shag where the children sit, the plaid couch for the parents. There, the site of our everyday violence turned each Sunday toward another target, unified, collective.

Beyond, the bathroom, where my father tries every so often to drown my mother. Beyond, the first guns of what will become his collection. Beyond, the dining room table from which my father and I will rise when I'm fourteen, when he lays hands on me in a way never to be made right.

My father is Métis, my father is all motion, my father teaches me about football, about the trapline. He teaches me about violence and destruction and despair. I grow up to teach my daughter some but not all, not all.

We are levitating the house so we can sell it, so we can move a few miles up the highway to the bigger town, Exira. Instead of a hundred or so people, this town holds almost a thousand. It holds my best girlfriend and basketball practice; it holds the library and school playground where the hoop has a net. This levitation is step one of the salvation miracle. And this morning, I want so very much to be saved.

A few miles down Highway 71, kitty-corner from our non-Catholic church, sits the elementary school gym, where practice soon will be under way. When I arrive later that morning, I watch my best girlfriend from the doorway as she shoots free throws too hard, slamming the ball off the backboard and rim, missing on purpose so she can chase down the ball and lay it up.

Webster's defines this move, normally done with two people, as the give-and-go, "a play in which a player passes to a teammate and immediately cuts toward the net or goal to receive a return pass." I am the usual passer. In my absence, she's performing a sort of singular give-and-go.

Her dark blond hair is cut short. She will have, then and always, wide shoulders and sharp cheekbones and such explosive stop-and-go power.

Before we lose her, she will run track in the Junior Olympics.

Her times will be close to qualifying her for the regular Olympics. Before we lose her, she will start with drinking and graduate to pills and return to drinking. Before we lose her, she will travel the world playing for the American Basketball League. Before we lose her, she will be the one I tell about my father, about what goes on inside our house. Before we lose her, she will be part and parcel of how I leave this place, and I will be complicit in how she does not. Before we lose her, I will be one of the first to take her to a party, to hand her a glass.

What does it mean to be unified, collective? What does it mean to remove yourself from a trinity, a family, a friendship? What does it mean to memorialize the dead? What does it mean to be present for the living?

When my best girlfriend and I are young, I ride my bicycle beside her on her training runs. I run and compete, too, sometimes in the same races, but this is how fast she is: I need the bicycle. We talk as we move, and the jokes she likes best are wordplay jokes. We trade them and laugh and keep pace up the hills and fly down. We trade them in the gym as she shoots and I rebound, and we start again.

My whole life this will be what I want from friendship, from love: movement in sync with language, language in sync with movement and laughter. My whole life I will want these pieces unified, together, a trinity most holy in its ordinary magic.

II.

According to Webster's, the word *shooter*, first used in the thirteenth century, is defined as "one that shoots, such as a: a person who fires a missile-discharging device (such as a rifle or bow), b:

the person who is shooting or whose turn it is to shoot, c: Photographer."

The first time someone shoots me, she's aiming at a frog. My best girlfriend and I are under a bridge, wading our way around a creek after school. We're right around twelve years old, and the day we shoot the frog, I am wearing new brown suede loafers that I have entirely forgotten, despite their soft presence on my feet.

We have another friend along, and we splash and talk and take turns with the BB gun. My best girlfriend unsurprisingly is the best shot, and I unsurprisingly am the worst.

When the BB ricochets off a creek rock near the frog, it finds its spot in the flesh above my left ankle. The frog executes a jump-dive move that frees it from our sight. We'd all been following it and now are following the BB's trajectory to its spot above my anklebone. It doesn't hurt that much, and I answer, "It's fine" and "Really" to the chorus of "I'm so sorry" and "Damn frog."

We are all in the back of our minds thinking that we shouldn't be shooting at frogs anyway. I, in particular, have been thinking this. I've been taught by my father, my uncles, my grandmother that you only shoot what you're going to eat. None of us has any intention of eating this frog—though I've eaten frog legs before that my cousins have shot.

I could not bring home a frog we'd shot and present it to my mother without explaining we were out shooting by ourselves. At twelve, I was still somewhat under my sister's supervision, at least technically, and I also did not want to drag her into the trouble. Even though it was only a BB gun, I would be grounded for weeks, maybe even from practice.

According to Webster's, the second definition of *shooter* is "something that is used in shooting: such as a: a marble shot from the hand" or "b: REVOLVER—usually used in combination // six-*shooter*."

Though marbles themselves have an earlier history among the pre-Columbians and in ancient Egypt, Rome, and Crete, marbles began as a sport in Germany. Nuremberg town officials are on record as limiting the playing of marbles in 1503, well after *shooter* came into the lexicon. So there were shooters in Nuremberg in early days.

In North America, people generally trace the origin of basketball to Canadian James Naismith's childhood game "duck on a rock." Naismith grew up to be credited for founding basketball, for making its rules, inspired by the childhood game, which involved players trying to knock a large stone off a tree stump. Naismith worked at a YMCA in 1891 where he perfected his rulebook before taking it to the University of Kansas. So perhaps the first North American basketball shooters began in Naismith's gym.

If all of the Americas are included, though, the shooters begin with Mayan players of pok-ta-pok or pokolpok. The game featured players, two hoops, and a five-pound rubber ball. The winners sometimes lost their heads as sacrifice.

Walking home from the creek, my suede loafers soaked and beginning to chafe, I'm not thinking of winning or even of shooting or getting shot. I'm thinking of nothing other than making it home before my mother. But it begins to rain and as I begin to hurry, a car honks its horn, and I see my mother has pulled our car alongside me.

She's picked up my baby brother from the sitter's, and I think his presence in the back might save me. But she swings open the passenger side door in the front, and so I climb in.

At the start of the day, the suede loafers had held a color somewhere between tan and brown, a rich color with some red to it. They were lovely, and they fit my feet, and they held a new suede smell, along with what I remember best—the soft nap, how I could not stop reaching down to touch it.

My hands on the door handle are cold.

"Those are new shoes," my mother says. "You're grounded."

But she does not mention practice.

That night, late, after dinner, after everyone's in bed, my ankle throbs like it's gained its own heartbeat. My bedroom has its own connecting door to the bathroom, but it's a squeaking door. I open it and close it behind me with exceptional care. In the bathroom, I use the fingernail scissors to dig the BB from under my skin, a procedure that is surprisingly uncomplicated. I cover the hole with rubbing alcohol. Then after the bleeding slows, I lay two Band-Aids crossways like X marks the spot.

My mother's last words to me before bed had been: "What were you thinking?"

I tuck myself back into bed, my heartbeat moved back to my actual heart. I'm thinking no one's said anything about practice. I'm thinking, This is not much different than a splinter.

III.

In high school, with other friends, my best girlfriend and I both start drinking like it's at least a part-time job. At Monday practice, sometimes the beer smell overwhelms the air as we sweat out the weekend. But for her, the weekend bleeds into the rest of the week. She comes to school in the mornings sometimes already a little drunk. After school, practice then includes a hangover.

One crisp fall night, during halftime of a football game, we girls take the field for a game of flag football. My best girlfriend and a few others have been drinking throughout the day. Even so, there, under the bright lights, she's faster than any of the boys were during the actual game.

In the eighth grade, my best girlfriend had tried out for the football team, was faster and stronger than the boys, was not allowed to play. Now we are on the field for fifteen minutes, and she scores three touchdowns. I block for her on two of them by grabbing the ankles of other girls and pulling them toward the ground.

On the flag football field, that night, she is all motion, all shoulders and churning legs, turning sharp. That night, on the field, she is the one in control of everything.

IV.

More than twenty years later, we'll be in a church, not our own, in the back pew, solid oak, and I'll be hanging on to it with both hands to correct my vertigo. I'll have driven more than fourteen hours to be here, in my hometown, to sit next to my mother, to memorialize my best girlfriend who has overdosed this winter on pills washed down with wine.

My high school classmates will be at the bar on Main Street having a pre-funeral drink. "Can you imagine?" my mother will say, and "This is not a class reunion," and "What are they thinking?"

I'm thinking about my father, how he is at a gun show in Des Moines. I'm thinking I'm grateful the family has chosen this larger, less familiar church. I'm grateful we're not in my child-hood church kitty-corner from the elementary school, where the gym once was. Instead of tearing down the school, a few years ago, the town burned it as part of a firefighting exercise. The lot now holds a Dollar General. This is rural America. This is where I'm from: a place that burns down its elementary school, asbestos and all; a place that memorializes an overdosed friend by pre-gaming her funeral.

Our funeral attire instructions include a note about wearing our team colors, our football jerseys, to honor how our friend was a Denver Broncos fan. I'm wearing a black dress at the funeral, am sober yet still dizzy, am home yet so very far out of place.

The return began in the rain, which persisted, state upon state, and it ends winding on Highway 71 past the once-levitated house, which each year sinks and slumps further into its frame.

In the longest stretch of rain, the end seemingly never coming, I stop over for the night at a hotel. The night before my best girlfriend's funeral, the Oklahoma City Thunder played the Pistons. Russell Westbrook triple-doubled, tying LeBron James's record. Though most Americans seem to prefer Kevin Durant with his long, loose limbs and beautiful jump shot, I have long been following Westbrook. He is all compact rage, all wide-shouldered motion. His body, in this, our America, is deemed less acceptable—the rage, the power, the sneer—the complete absence of apology. And I love him for all of it.

At the hotel, I prop myself up with all the room's pillows and watch the highlights—Westbrook's rebounding like gravity is myth only. I am sorry to have missed the game. I am sorry to be making this drive. I am sorry for how many years have passed since I heard my best girlfriend's voice, her laughter, for how many years there will be now without.

I am sorry our last interaction was so stupid and sad. On

social media, she'd posted a comment on an article I shared about violence against Indigenous women. She wrote: "You know, I'm part Kiowa." And I liked it, then unliked it, then liked it again. Of course, I knew she was Kiowa. Of course, I objected to the language, the "part." Which part? The back of the left knee? The curve of the right ankle? The crook of an elbow? How many ways do we carve ourselves up and portion out our parts, our bodies for other people's comfort? How can a body such as hers—once all flight, all power and motion—be reduced to the language of the partial?

Westbrook will go on this season to surpass LeBron and everyone else. He'll take the triple-double record from Oscar Robertson with a last-second three-point shot against the Denver Nuggets. The shot is from thirty-six feet. The farthest curve of the three-point line is set at just under twenty-four feet. So Westbrook shoots from more than twelve feet past the line. I don't miss this game. His face, as soon as he releases the shot: all sneer and focus that turns to roar and smile. But the sneer comes before the shot hits the net. He knows its trajectory. He knows who he is and what he's done.

Khelcey Barrs was Westbrook's childhood best friend, and Barrs died suddenly at sixteen of an enlarged heart. Westbrook was only fifteen years old. They were at practice. They spent every day together, walking to school, to practice, back.

Of the two, Westbrook then had the smaller frame and thus the smaller prospects. He grew five inches between junior and senior year. He transformed; he levitated. On Westbrook's levitating feet, on his shoes, each night, each game, he memorializes his friend with his initials.

Who I am is someone working toward a memorial. Who I am is sorry for how this working includes my shame and my lack, how I let the parsing of language get in the way of friendship. My childhood best girlfriend was Kiowa, and I am Métis, and we grew up together in a mostly white town, and I never came back, and she was the best of us, and she came back this season for good.

V.

In the last pew, my mother is talking about our childhood church, about my best girlfriend and others from our Sunday School class who've died, how many have died and so young, and "You girls," she keeps saying, "you girls are supposed to outlive us," and then she dabs at her eyes with her wrinkled Kleenex.

"You sang at her wedding," my mother says.

"No," I say, laughing a little.

"You did," she says.

"No," I say again, not laughing.

"'Wind Beneath My Wings,'" she says.

"God," I say, "I hate that song."

"Well, you sang it," she says. She sighs like what is wrong with me, why am I so difficult, so I stop talking and start trying to remember.

The teenage years are like this—full of gaps—some of which have developed into chasms. Webster's first defines *dissociation* as "the process by which a chemical combination breaks up into simpler constituents." It asks if I want to see *dissociant* in medical. I do.

When I click on it, though, I'm sent to *mutant*, so I try again, to be sent to *mutant* again, and a third try does not offer different results. Webster's medical defines *mutant* as "a mutant individual."

This is my first Webster's failure, my first Webster's humiliation.

My associative brain, my interest in Webster's, is caused, in part, by dissociation from childhood trauma, which perhaps makes me a dissociant, which perhaps makes me a mutant, or so says Webster's.

In any of these cases, my best girlfriend knew the how and the why of the dissociation. She offered sleepovers and laughter, bike rides up steep hills, and the steady rhythm of the ball against the backboard and into my hands, on repeat. She offered "I'm sorry" if I was hurting, "Damn frog" if we both needed to laugh.

Her timing, as in ball, as in shooting, was precise. I left those precise rhythms when the cost of homecoming became too great, when the cost of time in my father's presence became too great. I saved parts of myself that I believed then and now to be necessary parts, and I left behind both necessary parts and necessary people. This leaving, too, is a carving.

I spend my best girlfriend's funeral gripping the solid oak of the pew and remembering her wedding day. I have to focus, to replay that time like movie stills, like Polaroids ready for the sorting. The memory comes as the funeral unfolds.

In our childhood church basement, I help my friend into her white pumps. Her feet are swollen because she's pregnant, and I'm saying, "You could wear your high-tops instead." I'm saying, "We can leave right now. My car is parked by the playground." I'm saying, "You don't have to do this."

Upstairs, I sing "Wind Beneath My Wings." I touch my hands to my collarbone like I do when I'm nervous and try to stop doing it and do it again. These are the hands that will hold her baby boy the first time a nurse needs to draw his blood. These are the hands that touch his today, that reach around his shoulders to say "I'm sorry." He's so tall and handsome, with his mother's cheekbones and broad shoulders. These are the hands that put one of the first drinks into his mother's hands.

After the funeral, I stop my remembering and shift into the now. My mother drives home past the lot that once held the elementary school and gym, and I go to the bar with my classmates. I hold a glass in my hands.

Webster's third definition of *shooter* is: "a shot of hard liquor (such as whiskey or tequila) often diluted with something (such as soda), *also:* a bit of food (such as a raw oyster) served in a shot glass."

I have drunk down half my glass. Other people are continuing on to shots, but I have made all the small talk I know how. I am inching my way toward the door when I see my best girlfriend's sister waving in my direction. She is having a hard time standing. She is the one who found my best girlfriend, who called for help, who got the call when it came—that my best girlfriend, that her sister, died in the helicopter, in the Life Flight, midair, in motion.

When the sister's hands reach for mine, I am wanting only to be anywhere but here. I am wishing for the thud and fall of feet on a trail, the thud and fall of a ball on the hardwood. She puts her hands atop mine, looks into my face, and says, "I remember you," and I say, "I'm sorry—I'm so sorry." I stand there a little while longer, her weight resting on mine, her hands resting on mine. We're less than a half mile from the highway, from the trucks and their Jake brakes, and I have the impulse to do what I've practiced my whole life—to get in my car and go. But her hands are on mine, her weight is on mine, and so I hold her like that, and I keep back my sorrys, my damn all the frogs. I hold it and I hold it, and I don't let go.

FIVE

Carry

I.

In the memorial garden, my colleague Michael Heffernan bends to tend some short, once-green plants that, to my untrained eyes, remain mysterious. He is quiet and pours the water with care. He is so quiet. In this, the first week of classes, my first on this campus, I don't yet know Michael well, but already I know *quiet* to be, for him, the most unnatural of states.

The moment before, I was sitting in my office near his in our building, Kimpel Hall, and he was trying to exit the door next to my office, his hands filled with water glasses. I said, "Thirsty?" And he said, "Do you know about the garden?"

When I shook my head, he nodded toward the window, to a grassy patch, and I had work to do, new names to memorize, grading to finish already. Another colleague had just been in my office too, talking about a female graduate student, describing her as "a bag of snakes." At first, I'd misunderstood. "She *has* a bag of snakes?" I said. "In the building?"

On the topic of snakes, I'm surprisingly neutral. But if this student kept her snakes, say, in her office down the hall, I felt I perhaps should be prepared.

"No, no," said the colleague, "she *is* a bag of snakes." When I presented to him my blank-faced silence, he waved his hands around in my doorway as if clearing a swarm of bees and took himself back down the hall. I understood him fine, of course. He was trying to tell me the student is difficult, is trouble, is to be avoided. But the phrase "bag of snakes" and his casual delivery made me want to defend her. I thought, if this is how her faculty are, how brave she must be to have brought with her only one bag of snakes. I thought, She needs to go home on the weekend and collect the other three bags.

So when Michael holds out his water glasses, says "garden," I'm still thinking snakes and more snakes, and now I'm thinking Arkansas, Bible Belt, strangeness, and I don't want to follow. I don't. But Michael is more than seventy years old, and how will he open the door with glasses of water in both hands? So I take one of the glasses; I follow.

In the garden, after the careful tending of the plants, Michael tells me about his friend, John Locke, who was killed in our building, on this campus, the University of Arkansas, on the first day of classes in the fall of 2000. The memorial garden, like me, is new to campus in the fall of 2010.

After the tending, Michael and I sit on a concrete bench, the August sun heating the concrete, the concrete heating the backs of my legs. He tells me about his friend's life, as a father, as a professor of comparative literature for thirty-three years, as a teller of elaborate jokes, as a mentor.

"He could listen," Michael says. "He heard you."

Michael's eyes are wet behind his glasses, and we sit across from the memorial grass, the memorial koi pond, the small plaque. We sit like that, the sun on our heads, the concrete warming my legs, until Michael nods and pats me on the arm, and we head back inside, each of us carrying a water glass emptied.

After, I learn more details: a graduate student, recently expelled from the program, shot John Locke in his office, and then, a few minutes later, shot and killed himself. In the faculty vote on the student's expulsion, John Locke had been the only person to abstain, the student's only supporter. John Locke's office was Kimpel 231, and my new office down the hall is Kimpel 221.

This year, in spring 2018, in the first week of classes, according to a new law, anyone who's licensed can come to Kimpel Hall carrying a handgun, to my office, Kimpel 221, carrying a handgun, to my classroom carrying a handgun. The only stipulation is the license and the gun's concealment—in a purse or backpack, tucked under or over a shoulder, or in a holster under one's campus logo T-shirt. Similar laws exist in nine other states as well, affecting thousands of campuses, hundreds of thousands of students, faculty, and staff.

But on this, the campus that is supposed to be mine, I'm supposed to be concerned with the mine, with the now. As Americans, we're all supposed to be concerned with the now over the past, with the mine over the ours. So to consider the mine, the now, anyone with a license now can carry his gun and sit to warm himself on this concrete bench. Anyone with a license can look out, with his hand on his handgun, and enjoy the memorial garden.

II.

Most of the great state of Arkansas was once Quapaw land, but the northwestern corner where I reside—including the town, Fayetteville, and the university campus—was Osage territory, not formally ceded until 1818. This particular patch of territory had been long contested, first between the Osage and Quapaw and then between the Osage and Cherokee. So the earning of it had been hard fought, hard won. The eventual ceding of this territory to the United States government, of course, happened at the sharp point of the bayonet or down the wide barrel of the earliest muskets and long guns, known as Northwest guns, Mackinaws, fusils or fusees or Hudson's Bay fukes.

The southern border of this space we call campus, the University of Arkansas campus, is now called Martin Luther King Jr. Boulevard, but was once part of the route best known as the Trail of Tears.

From the Library of Congress to Wikipedia, through the history books in between, the language describing Removal is a study in power dynamics.

In 1830, President Andrew Jackson signed the Indian Removal Act and began the Era of Removal of the five southeastern tribes from their homelands to reservation land in Oklahoma.
The Choctaw were removed in 1831.
The Seminole were removed in 1832.
The Creek were removed in 1834.
The Chickasaw were removed in 1837.
The Cherokee were removed in 1838.

Note, in this, the language of the official record, how Jackson is the only one assigned an action, albeit a polite action: he signs; he begins. Note how passive is the language of Removal: "were removed," "were removed," "were removed." Note the absence of guns from this official record, official narrative. There is no mention, for example, of the seven thousand United States soldiers who arrived in Cherokee territory in 1838, who forced the removal of thousands of Cherokee people. There is no mention of how sharp the points of the soldiers' bayonets.

According to Webster's, the first known use of the word *campus* occurs in 1774. Definitions include:

1: the grounds and buildings of a university, college, or school
2: a university, college, or school viewed as an academic, social, or spiritual entity
3: grounds that resemble a campus // hospital *campus* // a landscaped corporate *campus*

As of 2020, there are ten states that allow guns on school campuses: Arkansas, Colorado, Georgia, Idaho, Kansas, Mississippi, Oregon, Texas, Utah, and Wisconsin. Though there are competing narratives about motive and means and though Utah's campus carry act was passed in 2004, all agree the campus carry movement really began after the 2007 shootings at Virginia Tech. In little more than a decade, the movement grew from one state, Utah, to ten, at roughly the rate or speed of one state added per year.

Though the University of Wyoming wouldn't open its doors until 1886, the first remains of the dinosaur known as *Camptosaurus* were found in Wyoming in fall 1879. The *Camptosaurus* is a plant-eating, beaked dinosaur of the Late Jurassic period, of western North America and possibly Europe. The name means "flexible lizard" or "flexible-backed lizard." Scientists believe a full-grown *Camptosaurus* could move at roughly the rate or speed of fifteen miles per hour.

To study a familiar moment in time: a woman tells someone how she met her husband through a mutual friend, at a restaurant, and that someone smiles politely. If the same woman tells that same someone how she met her husband while they were students together on a campus, the same someone smiles and sighs and says, "Oh, how nice." Their children will be encouraged to attend this campus, to be that charmed presence universities call legacy. Their children and their children's children and so on. Oh, how nice. To study the tangled history of this space considered campus is to study the sigh, the smile, the "Oh, how nice." To study the tangled, contested history of this space considered campus is to enter into a deep conversation about why some spaces are considered hallowed when they are, in fact, stolen.

III.

I'm teaching in Pittsburgh at Chatham College in 2007, at my first tenure-track job, when a college senior at Virginia Tech, an English major, brings his guns to campus and begins shooting. My friend Mimi is an MFA student, a teaching assistant at Virginia Tech. Mimi and I have been friends for years; I am the godmother of her teenage son, Daniel.

This year, I've become a parent myself. I have a newborn daughter. That morning, as the news blares from the living room television, I walk circles around my dining room table because this is a thing my daughter likes. The room holds stained-glass windows—red-, green-, and gold-patterned—and my daughter likes to follow the patterns they make on the hardwood floor, the wall, the table. So I walk and rock her, and she follows the patterns, and in between, I dial Mimi's number and I dial and I dial. I get busy signals, I get her cheerful voice, recorded, I get more busy, more signal.

It is late afternoon when I hear her voice, when I learn that Mimi has been in lockdown one building over from Norris Hall, the main site of the shooting. It is late afternoon when I learn she has spent her morning hearing shots, instructing her students not in the art of narrative forms, but in how to get down and stay down, in how to remain so very quiet.

In Pittsburgh, in the later afternoon, in my rental house, the light through the stained glass casts lovely, colorful shadows onto the hardwood. It is time to go to work, so I hand my daughter off to her father and leave the light to them.

Pittsburgh lies about three hundred miles north of Blacksburg, of Virginia Tech, by car. If the crow is flying, the distance is shorter and includes the hills known as the Allegheny Mountains and the Monongahela National Forest, which were long home to the Shawnee and to the Cherokee before Removal.

I don't drive to Blacksburg, though this is my impulse. Instead, I drive across Pittsburgh, its rivers and bridges, its hills and hollows, to the campus I'm supposed to consider mine.

To my graduate fiction class that night, I bring my wrecked face, my hair caked with baby spit, and my talk on the art of narrative forms. A student, Amy Fair, sits among the others in the group. Teachers are not supposed to have favorites, but in this private school space, on this private school campus, I do. Amy is from West Virginia, is tattooed, and swears like it's as necessary as breathing. She's not from money, either, or even from the middle class, and therefore she is as rare a creature on this campus as would be a *Camptosaurus*. She has brought the right amount of snakes.

Back in the fall semester, at the end of my pregnancy, when I had to miss a few classes to stay home and lie on my left side, Amy organized and co-led one workshop in my absence. Already, after one prior bed-rest episode, some students were complaining about my absence. Why, they wondered to the program administrator, could I not work right up until my due date? Why was I not there for them?

When I asked Amy to sub for me on what would be my second absence, she said, "Some of these bitches are going to hate that. Do you care?" "No," I said. "I trust you." "Good," she said, "perfect. Fuck those complaining bitches, anyway." Both our faces stretched wide a second before we looked away, before we examined with care the tops of our shoes.

Eight years later, in fall 2015, during the first week of that quarter's classes, when a student brings his guns to Umpqua Community College in Oregon, Amy is teaching an English class in that building, in Snyder Hall. She has just returned from a sabbatical. She is working on a book about the history of tattooed women.

Roseburg, Oregon, and the surrounding area are and were the territory of the Cow Creek Band of the Umpqua tribe, whose tribal headquarters are in Roseburg. The one hundred acres of the college campus is land taken from the Umpqua.

That fall day, 2015, the shooting begins in the room next door to Amy's classroom. One of her students in the front row is an Army veteran, Chris Mintz, who blocks the shared door between the classrooms with his body. Amy leads students, quiet, so quiet, out of Snyder Hall in one direction. Chris leads students out the other way, each of them knocking on doors along the way, quiet, so quiet, with their *get down*s, with their *follow me*s.

After, Chris is rightly valorized, and Amy happily ignored, because she tells all the reporters to go fuck themselves.

Which is to say, each of them lives, though Chris Mintz is shot five times helping evacuate fellow students from the campus library, and Amy takes a leave of absence to heal from post-traumatic stress. Each of them lives, but this is not a happy ending. There is no way to gerrymander this narrative into the frame of the simple, the jingoistic, the most American of our narratives.

IV.

My first campus is the University of South Dakota in Vermillion. Much of the Great Plains, including South Dakota, was and is Lakota, Dakota, and Nakota land. This corner of South Dakota, in particular, was Yankton Sioux or Dakota land. This word *vermillion* in Lakota means "the place where the red clay is gathered." All of which is to say, this campus sits on their land.

Before I left my no-stoplight hometown in rural Iowa for this campus, my sister had left for another, larger campus. When she went, she forgot her bag of snakes at home, or maybe she left them for me, knowing I would have a need. She didn't stay at school more than a semester. When it was my turn, the snakes went along, and I still was unprepared, but I stayed.

My first college roommate took one look at my father and then started working the phrase "Indians get" into every conversation, every corner of our room. "Indians get free computers." "Indians get free school." "Indians get all the scholarships." "You would know this," she said, "if you lived West River."

COLLECTED WORKS

Store hours:
Mon - Sat 8:00AM to 8:00PM
Sundays 8:00AM to 6:00PM
202 Galisteo Street, Santa Fe, NM 87501
(505) 988-4226

57092 Reg 1 9:31 am 10/13/20
REPRINTED RECEIPT

S CARRY	1 @	27.00	27.00
SUBTOTAL			27.00
SALES TAX - 8.4375%			2.28
TOTAL			29.28
~~CASH~~ PAYMENT			29.28

WEB

Thank you for shopping at
Collected Works Bookstore
Returns for Store Credit Only
with Receipt & within 30 days of sale
Sorry, NO cash refunds...

In South Dakota parlance, West River means west of the Missouri River, which divides the state, east/west, with most of the reservation lands on the western side. She is playing both sides—if I'm Indian, I'm a taker. If I'm not Indian, I should know the Indians are the takers. She is here to give me an education. I give her my blank face. I give her more and more time in the room without me. I give her no answers.

On this, my first campus, on my first visit to my faculty advisor to choose my classes, the woman is behind schedule, so I wait in the hall while student after student files into her office. Sometimes this professor flits by, all scarves and long, flowing skirts, on her way to fetch more coffee. The students remain in her office.

When my turn comes and I go in to schedule my classes, creative writing and Native literature, in which I'm planning to major, the professor comes back to her office with her full cup, and says in a voice not quiet—"Get out." She recovers herself and says, "I need a minute. Please wait in the hall."

I've been waiting in the hall, and I go back there. From inside the office, there are the sounds of shuffling and rifling.

When the door reopens and she waves me back in, her purse has been moved to the other side of her desk.

"I'm sorry," she says, by way of explanation, "but things have been taken lately from people's offices."

I sit through my advising session very carefully, my file in front of her, which includes my demographics. I think of my friend from Pine Ridge who's scheduled to come to this office the next day, and if this is how I'm treated with my light skin and blue eyes, how is it going to be for her? I'm thinking how I'll tell her the story—the scarves, the skirts, the crazy eyes. I'm thinking that we'll laugh, and so I sit in the chair but remain unadvised.

The next semester, I get a new roommate and a new advisor,

and the roommate is fine, and the second advisor, instead of proffering advice, offers his hand on my knee, his traveling hand, and I leave the building again unadvised and go back to my room to tend my snakes.

V.

I'm attending this campus on a scholarship, and my scholarship advisor is a woman who swears and paces, and I love her and fear her in equal measure until the day she trusts me with the story of her son, a grown man, accused of sexual assault in Nebraska. He has to go to court, she says. It's such bullshit. He wouldn't do that.

At a party, a half block off campus, this man, the son of my advisor, drinks and drinks. One night, just before this conversation, I'm there, drinking and drinking. The house belongs to a good friend who falls asleep snoring, and this man—we'll call him Doug—chases me around and around the futon couch like we're playing some terrible game of duck-duck-goose. There are no snakes present, no *Camptosaurus*, and my friend is asleep, is snoring from his recliner, and where have all the other people gone?

The way I get away from Doug is because I'm small. The futon has a large wooden frame, and there are meant to be soft, comfortable pillows on the back, but they are absent, and I make use of their absence. Which is to say, I've lost the game of duck-duck-goose. I'm on the futon with Doug, and I only get to leave because the pillows are missing, and I wiggle out the gap and shake awake my friend, who walks me home, to my apartment just off this place considered campus. My snakes are waiting, and I think perhaps I will, this day forward, carry them with me in that space we call *always*.

The next week, I learn Doug will be acquitted on all charges in Nebraska. The next week, one of my friends tells me he raped her at another party. I don't tell my advisor: she is in charge of my scholarship; she is happy her son is acquitted. Later that year when he is going through his twelve steps, Doug follows me around town, apologizing. At the bookstore: apology. At the bar: apology. At the diner: apology.

I tell him to move on to his next step without my forgiveness. I tell him I work the police beat now, and I mention the statute of limitations, and he grows quiet, so quiet, and he moves on to the next step or does not, but he stops enacting the act we call *apology*.

This story is an ordinary, everyday-violence story from a space considered campus. It is hard to see this space as hallowed when it is filled with so much ordinary, everyday violence. It is hard to see this space as hallowed when it has been filled since the start with such ordinary, everyday violence. It is hard to see this space, this campus, as mine when it so clearly is not, when it so clearly never was. It is hard not to ask the question: Who benefits from having an armed presence on a place considered campus? It is hard not to answer it with the negative, with the absence: not the girls who become women while they tend their snakes.

They are waiting in the campus halls for someone to offer advice. They are waiting still.

SIX

Route

I.

At the Hill Top Motel, a man with a tidy mustache walks me down the narrow hall, pausing at the door to Room 119. "That's the Tim McVeigh Room," he says. "Sure you don't want to switch?"

The placard on the door had already alerted me to the room's special status. I assure the man, who's co-owner of the hotel, that my room will be fine. Dennis Schroeder has a dark tan, light eyes, and sandy brown hair. His mustache is trimmed tight, his gray T-shirt stretched over his belly, which angles downward, toward his knee-high dress socks and new tennis shoes.

"That McVeigh?" Schroeder says, nodding to the placard and pausing for dramatic effect. "He plotted the whole thing right here." He wiggles his fingers and the keys to my actual room, which I am hoping lies farther down the hall. He has the key to my room in one hand, has insisted on carrying my small suitcase in the other.

It's summer 1996, when room keys still sometimes come attached to key rings, octagonal-shaped or oval, discreet black or neon plastic. It's one year after the Oklahoma City bombing, of which Timothy McVeigh was convicted and for which he was later put to death. I'm in Kingman, Arizona, because I've left Vermillion and the University of South Dakota, having just finished my master's degree. I'm to teach composition, public speaking, creative writing, and whatever else anyone might need at Mohave Community College here in Kingman. I know no one here. I'm twenty-five years old. It's my first real, professional job.

My key ring is the shade of green known as Kelly. Webster's says we've been calling this color Kelly green since 1927, that the term stems from the color's association with Ireland, where Kelly is a common surname.

I know about the Oklahoma City bombing, of course, but I somehow had missed Kingman's connection to McVeigh. During the two years prior, I'd spent little time watching television, had been living in South Dakota and researching another crime, the murder of a Lakota man, Clifford Hirocke, outside Vermillion at a former scout camp called Camp Happiness. For my master's thesis project, I wrote a documentary play about Cliff's death, and then, soon after, just a few weeks after the bombing, I left America for Wales, where I worked waiting tables for almost a year, where I missed most American news and was happier for it.

But most of America in this time had been following the coverage of the bombing and subsequent reporting on Tim McVeigh and his partner in crime, Terry Nichols, as well as his friend-turned-informant Michael Fortier. On April 19, 1995, little more than a year before I arrived in Kingman, McVeigh pulled his rented Ryder truck in front of the Alfred P. Murrah Federal Building in downtown Oklahoma City and detonated the bomb. It killed 168 people, including 19 children, and more than 500 people were injured.

Before 9/11, it was counted in the official record as the worst domestic act of terrorism in our country's history. You don't have to leave the state of Oklahoma to find other examples, though—the Greenwood Massacre on what was called Black Wall Street in nearby Tulsa, in which an estimated 100–300 Black men, women, and children were murdered and up to 800 injured in 1921, or the 8,700–17,000 Choctaw, Creek, Chickasaw, Cherokee, and Seminole people who died during the Removal Era.

The placard's gold stars are set around McVeigh's name like it's a miniature Hollywood Walk of Fame, right here, just for me, or for any other traveler who's tired and has stopped for the night. Dennis Schroeder still talks and talks, gesturing over-large for such a narrow hall, asking me again if I'm sure I don't want to switch rooms, saying, "It's a rare opportunity. It's usually occupied." Just a few years before, in 1990, McVeigh had been in the Army, part of our occupying force against Iraq in Operation Desert Storm. Nichols, Fortier, and McVeigh met in basic training in the Army.

For his actions in combat in Operation Desert Storm, McVeigh earned a Bronze Star, with a V-for-valor device on the ribbon, and I wonder what that means now, what any of it means. I wonder what sort of place it is in which I've landed.

Just off Route 66, as the song will tell you, and just off I-40, Kingman is the sort of place where people stop for a night and then drive, drive, drive. I'm not people, though. I've taken a job here, my very first professional full-time job teaching. I'm staying.

When I finally enter it, my room holds a floral polyester bedspread and cinder-block walls with off-white paint. A vintage dining table sits in the corner, and I set my bag down on it. It holds the sort of finish on which a glass won't leave a ring, Formica, maybe, but with a wood look, a simulation.

I listen at the door until Schroeder's footsteps recede. He's not creepy, exactly, but I'm about to go outside to my truck, to bring in my husky, Lucy, who is protective, who's been waiting.

In the parking lot, I'm relieved to see the truck's still running. I left it locked but turned on for the air-conditioning because June in Kingman is too hot already to behave otherwise. Beyond the parking lot and swimming pool, the view is beautiful in an O'Keeffe painting sort of way. Tall cliff faces in tans and deeper browns hold dots of dark and silver green, cactus and trees I will later learn to name: cholla called buckhorn and teddy bear and Christmas, hedgehog and barrel cactus, Manzanita and Joshua trees, prickly pear of all sorts.

The sky holds only sharp blue, no clouds, over the Cerbat Mountains in the distance. The wind picks up, begins the dust swirl with which I will become so familiar, and Lucy and I hurry into the Hill Top, past the McVeigh Room, to ours. I sleep a deep traveler's sleep, and Lucy patrols in front of the door, silent as huskies are prone to be when on watch, alert, though, prepared.

II.

My first morning in Kingman, I leave the Hill Top to meet Peggy Bivins, my prospective landlady. She's wearing slippers and a floral housedress or muumuu covered in enormous pink and green flowers. She waves cheerfully as she walks across the street from her family's home to the white clapboard house I hope to rent from her and her husband.

She pets Lucy, ruffles the dark fur around her collar, and Lucy swings her tail in apparent joy. I start my job the next day. I'm hoping this will work. I'm extra chatty with Peggy, telling her about my stay at the Hill Top, the McVeigh Room, the plaque.

"We rented to them, too," she says. "Those boys."

"This house?" I say.

We're not through the threshold yet, but now I'm wondering what lies beyond the white clapboard façade, the windows rimmed in ordinary, everyday shutters. Peggy is at the front door, framed by those red shutters, which now seem either jaunty or murderous.

"This house?" I say again.

I'm not so much considering if I can live in a house where such a thing has been plotted, but how. All my possessions are either in storage in my mother's attic or in the truck that sits in the driveway as if it's already home.

She turns and squints at me. "No," she says, "the other one."

"Oh," I say. "So you knew him?"

"He paid his rent on time," she says. "Didn't give us any trouble."

I nod, but I do not manage a smile.

"No trouble," she says, looking me up and down. "No trouble of any kind."

Later, I'll find it's easy to verify McVeigh stayed at the Hill Top for four days right before the bombing; his motel registration card is entered into evidence during his trial. It's less easy to verify he or Fortier ever were tenants of my landlords, the

Bivinses, though I check and work to cross-check references and addresses. They did own multiple rental houses, so it's plausible Fortier, in particular, may have lived in one at one time, or even McVeigh, perhaps. But in the time leading up to the bombing, Fortier and his wife and McVeigh all lived together in the Fortiers' trailer.

It's difficult to imagine anyone would fabricate such a fact only to dismiss its sensational value, only to render the fact and the men so ordinary, so everyday. Over time, I'll come to associate this trait with the place—an understated delivery of a startling circumstance, an underplaying of the extraordinary and the strange.

Since then, we've seen a resurgence of this sort of affect, this sort of underplaying of extraordinary violence. The president calls tiki-torch-wielding men in Charlottesville "very fine people," even as Heather Heyer dies. At Standing Rock, hired security shoot rubber bullets into a peaceful crowd, blinding a woman. In an Arizona hotel, a police officer shoots to death a man while he's prone, while he's already facedown on the ground. In Minneapolis, police officer Derek Chauvin kneels on the neck of George Floyd for eight minutes and forty-six seconds, and Floyd dies, there on the ground, after asking repeatedly for his mother.

That day, back in the nineties, I've been in Kingman less than twenty-four hours. I sign the lease. I unpack my one set of sheets, my books, my handful of dishes. I walk Lucy along neighborhood streets rimmed with stone and ranch-style houses. I work to imagine a life for us here. At bedtime, I lock the front and back doors and check them again and stop myself from checking a third time.

III.

Mohave Community College, where I work in Kingman, opened in 1971. The land for the campus, the 160 acres that sit just outside town, was donated by John Leonard and Grace Neal. John Leonard Neal was a rancher, married in the 1930s. He was from a prominent local ranching family who owed their fortune and fame, in part, to the time during World War II when, according to author and Route 66 historian Jim Hinckley, "a large swath of the Neal ranch in the Hualapai Valley became one of the largest flexible gunnery schools in the nation with assistance from the Herculean efforts of construction crews pulled from the Davis Dam project on the Colorado River." Hinckley adds, "Listed among the thousands of men trained at the Kingman Army Airfield is Clayton Moore, best known for his role as the Lone Ranger."

Earlier generations of Neals also owned land in the area around the historic springs that were important to the history of the town, near Fort Mohave. The springs were a source for year-round water, important in this high desert region, and were named for Lieutenant Edward Beale, who surveyed the road to connect Fort Mohave with another fort in New Mexico. According to Jim Hinckley, Beale's road expedition also was to serve a secondary purpose, "testing the viability of camel transport for military application in the desert southwest."

I learn about the Neals and Beales straightaway, but it takes longer for anyone to talk about or explain the history of the tribe with the closest reservation, the Hualapai. According to their tribe's website, the name comes from their words for ponderosa pines and for people, meaning "people of the tall pines," and their original territory encompassed around five million acres.

The Hualapai War started in 1865 when their leader Anasa was killed by a white man. The Hualapai retaliated and also closed a nearby trading route to white traders. Raiding and killing and more retaliation followed until the U.S. government sent the cavalry in after killing yet another Hualapai chief. After their surrender, the remaining Hualapai were forced to walk nearly two hundred miles to near Parker, Arizona, to an internment camp called La Paz. The La Paz Trail of Tears, much like the better-known Cherokee Trail of Tears or the Bosque Redondo of the Navajo, is commemorated annually by the Hualapai descendants of those who survived the long walk and the internment and then managed to escape.

Already in my earliest days in Mohave County, I know Kingman to be a place of strange facts and oddities, a place that prepares for war camels and the Lone Ranger alike. Already in my earliest days in town, I know Neal and Beale to be considered important names. Already in my earliest days, I know war and enterprise to be intrinsically linked in the mythos of the place, that my ideas of heroism involve walking those two hundred miles versus riding them on horseback, that my allegiance goes, as is usually so, to those who were not armed.

IV.

In my first semester of my first real, grown-up job, teaching English at Mohave Community College, one night, in composition class, a man—I'll call him Greg—paces the back of the room, sits back down, and then returns to his pacing. He's over fifty or at least looks over fifty. His eyes dart around the room, never landing on any of the rest of us. His tan, weathered skin holds a light sheen that he seems to want to scratch off the sides of his face.

I do not get close enough to smell him, so I can't say for certain whether he's drunk or high or some combination. He has thick-textured salt-and-pepper hair with waves that fan up and out, through which he can't stop running his hands. He can't keep them still.

He might be considered good-looking on a better day. My guess, if I had to say, would be that he's high on meth. A good many people here are.

Since I grew up in a house with a violent, drunken father, I know the voice to use. I know how to say, "That's interesting," and "You should talk more about that once Angela's done," and "I can hear you better from the chair, though. It's closer."

The combination of soothing voice and flattery works for about thirty-five minutes, and the class is three hours long. We don't usually break till the ninety-minute mark, but some of the women's bodies are stiffening. Some look at their shoes; some begin to get that faraway look on their faces, the dissociated look—though I don't know that anyone was calling it that back then.

This class, like many I teach there, is a night class geared primarily toward women aged thirty to fifty-five whose lives have changed through divorce or being fired from their jobs or worse. They're parents or grandparents. They want jobs or better jobs. They do their homework and bring their best selves to class.

At twenty-five years old, I'm often the youngest person in my classroom. Still, they all treat me with dignity and respect. I have not one but two degrees. They're impressed by this— something I've almost never encountered since.

Our classroom is in a modular building, otherwise known as a trailer. This is before cellphones are common, and there's no wall phone either since the trailers are supposed to be temporary.

I call break early. I say I'm hungry and can use a candy bar. I smile at the aggressive student. I make prolonged eye contact with all the women in the class who are paying attention, and together we head straight for the main building, the commons building.

All the women in the class know what to do—they read my eye contact correctly. They get up and head out to break, walking fast and efficient. No one gawks at Greg or speaks with him; no one acts like our early break is in any way irregular.

Mary is working at the front desk at the commons. She's middle-aged and both competent and kind. I like her very much and am grateful to see her.

"Call security," I say, and she does not hesitate. I buy a Snickers and go out in the hall to check for Greg, to check on the other students.

Greg does not return to class when we return from break. The security guard patrols around more than usual and close to our trailer. We continue our class, each of us positioned to keep one eye on the door, but Greg doesn't return that night.

The next day, I learn Greg had enrolled in the class under a false name. A few years back, he'd brought a gun onto campus— he'd made threats. He was not supposed to be there in my class, or in any other class, having been permanently barred from the college.

After, from the administrators to the staff to the students, everyone is kind. Everyone praises my handling of the situation in a quiet way, using humor or their own stories. Everyone is competent. We all go about our business.

If he had come back into our classroom that night, I suppose it would have been considered or labeled a school shooting, but it also would have been for me a workplace shooting. It's my first real workplace, and I feel protective over it, over the people who share the space with me.

I know, though, if Greg had come back with his gun, what likely would have happened also would have been a shooting in a place with connections to one of the worst acts of domestic terrorism, the Oklahoma City bombing. Michael Fortier had taken classes here in the years before, as his friends planned the bombing. And just like with Greg's return to campus, no one had any idea what Fortier knew; no one had any idea what was being planned at his trailer outside town.

Already, I love the people here and the landscape, especially at night when the stars come out on campus and the coyotes call to each other through the desert. Already, I'm learning to be wary of giving away too much of this love, this good feeling, to a place that seems to embrace or, at least, to not wholly shun all these men whose lives partake in both everyday and extraordinary violence.

V.

We're hiking with the dogs, a friend and I, just outside Kingman, on a sunny weekend day. The landscape still is novel to me—the land so flat and wide, broken only by tall rocks and cliff faces, the twisting spines of cholla or long-limbed cottonwood, the bright blue sky the stuff of picture books.

Our path curves left, and we walk along a tall row of rock

facing before we curve further and come upon the men. The rocks till that moment had obscured them from us, us from them.

It's clear they've just finished setting up their targets, have just finished jerking off. One zips his fly, and the other rips a picture from a magazine, a woman with enormous breasts, her legs positioned into a sharp V.

Jack, the bigger and newer of the two dogs, snarls and yanks his leash, and I nod to the man nearest me—the one who's just tucked himself in—making eye contact, before I pull the dogs past.

There isn't another way to exit, except back the way we came, so we keep walking. We talk low to each other, my friend more unnerved than I am, but neither of us surprised. As we walk, our view consists mainly of cholla and prickly pear, the sky shifting from its brightest blue to blue streaked with pink. My friend points out interesting cactus, lizards, and what she says is the tail feather of a roadrunner. We walk also accompanied by the distant sound of the men shooting their guns.

We walk until we're tired, until the gunshots stop. We sit and drink water on a rock, and when we make our way back, Lucy, the smarter dog, the quiet one, has her hackles raised as we near their campsite. But even their camp chairs are gone.

They've left behind only the spent shell casings and bits of target magazine girls.

I come into the desert that day with only the most rudimentary knowledge of its plants and insects, its snakes and storms. I leave having acquired so much knowledge of the flora and fauna. I leave having confirmed so much unwanted knowledge about men.

My time in Kingman, all three years, is spent like this, on deciding. How does a person live a life filled with these sorts of interactions with men like these—in the world, in the wild, in the classroom. I write "men like these," but Kingman also will be the place where I learn to trust wholly my instincts about when "men like these" can be abbreviated to "men."

VI.

I date three men in my three years in Kingman, and two of them are good men, and all are affected by guns and difficult fathers and this place—either a pull to stay or a pull toward fleeing.

The one who's not a good man is also someone I work with, so work now shifts from enjoyment toward apprehension.

To work, James wears a tie and button-down shirt, ironed with care, a pair of wire-framed glasses that need to be tightened. He has a bony yet boyish face and can't stop pushing up his glasses. Still, there's probably something attractive in the bone structure, the high cheekbones or his bright green eyes. He works in the administration building—something to do with technology—and I don't know him even a little bit, have maybe said hello once.

I am almost never attracted to blond men. I don't notice them in crowds, at least not in good ways. When he comes into my office the first time and stands almost at military attention, I wonder if I've broken a computer rule or protocol, or if he's there to fix something I'm not yet aware is broken.

All of which is to say, I'm not interested in him. I can't imagine he's there in the doorway for reasons other than work. Also, looking back, it's possible I'm made uneasy by how he comes into my office and lingers there, a tall, hovering presence, not getting to the point, making very awkward small talk while my hands pause over my keyboard, ready to resume typing.

Eventually, I grow to understand this is a social call, of a sort. I put my hands at my sides but still have the impulse to resume typing. I have a desire to be polite in a new workplace environment, but I grow impatient. Eventually I ask if I can help him with something, and he stumbles out an invitation, and I say I'm busy that night and when he proposes another night, oh, well, I'm busy that night, too.

When he leaves, he smiles and says he'll try again, and I say, "Oh," and this makes him laugh softly.

There's nothing sinister in the exchange, exactly, but also there is no way for him to have interpreted anything I said or did as encouragement. Men in workplaces all across America, more than twenty years later, still are getting this wrong. If women at work give no clear signals, if there's no flirting, no interaction of any sort, then why would a person end an exchange with "I'll try again"?

I dismiss the interchange, but he does, in fact, try again a few more times, and eventually, he sits down in the chair in my office, and we talk awhile, and after a few times of that, I agree to go to dinner.

There's a world in which this means he's worn me down, and I suppose that's part of it. But also, I'm lonely and in a new place, and he seems lonely and also harmless.

We go out a few times, and I spend a lot of my free time thinking of ways to break up with him, but I don't do any of them. His behavior swings from overly conciliatory and sad to somewhat aggressive. I feel too off-balance to know the easiest way to extricate myself.

During this time, I leave the Bivinses' rental house and buy a house of my own.

I'm not in a newer subdivision like many of my colleagues but in a mixed part of town that includes older and newer construction. My house is new, brand-new. It's the first house I've ever owned, the first the builder's ever made, and I'm the first to live in it. It's small, with mauve stucco, three bedrooms and two baths, with a good layout and a fenced-in dirt yard for the dogs.

I have good neighbors, including the middle-aged couple next door whose son, Ben, is a little younger than I am, who comes home to visit them most weekends.

According to NeighborhoodScout, "With a crime rate of 43 per one thousand residents, Kingman has one of the highest crime rates in America compared to all communities of all sizes—from the smallest towns to the very largest cities. One's chance of becoming a victim of either violent or property crime here is one in 23."

It was higher, even, when I lived there, and so though it's true Kingman then and now has a high crime rate and was known then as being a rough town, I mainly experience violence there that could be classified as interpersonal or domestic.

One weekend, when Ben is home visiting, a group of us agree to go out hiking together—James, his younger sister, Deanne, another friend of theirs, Ben, and me. There are perhaps too many of us for one vehicle or there's some other complication, but in any case, the younger sister and Ben end up riding together alone in his truck and the rest of us follow in a car.

Ben leads because he knows the area, knows the spot he wants to show us.

James is quiet on the way out of town and, when we reach the city limits, begins muttering to himself. His friend sits up front, and I'm in the back, and both the friend and I ask what's wrong, and he only shakes his head, saying, "I don't like it."

I have no idea what the "it" is to which he's referring. Up until now, the day has been regular and fine. The sky is its ordinary bright blue, and though James had been talking fast, making arrangements and gathering gear, while the rest of us sat around, I had thought he was perhaps just a little jealous of Ben.

Ben's broad-shouldered and good-looking, with an easy smile and a genuine interest in other people and their histories. If he were a dog, he'd be a golden retriever or a chocolate Lab— easygoing and personable and good to be around.

Before we'd left, he'd tried repeatedly to engage James in conversation, but James had answered in brief phrases, terse sentences.

As town gives way to desert, the pavement gives way to dirt, and Ben's truck accelerates, so we drive faster, as well. The dust his truck kicks up makes it difficult to follow, and soon we're fishtailing around bend after bend.

"Slow down," I say over and over. "What do you think is going to happen?"

"We don't know him," he says. "He's got Deanne. We don't know what he's capable of."

I tell him repeatedly that I do know Ben—that there's nothing wrong with him, that he's not going to do anything to Deanne. But James drives faster and faster, until we come around a bend and have to slam on the brakes because the truck is parked there, right in front of us.

James gets out of the car so fast that both his friend and I have to scramble to keep up. It's a two-door car, and by the time I extricate myself from the back seat, James is already out on the road, yelling at Ben, and I as run closer, I see James is holding a knife to Ben's neck.

Deanne, the friend, and I all work to talk him down, and it

takes a few long minutes, but he does put down the knife, and his friend picks it up, and Ben backs away toward his truck, red-faced and shaking. I follow him.

"I'm so sorry," I say. "I had no idea he would do something like this."

Deanne is telling her brother how ridiculous he is, asking him over and over what's wrong with him, but her tone is off, is like she's scolding a child, a bad boy, rather than a grown man who's just held a knife to another man's throat for no reason.

We drive back to town, Ben on his own in the truck now, the rest of us crammed into the car. Deanne berates her brother in the same singsong voice, like none of this is serious or real, like, oh, how silly. Nausea rises inside me, and I breathe slow and deep to keep it down.

Back in town, I arrange all of them in my living room and put them into a sit-stay position like they're dogs. I instruct the friend to give everyone glasses of water. I instruct James that if he wants to stay out of jail, he should start working on an apology.

Next door, the neighbors and Ben look shaken. I talk them down from calling the police, and later of course will wish I hadn't. I grew up in a house where I heard *no good comes from calling the police; no good comes from calling social services—no good, no good,* on repeat.

It's still ingrained. It's a flawed way to think in some circumstances but is sound advice, sound thinking, of course, in others.

That day, I go back to my house and get Deanne and James. Deanne apologizes for her brother, so now both of us are doing his job for him. She says he's protective of her, that since he's gotten out of the military, sometimes he's overprotective—sometimes he overreacts.

It's true he was in the military; there's a framed picture of him in uniform on the wall of his house. But he hasn't been to war, and he hasn't given any signs of this level of volatility before this day.

James follows his sister's lead and apologizes and talks about the military, about "his training taking over," and I feel entirely nauseous now—how well these two are reading the neighbors, who are good, everyday people, who will not want to call the police on a veteran who's not been home long, who's having some trouble adapting.

Never mind that he's been out of the service for years. Never mind that he never went to a war.

I'm exhausted now and just want the day to end. Back home, James stands in my driveway, trying to convince me to come over to his house, to let him apologize more, and I tell him I'm much too tired. I say no—I say it many times—and when I shut the door, I lock it behind me, and he's still standing there.

It's not much longer, of course, until I break it off with him. I wait a few days, hoping his mood will stabilize, and when he seems a little calmer, I let him know to stop calling me, to stop dropping by my office, to stop.

He calls me, alternately crying and threatening, every other night for weeks, until I change my phone number. After, he drives by my house with about the same regularity, until one night he comes to the door and rings the bell.

He's out front, crying loudly and apologizing to the front door, and the last thing I want is for the neighbors to think they have to intervene.

He comes inside, and by this, I mean I let him inside my house.

He sits in my living room on my new couch, crying and shaking, taking off his wire-rimmed glasses and running his hands through his hair.

"I'm sorry about the knife," he keeps saying. He's rocking back and forth a little, holding onto himself, repeating it.

Jack sits near his feet, expecting treats or pets. I'm in a dining room chair across the room, and Lucy has positioned herself in between James and me, and her hackles are raised, her whole body at attention. She's never liked him, has often sat in between us, watchful, wary.

Huskies don't generally make any sound before they attack, and I've only seen her act this exact way one other time—when a man tried to break in through the back door of our apartment the first year she came to live with me. He picked the back door's lock, and as it was swinging open, she sped through the gap, and there was a small scream and then running feet, and I called to her and called, out into the dark.

When she came back, she had a small, torn piece of light denim in her mouth, which she presented to me. I gave her two pieces of lunch meat and a steady stream of praise. I pushed the dresser in front of the back door, the recliner in front of the front door, and we slept together that night on the couch. *No good ever comes from calling the police.*

This night, though James has no idea, she's coiled and entirely ready.

I've been thinking instead of listening, and he's stopped shaking as much but is saying something different—"I'm sorry I brought the knife."

And I say, "What?" and he says, "I'm sorry," and I say,

"Where is the knife?" and when he doesn't reply, I say, "What did you do with the knife?"

I say it slowly, and I click my fingers for Jack, and he comes to me.

James is all alone on the sofa now, except for how, maybe, he's brought along his knife.

I rise and keep my hand on the kitchen chair. It's not a particularly easy weapon but is solid wood, is plausible. I've also just bought these chairs—mid-century, teak—and I'm cold all over with the idea of having to break one.

"Did you bring a knife," I say, "into my house?" I'm angry now and no longer as aware as I should be of my tone, of keeping myself together.

I've crossed the space of the living room, am two or three steps from him, still carrying the chair, standing next to my dog, thinking, if worse comes to worst, I can throw the chair into the window beside his head and run.

"No," he says. "I wouldn't do that."

I back up then and walk toward the door, but I keep my face turned to his.

"It's in the car," he says—like this is a good and reasonable answer.

"Why," I say, "did you bring a knife?"

"Because I don't have the gun anymore," he says.

"Get in the car," I say.

"What?" he says.

"You're going to get in your car now, and you're going to drive."

I don't know what it is about my voice—perhaps it's the nature of the direct order or the dog beside me—but he goes to the door and he gets in his car and he drives.

He calls me a few nights later, and I remind him that the gym I work out in is the cop gym, and I say if he calls me again, I'll have two or three of those guys at his door every night, and though I don't actually know the name of a single cop at my gym, have never spoken to any of them, the threat works, and this is the last time I hear from him.

If, that night, he had brought into my home his knife or a gun, would this have been domestic or workplace violence? Would he have argued this violence was related to his time in the military, for sympathy or because, in some way, it was? Is this violence related to this place's history, to its roots in taking land from the Hualapai, in how its ranchers got rich off both theft and war profit?

I am not prone to making bets, but if I were, I'd put my money on the chip marked domestic. And perhaps it doesn't matter in the end what you call this sort of everyday American violence. But simplifying violence like this, demoting it down to the world of the domestic, is a lessening, a looking away.

I know I would not ever have gone on a date with James if we hadn't worked together. I know I felt some pressure to be nice, to be accommodating, to give him that thing we call *a chance*.

I'm suggesting that the ways in which our violence is connected layer—they twist and turn like a car chasing a truck down a dirt road, kicking up dust, making it difficult to see where one part begins and the other ends.

VII.

Sometimes, after, on the weekends, I arrange camping trips with my hiking friend and stay over at her house in Lake Havasu City. A roadrunner lives in her cul-de-sac and likes to race back and forth by the mailboxes in the early mornings. I drink coffee and watch its gliding and leaping stride, the tuft or crest on the top of its head making me want to call it dapper. Sometimes it makes a cooing noise and other times it will race alongside me if I run back and forth on the circular drive.

I like this fun better before my friend tells me the roadrunner most likely is hunting the small, Kelly green lizards that also live down by the mailboxes.

By the time I leave Kingman, Michael Fortier will have left, too, having become a witness against Nichols and McVeigh, having gone into witness protection with his wife.

I've read almost everything that's been published on Fortier. McVeigh and Nichols lived at Fortier's trailer, and McVeigh used soup cans to demonstrate to Fortier and his wife how he was going to blow up the Federal Building in Oklahoma City. They saw his violence; they saw his plan, but in a place like this, it seemed to them to be all talk, to be regular talk. They did not recognize any of it as extraordinary.

This story seems to me to embody the how and why of Kingman's strangeness, of the tendency its citizens have not to flinch or look away in the face of violence, but not to see the depth or breadth of it coming, either.

I lived in Mohave County maybe just the right amount of time to feel like I was beginning to belong. But the everyday violence tallied against any such certainty, soup can atop soup can, precarious and ever shifting and certain to fall. I left there for a job back closer to home, on the Rosebud Reservation in South Dakota. I left there with the mountains held close, with an enduring love for the big sky. I left there maybe just in time to carry it all with me, to know you can love a place and still never want to return.

SEVEN

Dog Days

I.

When my daughter is seven years old, we are at my father's house, which sits on an acreage only a few miles outside Exira. We're back visiting for his birthday, and he is telling the story of trying to hit a four-year-old girl. June is the month of marriage, the height of summer, flowers at full enchantment, the sky as blue as it will ever be. It's not quite the Fourth of July, not yet anywhere near the dog days of August, not anywhere near the summer's end.

Webster's defines *dog days* as "the period between early July and early September when the hot sultry weather of summer usually occurs in the northern hemisphere" or, secondarily, "a period of stagnation or inactivity."

My father's brain hasn't yet devolved into stagnation or inactivity. He doesn't yet have dementia—it will be a few years still before the diagnosis, Lewy body dementia, the second most common kind of progressive dementia. So this day in June represents my father at full power.

The girl he's tried to hit had been a foster child living with one of my stepmother's relatives. The girl ran around the living room of the house they were visiting, pursing her lips and blowing little spit bubbles, making little spit noises as children that age are prone to do, as my daughter had been prone to doing just a few short years gone.

"You better not spit on me," my father reports saying. "You better not, you little shit."

I know the voice he uses for that phrase, of course. I know how tight his eyes get, how his face stretches into a grimace-smile. The little girl, though, doesn't know how to read his oversized expression. She moves closer and closer to him, most likely mistaking the face for a teasing one. She blows her little spit bubbles, spit, spit, spit.

"And then," he says, making his grimace-smile face, "she spits, right on me."

We're in the new addition room, and outside, on the new deck, my daughter runs back and forth, helping my stepmother with the flowers, checking on the birds. Really, the birds are the impetus for the new deck. My father and stepmother like to sit outside and watch the birds—cardinals and blue jays that fight over the birdseed, songbirds once the winter's ended. Both my daughter and my stepmother have been in and outside, back and forth, and I'm grateful, as my father continues, that this, for them, is an outside moment.

"So I snatched her up," my father says. "I snatched up that little shit and put her across my knee—" He pauses here to grin a real grin, to shake his head and then make good eye contact, storyteller-style. "And I raised my hand up—" He shows us, his hand and arm raised high. "And you should have the seen the look on her face—"

My stepmother comes back inside at this moment, and says, "Are you telling that story again?" She is the one to shake her head now.

"I came in the room," she says, "and stopped him just in time." The look she gives him is a rare one. Generally, they get along well. In more than twenty years of their marriage, I've never seen the look she's giving him now.

He puts down his hand.

It's his birthday, so next we sing the happy birthday song, and people eat cake.

My daughter's father, my then-husband, has enormous dark brown eyes that he holds over-wide when trying to make a point, when he's afraid, when he's working toward focus or trying to sort through a problem. His eyes are over-wide as the candles are lit and then blown out.

Later, my stepmother will tell me the girl had been in an abusive home, had not had anywhere to go, and so was taken in by one of her relatives who knew the parents a little.

I don't know where to put this information in my body, but I feel it everywhere. My arms feel weak and shaky like they do in illness, and the bad feeling settles along my collarbones where I'm sure it's working to steal my voice.

I'm glad I can't eat the cake because of my celiac disease. This is a first for being glad. I'm glad we leave soon. Or at least, in the moment, I am. I am thinking this will be the low point of the day, but days, of course, have ways of heaping surprise upon surprise.

In the car on the way back to my mother's house, my childhood home, my then-husband drives with much more than the usual care, hands at ten and two o'clock, his eyes fixed on the road ahead. In the back seat, our daughter is nearly asleep, having run herself out on the deck and in the yard. By the time we make the turn onto the highway, her eyes are closed, her breathing thick and settled. Once he realizes she's sleeping, her father turns his face to me.

"Jesus Christ," he says, and then he says it again. He's shaken—it's clear in his grip, his face, his failure to form other words, to form a complete sentence.

"I can't really believe it," he says after a mile or so has passed. "Jesus."

During the eating of the cake, he had not been able to meet my eyes. In the moment, I hadn't wanted to think too long about what this inability might mean. But it's clear now: all the times I had told him about my father, he had not believed me, not really.

On this day, we've known each other for more than a decade, have shared a house, a bed, for almost that long. He's heard all my stories. He knows how I have to turn and twist to fall asleep most nights, how the spot on my rib cage, on my left side, prohibits easy sleep. He knows the story of the injury when I was fourteen, how it happened. He knows the other stories, too. Or at least he's been told.

The look on my then-husband's face, his *Jesus Christs*, become a point on the continuum to how he becomes my ex-husband. He believes me now. But he didn't before. It is all over his face—the wonder and shock, the sympathy with a tinge of embarrassment.

This moment conjures others. When our daughter was not yet one year old, her father's hand on her car seat handle, his tight grip, his body over mine when I say, I'm leaving, and he says, Fine, but you're not taking her.

I turn my face to the window, to its cool surface, to field after field of passing corn. The car is quiet. We drive on.

II.

When I'm in my twenties, I live for a year in Valentine, Nebraska, a town of not quite 2,600 people, which is surrounded by wilderness. I teach just over the border in South Dakota at a tribal university. Despite the myth of the vanishing Indian, the reality is that there's a housing shortage on the Rosebud Reservation. So I live in Valentine and drive the half hour to and from work each day.

It's a beautiful landscape—the rise and fall of the Sandhills' gentle slopes and dunes, the sunlight catching the sharper hills and cliffs surrounding the Niobrara River and its National Wildlife Refuge. The area is lush with water, with tall-grass and mixed-grass prairie, which house elk and deer and many birds, including Western meadowlarks, sharp-tailed grouse, prairie chickens, pheasants, and Merriam's turkeys.

My father hasn't hunted deer since I was a child, but he likes to hunt birds. He hunts pheasants at home and visits primarily to see if he can get a sharp-tailed grouse. Really, I think he likes studying them as much as shooting them. They're new to him, and he likes reporting to me their movements, the noises they make. My father visits several times while I live there, bringing along his bird dog, a yellow Lab named Frisco.

He brings his dog and his gun, and he arrives with a couple bottles of discount wine. Part of the fun is how I'm supposed to guess each bottle's original price and then how much he paid for it. It is usually a bottle of wine that once cost $8 to $12 and that he'd bought on sale at the pharmacy for $2 to $4. The discount tickles him, as does the game, and we have a glass of wine with dinner but not much more than one because he wants to be up early to go hunting.

One glass of wine, too, serves for each of us as indicator— the ability to enjoy ourselves a little, the ability to stop. According to Webster's, the first known use of *indicator* comes in 1666, under the primary definition—"one that indicates: such as an index hand (as on a dial)," or, of course, as on the trigger of a gun.

Other definitions include:

> 2: any of a group of statistical values (such as level of employment) that taken together give an indication of the health of the economy
> 4: an organism or ecological community so strictly associated with particular environmental conditions that its presence is indicative of the existence of these conditions

These visits with my father occur in the time I think of as the post-apology years. He has said he was sorry to me for the physical abuse of my childhood, for a few incidents from my early teen years, in particular.

We have made a sort of peace with each other. I don't necessarily consider whether or not this peace will be lasting. I do consider this time to be a good indicator, definition two, for the health of each of us as individual people, if not for us as part of a collective, as part of that thing we call family.

I enjoy these visits and this new peace. I enjoy the look he gets on his face when I get close to guessing the right amount for the wine—how it's the same look he'd get when I was a child and we'd skip church sometimes and stay home without my mother. He, my sister, and I would play games and watch television.

I liked church, in particular the way the light filtered through the stained glass, the smell of the polished woodwork and pews, the singing. Singing was something I could do, was something my dad could do, also, and I looked forward to our voices rising together on Sundays.

But we had church to look forward to each and every Sunday.

I can only think of two or three times we stayed home from church without our mother—we overslept, perhaps, or one of us had a fever but was not very sick. That window—well enough to play but not well enough to be out in public—was such a delicious sliver, such stolen time. It was special for its rarity—our father happy and playing with us.

The most usual game is hide-and-seek, and the two-story house offers plenty of nooks and small spaces. This is before my brother is born, so I am the smallest. Most often, I hide in the white wicker hamper. If it's full of laundry, I leave the laundry in a careful pile, hidden but nearby.

It takes a long time for my sister and my father to find me. They call my name in a singsong way I like, and my father sometimes makes my name into a silly song. It will be a long time before I figure out they know I'm in there all along—that the search is a faux one.

Years later, I will teach my brother to hide in the hamper, too, and then I will turn his name into a song. I will be in on the fun of letting him hide longest.

Those hide-and-seek moments are few, and maybe that's why I remember them so precisely. In those years, we're coming into the Reagan era, right before the bottom falls out of the local economy, the state economy, the regional economy. We're coming to the end of life as everyone's known it who farms or makes a living off farmers, which, here in rural Iowa, is everyone.

The farm crisis of the 1980s included record foreclosures on farms, small farms in particular; it was the worst financial crisis in rural America since the Great Depression. The Department of Agriculture had encouraged everyone to buy more land and more equipment, to plant more crops or to get out of farming altogether. So the number of acres of corn planted, for example, rose dramatically in the late seventies, peaked in 1980, and then plummeted a few short years later.

So many families lost their farms. So many families lost their land.

Of course, all the land I mention is land first stolen or bought at an extraordinarily discounted price—from the Ho-Chunk, Ioway, Otoe, Omaha, Dakota, Lakota, Mandan, Osage, and Ponca. The Meskwaki, Sauk, Kickapoo, Ojibwe, and Potawatomi were some of the last tribes to make Iowa home; many Métis lived there, too, then and now, though not all mark themselves "Native" on the census. Today, the Meskwaki Nation is the only one to have a formal land base still in the state. The state's Native population at the last census was 0.5 percent.

For my father, who grew up on his parents' farm, who grew up hunting and fishing and trapping, there is no other place.

When the foreclosures began, in addition to the loss of land, so many others lost their jobs, including my father. My father sold MoorMan brand animal feed to area farmers, and he was laid off like many workers during the farm crisis. He enjoyed driving the rural roads, farm to farm, talking to farmers and their families.

After the firing, for a year or more, he didn't get another job.

Instead, he hunted birds in the fall and trapped in the winter. He'd always done both these things, but now what he made was no longer extra. He trapped and sold the pelts from otter and mink, beaver and raccoon, and sometimes muskrat.

The late seventies and early eighties brought the height of prices for pelts, and their subsequent fall in value was accelerated by the stock market crash on Black Monday in 1987. Russia had been driving the fur market prices until then, along with demand from Japan, Great Britain, and the Netherlands. PETA, formed in 1980, also began to put pressure on the market.

My mother began to put pressure on my father, as well, especially once we moved to town. It was an embarrassment for my mother, having fur pelts strung out on the lawn and in the basement. There also was less money in those years, and even before, there had never quite been enough.

In those years, my childhood, my mother and father began to argue increasingly about so many things—money and politics and what it meant to make a good life. My father and many others in the region who'd always voted Democrat voted Republican, voted for Reagan in the 1980 election.

These men were out of work or had lost their farms. They listened to other men like radio host Paul Harvey, a precursor to Rush Limbaugh, who would come onto the air in the late 1980s. Harvey was there first, in those recession years. In Harvey's *New York Times* obituary, he was described as someone who "personalized the radio news with his rightist opinions, but laced them with his own trademarks: a hypnotic timbre, extended pauses for effect, heart-warming tales of average Americans and folksy observations that evoked the heartland, family values and the old-fashioned plain talk one heard around the dinner table on Sunday." He also was known for railing against the unemployed

and unwed mothers, for being good friends with both J. Edgar
Hoover and Joseph McCarthy.

In my father's blue Chevy LUV pickup, we bounced the hills
and curves of local roads, on the way to the turkey timber, the
traplines, my grandparents' farmstead. The truck needed new
shocks, but there was no money for new things. A truck's shocks
and struts keep it in contact with the road by mitigating the
transfer of energy, especially on bumpy roads. We bounced
through potholes and sharp curves, the old, loose seatbelt allow-
ing enough give for my body to rise up, for my head to touch the
ceiling. My father made "whee" sounds like we were on a roller
coaster, like this was all some grand adventure. And sometimes
it was or seemed to be.

And sometimes on a particularly sharp curve or deep hole,
my head made too much contact, made a sharp whack, and my
father's eyes made contact with mine, and the fun left, the warning beginning. His face conveyed so clearly that I'd better not
cry. I learned to hold my body more tightly, clenching my muscles and grabbing hold of the bench seat's edge, and I did not
cry, and everything hurt after.

My father turned the truck radio up the loudest for Paul
Harvey. His program, *The Rest of the Story*, ended each time with
the catchphrase "And now you know . . . the rest of the story,"
with "rest" being made emphatic, being dragged into almost
bisyllabic territory. I remember the cadence and the volume
more than the content. But the content—gun ownership, men
as strong heads of households, men as protectors of their homes—
clearly had an impact on my father and those like him, who were
out of work, feeling disrespected, longing for what they'd had
only a minute or year ago, driving in control over their hills and
back roads versus bouncing over them.

The Paul Harvey years started before and bled into 1987 when the Fairness Doctrine was repealed. The Fairness Doctrine policy had ensured radio coverage of controversial issues was "honest, equitable and balanced." Mark Fowler, the Federal Communications Commission chairman at the time of the repeal, had first been a staffer on Ronald Reagan's presidential campaign. So the repeal made way for conservative talk radio to begin officially, for voices like Harvey's to grow more radical, for Rush Limbaugh and his compatriots to begin spinning without any counterbalance their particular narratives about America.

In the same time frame, the seventies and eighties of my childhood, the National Rifle Association backed a presidential candidate for the first time since it began in 1871, choosing Ronald Reagan over Jimmy Carter. Pre-1970s, the NRA had no political action committee, no lobbying arm.

The before-and-after nature of the organization's focus can be seen clearly through the covers of its primary magazine, *American Rifleman*. Before the 1970s, covers mostly featured wildlife, nature scenes, and many, many scenes of trees and hills with a hunter and dog duo or a lone hunter, depicted as much smaller than the rest of the natural world, the hunter's face not featured or necessarily discernible, the hunter's face not a primary focus.

In the 1970s, the covers shift to put the lone hunter in focus in the hunting scenes, and by the 1980s, the hunting scenes make way for the more overtly political. Ronald Reagan makes the cover in 1982, 1983, and 1985. A 1994 cover features the headline "Too Many Politicians Show Their Stripes" with the accompanying image of a man's back with a painted yellow stripe running between the last two words of the caption. For the NRA, apparently, Reagan was the last in-favor president of the century. He also was the last president to date to carry a gun in office.

In voting for Reagan during those years, my father switched not only parties but alliances. He remained a sportsman, a hunter who valued gun safety and eating what you killed, but he also began in those years for the first time to espouse the rhetoric of using guns for protection. Men needed their guns to protect their families. His guns in our home, kept locked on the highest shelf in those years, came down more often whether we were going hunting or to the trapline or to the grocery store. My father in those years shifted from someone who used a gun for shooting birds, which we then ate, to someone who believed the gun was to protect what was his. We were his, apparently. We were to be protected. Never mind the only one who menaced us was him.

Overseeing the NRA during the Reagan years was a man named Harlon Carter. Born *Harlan* Carter in Granbury, Texas, Carter later moved with his family to Laredo, where his father worked for the U.S. Border Patrol. In 1931, Harlan was convicted of the murder of a fifteen-year-old, Ramón Casiano. The family's car had been stolen a few weeks prior to the murder, and Carter's mother had seen "three Mexican youths loitering" near their house. A confrontation ensued, and Carter, the only one armed with a gun, shot and killed Casiano. Carter pled self-defense since Casiano had held a knife. But Carter was convicted; he served two years in prison for taking Casiano's life before the Carter family's work to overturn his conviction was successful. He changed the spelling of his first name after he left prison but before he became the president of the NRA.

It's easy to get lost in the craziness of Carter's story. It's harder, perhaps, to avoid seeing how that time laid the ground-work for our present day. It's harder, perhaps, to ignore the par-allels between that time and our current moment.

If this world, this time, seems familiar, it's because there are so many points of overlap with present-day America. In 2020, Rush Limbaugh, Harvey's airwaves heir, is awarded the Presi-dential Medal of Freedom, despite how his rhetoric espouses the opposite of freedom or honor for all. For rural American men then and now, for those who want to believe and belong, the rhetoric promises belonging. But at what cost? So often, then and now, these notions of freedom, of belonging have been linked also to gun ownership.

For all the considerable rhetoric comparing Donald Trump to Adolf Hitler, there's not enough substantive consideration of the more recent past. We're not looking hard enough at how the recent past was made, how policy or the repealing of policy affected everyday Americans. We act as if it's difficult to trace where Trump's base comes from—it isn't. The base is filled with those shifted in the Reagan era, who are older now, of course, and even more afraid their way of life is shifting yet again. The base also includes the sons and daughters of those men, who are shaped by the memories of their childhoods and by news head-lines invoking fear about immigration, healthcare, flooding in farm country, and, of course, guns.

I am not meaning here to make excuses for my father or those with beliefs like his—past or present. I mean only to explore and explain how they're crafted, how they're made. Their stories are as American as any of our stories. In our coun-try, the myth of individualism pushes us to ignore structures that create tensions and pressures in individuals, yes, but also in fami-lies, in communities. But that's not how people are made, in isolation, with only some notion of character or goodness to form them.

I'm intending, then, not to be an excuse-maker or a victim, but rather to show the whole view of how a person like my father becomes who he is. This view includes the external pressures that were and are far outside the control of everyday Americans.

How all these men, then and now, take up their guns in anger is not entirely individual—it is at least in part structural. The myth of individualism leaves each person alone to thrive or die, to be harmed or to do harm.

III.

Unlike the intricate, long-lasting legacies of the Reagan years, my father's post-apology years are brief, their legacy perhaps less lasting.

One year, when my daughter is around four years old, we're back visiting in the summer, and she wants to see a pig—a baby pig, preferably, but really any up-close pig would do. My mother knows literally everyone in my hometown of around nine hundred people. She knows a good many of the people in the surrounding towns, too.

On my daughter's behalf, my mother consults friends, makes phone calls. The next-door neighbor's brother, an oversized man in farmer's striped overalls, can't think of anyone either. All the pigs are locked up tight in their hog confinement facilities. None are farm pigs. All the pigs are corporate owned.

My daughter overhears enough of these conversations to report to anyone who will listen that she had thought she might see a pig, but, "As it turns out, they're all locked up."

"As it turns out" is reported with wide eyes—I'm sure she's

imagining prison pigs in prison stripes. She charms and amuses nearly everyone to whom she reports the news. But there's another expression alongside their amusement—sadness, befuddlement. How is it possible, in a state with literally more pigs than people, that nobody can produce even one?

It's hot this summer though it's not yet August. Webster's reports that the phrase *dog days,* whose first known use occurs in 1538, originates from both the heat and the stars: "The dog here is actually the Dog Star, which is also called *Sirius.* The star has long been associated with sultry weather in the northern hemisphere because it rises simultaneously with the sun during the hottest days of summer."

That year, my daughter does not get to see a pig. That year, in a rare occurrence, we're all at my mother's, all sitting together in her yard. I come outside to claim my lawn chair, and my father is telling the story of the last time he put his hands on me and left a mark. I'm on the bottom stair of the back porch, and I grab the railing for support.

Everyone sits in a semicircle on the lawn. I pause there, on the step. People had been smiling, but now no one seems to know where to look. Though my mother still is smiling, my brother is studying the tops of his shoes.

My father's face is doing something complex. He had, after all, started the story before I came outside. He's caught now— between the audience, between finishing the story and how I'm watching him decide. He's been drinking and so has my mother.

"You were such a willful little shit," my father says, and my mother nods her head, and I stand like that on the last step and watch the apology years come to a close.

IV.

When my daughter is eight, my father has a cancer scare and, after treatment, is declared in remission. We're back visiting, sitting out on his deck, watching the birds who come and go from the feeder, and we're petting their new dog, Sadie, a black Lab.

We're still visiting every year or almost every year, but not more than that. It's difficult to explain to some—the why of the visits, given the history. In my culture, it's considered shameful to abandon family members, to withhold from them whatever care or affection you have to give. I still have some to give. But I will admit it's not a steady or regular supply. I can't count on it like I can the love for my daughter. I can't trust it.

Sadie the dog bounces around, wanting attention and food, bumping her head into my arm repeatedly until I make her sit and begin petting her.

"I had her so well trained," my stepmother says, "until I got laid up."

During my father's health crisis, she'd taken care of the dog, and then when she had a health scare of her own, my father began caring for the dog himself.

That day, Sadie displays clear confusion over who's in charge and how to behave. She will sit and behave if spoken to in a calm voice. If anyone raises a voice in excitement or anger, she reacts by bounding or thrashing around. Still, she's that thing we call "a good dog." She'd been allowed in the house and then banished to the barn with the older dog. It's understandable that she doesn't know what's happening.

"She just howls," my father reports. "Down at the barn—howls and howls and howls."

He wrestles his arms around her head and shoulders and

neck, playing rough, and when she puts her mouth on his arm, he smacks her nose, lightly at first and then harder and then much too hard still to call it a smack. He hits the dog, who bucks and tries to get at him with her mouth. My daughter watches from over by the bird feeder.

It is like a primer in how to make a dog mean. It is like a primer in how to make this visit a short one.

Before the visit, I've had a months-long primer in how I'm supposed to act if I'm to be considered a good sister, a good daughter. The last few months have featured call after call from my sister—who seems to want to debate endlessly whether she should go help my father with his cancer treatment in person or whether she is able or whether there is another way to help. Her world is more complicated than mine in all ways, perhaps. Or perhaps it's as simple as how I made this decision long ago or how my father's behavior made it for me.

He's still in my life because I think that's right, because our culture is clear about not throwing people away. Our culture is clear that you should do your best to stay connected. So I have. I am. But I'm not going to pretend I'm interested in or willing to show up for the physical labor of caring for my father. There's no part of me that's able to do it. In order to stay connected, I've had to set up boundaries and maintain them. It's imperfect. It causes strain—in my mind, my body, my heart.

We're all there when he hits Sadie the dog, who is a good dog, as I am, in my own way, a good daughter. We are good enough, in any case, to deserve something else.

When we leave later that day, my daughter presses her face to the car window's glass. "Can't we go back?" she says. "We can't leave her. We have to go back."

She begs and begs to go back for the dog, and if I thought

anyone would let us take the dog, we could, we would. I tell her this. I tell her I'm sorry. Her father agrees. He's driving and looks only at the road, and this makes me wish I were driving.

I know my father well enough to know both that he won't let us take the dog and also that he will treat the dog worse, that he will take out his anger and embarrassment on her, if he realizes we think he mistreats her. It's delicate. It's awful. We drive on.

This past year, more and more governmental agencies are recognizing that people who abuse their pets also often then abuse their families. Animal control officers in select cities and states are being instructed to contact the police or sheriff's departments in cases of animal abuse, so they can follow up with family members when the suspected abuser is not at home.

I don't know why I'm working so hard here toward gender-neutral language. Yes, women sometimes are abusers, absolutely. But the statistics from the FBI's Uniform Crime Reporting Program are clear. They are definitive. The following statistics, pulled by researcher Jackson Katz from the FBI's statistics, all are related to crimes committed by men:

- 86 percent of armed robberies
- 77 percent of aggravated assaults
- 87 percent of stalkings
- 86 percent of domestic violence incidents resulting in physical injury
- 99 percent of rapes
- Almost 90 percent of murders
- Almost all mass shootings in the past thirty years

There is little need, then, for striving toward language that leaves out an actor, that leaves out an actor's gender. Men hit—their dogs and wives and children. Men rape and rob and stalk and use their guns against each other and against their families and against the masses. I'm not trying to place blame here where it doesn't belong, but what good comes from our everyday obfuscation? Who is served by our everyday American procedure of rendering general and passive our language about violence?

In addition to how some animal control agencies now report animal abuse to police for follow-up, on their website in 2018, the National Sheriffs' Association has posted a FACT/MYTH sheet about animal cruelty and this violence we call domestic.

They cite a 2017 study that shows 89 percent of women who have pets during an abusive relationship report their pets were "threatened, harmed, or killed by their abusive partner."

Their facts include the following:

- Domestic violence, child abuse, and animal abuse frequently occur simultaneously in a family.
- Women with pets may delay leaving a dangerous environment for fear of their pets' safety.
- Individuals who commit pet abuse are more likely to become batterers.
- Animal abuse often is linked to the severity of IPV (Intimate Partner Violence).
- Safe havens for pets—offering assistance either with direct service or information to survivors of domestic violence about housing their pets safely—have grown nationally.

Their myths include the following:

- Animal abusers represent a distinct type of offender.
- A safe haven for pets of domestic violence victims is always

a place where the pets of domestic violence victims are sheltered in the same area as the family.

Other studies, too, show animal or pet abuse as one of the early prime indicators of violence. In my family, I'm meant to believe in the ways others believe my father has changed. But I don't. I believe in his past and present behaviors. I believe in the patterns. I would like to hold more hope toward change, but I'm not willing to risk anyone's safety on myth when there are so many facts, when the pattern is so clear.

We do not go back for Sadie the dog, and she lives at the barn with the other dog, and she is prone these years later to jumping up and knocking people down by way of a greeting. She is still a good dog. She's also attention-starved. On one of our last visits, she knocks down my daughter, and when I ask if she's okay, I ask in a quiet voice. "Mom," she says, "I'm fine." And physically, she is. But I can see in her face we're both thinking back to the earlier day—we're both still in the car, wanting to turn it around, wanting to go back.

V.

It's Christmas Eve, 2018, and we are halfway through dinner when I learn that only moments before our arrival, my father has been hitting the dog. She's a rescue dog, this girl, Ellie, a black Lab mix with a fondness for being scratched under her chin and left ear, with an even greater fondness for treats. She sits nicely for pets, rubs her head against your thigh. She's of the type we so often label good—a good dog, a pleaser, a love.

She's the dog of my stepbrother and his long-time girlfriend. She's well behaved, is easy to be around.

This is only my second Christmas back here in the last thirteen or fourteen years. After my daughter's father and I get divorced, she most often goes with him to Texas to his family's for Christmas. So I've been heading to Iowa. I've been performing the act we call "making an effort."

My father's diagnosis—Lewy body dementia—makes making an effort seem more urgent. The disease is named after Dr. Frederic Lewy, a German-born neurologist, who in 1912 discovered the existence of the protein deposits that cause the disease. According to the Lewy Body Dementia Association, "the protein deposits develop in nerve cells and cause neuron death in the brain. Lewy bodies interrupt normal messaging to the brain. The specific set of symptoms will depend on the area of protein deposit growth in the brain." Lewy body dementia was Robin Williams's diagnosis after he committed suicide.

The disease thus far has left my father many times confused about who we are or unable to come up with our names. These periods so far are not lasting. His hands sometimes hold tremors. He sometimes forgets common words or phrases. It's the most awful when he forgets something he's known his whole life— how to bait a fishing hook, for example, or familiar place names. He most often can come up with the name of the nearest tribe to a place, and then it's a guessing game from there—which direction? Are we working toward a city or town? Where is it, exactly, that we're going?

But this dog is part of the now. The look in the girlfriend's eyes as she leans over and tells me during dinner is part of the now.

When she smiles through the holiday meal, when she lowers her voice to tell me about the hitting, about the dog, she's also working toward this ideal we call *good*.

What does it mean to be a good daughter, a good mother, a good girlfriend or wife? Where in this ideal, this notion of good, is the room for honest emotion? Where in this ideal is room for struggle or for a graceful exit?

I tell the girlfriend she's done a good job with Ellie the dog, who seems like herself, who seems fine. She really does. I'm so angry, but I'm also so glad she seems unharmed or to have made a quick recovery.

"It's hard," she whisper-says. "Because of where she came from, we are very careful to be gentle with her."

I nod. I say again, "You're doing a very good job with her. She's a wonderful dog."

We drink more wine, she and I. After, we clear the table. Even in the most evolved of company, women most often clear the table. Women most often cook the food that's on the table. Women most often shop for or grow themselves the food that's on the table. Women most often plan what food to put on the table, not to mention what the table itself looks like, where it is placed in the room, what plates are atop it, what napkins and forks and knives.

In 2020, women often earn the money to buy the actual table, to buy the attendant glasses and plates, the shining knives. If they don't smile while planning and buying and setting and cooking and serving, they're not as good a daughter, girlfriend, mother, wife. When we police a woman's affect, when we privilege it or equate it with her actions, with what she actually does, we're engaging in our most pervasive and yet our most quiet form of sexism, our most quiet form of everyday violence.

If a man sets a table, he is praised for the doing, for the action. Imagine telling a man to smile while he sets the table. Imagine that at a holiday meal.

In the near future, the girlfriend will break up with my step-brother. Her social media posts indicate happiness—a bright face, new adventures, a moving on. I click and click and click until I see a picture with Ellie the dog, who looks happy and well.

Back in the now, back in Christmas Eve, we have opened our presents, and my father is trying to tell a story. He's trying to remember the name of the mountain outside the Mescalero Apache Reservation in New Mexico, which is not far from where I lived when I lived in West Texas. He has been through there many times. He is trying to tell a story about a time when he visited me.

"Where the Apache live?" he says—his voice rising, making a question.

"Sierra Blanca," I say. "I think that's it."

And then together we say, "Mescalero Apache," and we laugh a little.

He still sees the world in the same way most of the time—through orientation by land and people—which is a good thing turned bad in the losing of it. It is all heartbreak, at least if you've given over your heart.

Where we open presents is upstairs in the living room. My niece runs around barefoot as she likes to do, even though it's winter, as her father liked to do before her.

My father's house, a two-story ranch with a basement, was built into a hill, and sits on a small acreage just outside the small town in which I was raised. The basement used to hold all my father's guns—dozens upon dozens of them—what some of us in the family called "the arsenal."

My daughter is in Texas, and I watch my barefoot niece closely while we're there. She's three years old, and I am alarmed each time my brother or my stepmother encourages her to interact with my father. It makes my heart beat faster. I watch my niece with meticulous care and now I watch the dog, too, making sure neither is alone with my father while I'm there.

I've never left my daughter alone with my father, not once, though she's twelve years old. I never will.

In my family, we want to speak of my father like his dementia leaves him diminished and will also then leave him gentled. But this is not the pattern so far, nor is it the norm for people with dementia. According to the Alzheimer's Society, "Aggression may be linked to the person's personality and behavior before they developed dementia. However, people who have never been aggressive before may also develop this type of behavior."

I hope for the best for my father, who is the son of my grandmother, a woman I loved more than anyone. But my grandmother has passed on, and then my daughter was born. I love her best now. I will always love her best. I will always consider first what is good for her and second what is good more broadly.

I still am guided, too, by what my grandmother would have wanted, to honor what she taught me, and I try to quiet my mind enough to hear it, to know it. She bore six sons, trying toward a girl. She treasured my sister and me and my girl cousins. She would have delighted in my daughter, who is named for her mother.

Everything I've been taught makes the holding out of my arms to the past, to her, and also to my daughter, to the future, a necessary act. My father was her child. So I work hard to keep him in my life. I don't know how to be a whole person otherwise.

Because it's Christmas, I want to include here a hosanna. I want to include here a saving grace. I want to say, the dog seems fine. I want to say, the dog is not even my dog. But Ellie the dog looks like approximately two-thirds of my childhood dogs, closer to three-quarters of the dogs my father's ever owned. Whether he knows which dog, whether he knows which year, he's done this thing, hit the dog, and we're working toward the usual sort of holiday precipice, the edge of the cliff known as "to make a scene" or "not to make a scene," to say something or to keep quiet.

So far, the girlfriend and I are keeping quiet.

I have, back home in my house right now, sleeping on my sofa, a very large dog named Bella Marie. She's tan with black hairs interspersed in the fuzz. She sports a black, drooly muzzle and hazel, inquisitive eyes. She's part Anatolian Shepherd and part Saint Bernard, we're told, or maybe is a Leonberger. In either case, she's fuzzy and decent and weighs in at around 120 pounds. She wants more than anything to understand what she's supposed to be doing and then to do it. And then she wants only to collect her pets and perhaps a treat before lying down on the rug or sofa. She wants to play with our small dog, who is not very nice, but who has been won over by her dogged good cheer.

In Bella's first three years, before she came to live at my house, she was not a pet, was instead the thing we call a breeding dog. She and her breeding partner lived in Oklahoma, in some man's yard. She gave birth to two litters of puppies, who were then sold to other people.

The man didn't feed Bella or her partner very much. He didn't groom them or speak kindly to them or pet them. When she first arrived at our house, from how she ducked, it was clear he used something leash-like as a whip or maybe lasso. Eventually, neighbors grew concerned over how little food, how little water, and Bella and her partner were adopted by a shelter who placed her with a foster family. Claudia and her husband are the kind of people who say things like "We really want to keep her, but we already have too many," while petting her head nonstop. They did such good work with her.

She's the kind of gentle dog who ducks or hides, watchful, or gives you her belly when she's unsure. Dogs aren't born that way, of course, they're made. Claudia and her husband did good work to unmake the ducking, the watchfulness. It takes a week or two before Bella is certain our house will be as good as theirs.

What I'm trying to say is that if my father had hit her, I would have had the impulse to kill him. When I get an impulse like that, my narrative brain goes to work so quickly, and I'm thinking already of the new deck they built out front, how unsteady he can be now with his balance. How easy. How easy.

What I'm trying to say is that I would have ruined Christmas with, at best, shouting and leaving. What I'm trying to say is that my first impulse would have been toward violence. What I'm trying to say is that no part of me is proud of this impulse. It leaves me sick. It leaves me shaky. What I'm trying to say is I'm still in so many ways my father's daughter.

VI.

My Christmas Eve wish is that my father will not hit another dog. There is a past version of me that would have wished my father not be allowed to hit another dog. That's the wish of the present tense. What I want for Christmas is for my father not to hit another dog. It's so close to wishing him dead, but that's not how I mean it, either. I feel no malice, no sorrow.

I feel reasonable and calm now, and I pet this dog, Ellie, whose wavy, black fur is soft. And I remind my niece how to pet a dog by showing her, and she's good. She keeps calling her Bear, which is my little dog's name, and she keeps petting and petting.

When I was around my niece's age, when I was three or four, we had a dog named Betsy with wavy, black fur and the body of a Lab but not the boxy, square head. Once, I'd been at my grandparents' house overnight, and upon my return, upon our reunion, Betsy and I ran headfirst into each other, and I earned a concussion.

Another time, when I was around the same age, I climbed the tall, white cabinets in the kitchen to the one nearest the ceiling, and I retrieved a bottle my mother had put there in what she thought was a secret act. But I had seen its bright contents, which looked to me like candy. When I retrieved the bottle and could not free the contents from the childproof cap, I handed it to Betsy, the dog, and we again collaborated.

How much I loved candy then cannot be overstated. I could not be trusted around it. Candy was usually present only on holidays—and I was certain the bottle's bright pills, hidden on the highest shelf, must be candy.

As a grown person, I've tried enough candy to have grown indifferent to some of it. But I still can't have Skittles or Hot Tamales in the house without eating the whole of the box or bag or bag of boxes.

My mom's pills were tranquilizers, and though this story has been told in my family dozens of times, no one ever addresses the tranquilizer elephant. Or maybe it's obvious. My mother had a bottle of brightly colored tranquilizers because she lived in a house with my father.

Because to live in a house with my father, a person would want that, would require it, would consume the candy-colored pills like Skittles or Hot Tamales, except, I imagine, with shame attached and without the attendant chewing of sugar, which is for me shame-free, which is pure pleasure only.

That day, after I climbed the cabinets, after Betsy opened the bottle, after we'd both eaten many pills, my mother came out of the bathroom where she had been taking a shower. She dressed and got both of us into the car and drove us to the hospital, where the doctor pumped my stomach, where upon hearing the story, the doctor said to my mother, "What, did you drive the dog to the vet first?" It was winter. She had icicles in her Dorothy Hamill hair. She despised that doctor thereafter.

I don't remember well that doctor or many of the people from my childhood, but the dogs of childhood were: Betsy, Daisy, Schmitty, Pup, and MacDuff.

Back at Christmas Eve, in my stepmother's kitchen, we are putting away a few last dishes. My stepmother asks, "How does he seem to you?"

"Up and down," I say, roller-coasting with my right hand.

"That's about right," she says. "That's how it is."

That's been my overall experience with him in the last year, one of roller-coasting. When he called my daughter a few days ago, on her birthday, her name was a question in his mouth. But then once I handed her the phone, he sang her "Happy Birthday" in his beautiful tenor voice.

Later, when I asked her about the conversation, she said, "He was on topic."

This is one of our euphemisms now, "on" or "off topic."

At the end of this Christmas Eve, my father is trying to remember which dog he brought with him when he visited me to go bird-hunting back in Valentine, Nebraska.

"Frisco," I say. I remember then how Frisco wasn't house-trained and had to sleep in the screened porch, how I worried over whether he'd be cold until my father reminded me that at home, he slept in the barn.

"Frisco," I say again, and my father replies that of the hunting dogs, Shelby was "just about the best." We have not been discussing Shelby, but I nod.

When my father came to visit me in Valentine, I still had Jack and Lucy, who liked to run free through the same nature preserves and parks where my father and Frisco hunted birds.

Sometimes when my dogs and I went out into nature, we left with their fur covered in ticks or porcupine quills. Sometimes Jack and I had to sit in the car and honk the horn over and over and over for Lucy to come back to us. Huskies are often part wild. She loved us, me in particular. She really did. And she loved being wild some days just a little bit more.

One time, at the nature preserve, in the winter, three deer appeared across a large pond, and without hesitation, she took off after them, straight across the ice, and Jack followed.

It was early winter, and I was not at all certain about the ice. I first had the impulse to take the fastest route, to chase them straight across, but I knew we were all doomed if I fell through. I held my breath as they made it across, even Jack at about ninety pounds, who galumphed when he ran, who was not fleet-footed and graceful like Lucy.

I ran around the pond, hoping they would chase and chase the deer, hoping they would not run back across before I reached the other side. It is hard to run fast in that kind of cold unless you're a husky, but I did my best. I galumphed, stiff-legged, around the pond. I did not think my heart could take watching them try to make it back across.

This is what it would be like, day-to-day now, with my father if my heart were a different heart. If we loved each other differently. Each day I would watch him cross and hold my breath and hold my heart steady and I would walk around to meet him. Or maybe I would run. Or maybe I would walk across.

EIGHT

In the Neighborhood

I.

The year I turn thirty I buy a house in a nice neighborhood in Saint Paul, Minnesota, and I live there with five young men, all college students, one of them my brother. The house has five bedrooms and an efficiency apartment above the garage, and the boys, as I thought of them then, as I think of them now, pay me rent, and this is how I afford to buy a house in Macalester-Groveland, one of the most sought-after neighborhoods in the Twin Cities.

This is the summer of 2000, twenty years before George Floyd dies while police officer Derek Chauvin kneels on his neck, twenty years before protestors take to the streets of Minneapolis and Saint Paul and then to city after city, town after town, all over America. If anyone had asked me then, I would have said Minneapolis would be an unlikely starting point for such an uprising. It was, then and now, a place with considerable violence and inequity but also a place with strong multiethnic neighborhoods, effective grassroots organizations, and progressive laws.

But the American Indian Movement started here in the summer of 1968 to combat both the poverty of Native people in the area and police brutality against them. In spring of 2020, the unemployment rate nears 15 percent. The *Star Tribune* reports that between January 2000 and May 2020, of the 195 people in Minnesota who died after a physical confrontation with law enforcement, 27 percent were Black; as of the last census, in 2010, only 6.19 percent of people in the state checked the box marked Black or African American. It's not difficult to understand, then, how this place becomes the starting place.

Back in the summer of 2000, on my own, I'm not able to buy a house in any neighborhood of this city. I have just moved from Valentine, Nebraska, from my rental house near where I was teaching on the Rosebud Reservation. I have a new job as a technical writer, despite not understanding much about technology. My salary puts me over the poverty line, but the line still is in spitting distance. No one in my new neighborhood uses phrases like *spitting distance*.

But this is pre-2008, the bottom not yet falling out of the housing market, mortgage brokers still filling out paperwork with peak creativity. So I buy a house in the neighborhood, and we all move in, despite how it's a speculative venture, at best, despite how I'm still poor.

I buy the house for sale by owner. One summer day, I'm circling the neighborhood, street by tree-lined street, driving slowly, trying to imagine myself living there. The trees, tall maples and oaks, sit next to two-story or one-and-a-half-story houses built mainly in the 1920s and '30s. Craftsman bungalows and Tudors, Colonial Revival and Prairie Style homes made of brick or painted cheerful colors.

The neighborhood is within walking distance of the boys' college, and already, on my way down the third street, I'm in love with the bungalows, the tidy yards and potted flowers in full bloom.

On that third street, Sargent Avenue, a woman exits a Craftsman-style house with a sign almost as tall as she is. She begins working its post into the patch of lawn between the sidewalk and street. She's tan, with light brown hair, and looks as strong as she is tall, that build and shape sometimes called rangy. I'm hovering, my car idling, and she waves me to pull over, so I park in front of the house, near the patch of grass that's about to hold the sign.

I never know what to call that patch of grass or dirt. I think of it most often as a no-man's-land, a space not belonging to the homeowner, exactly, but one for which the homeowner is still held responsible. According to Webster's, the phrase *no-man's-land* was first used in the fourteenth century and originally meant "an area of unowned, unclaimed, or uninhabited land." Other definitions include "1b: an unoccupied area between opposing armies," "1c: an area not suitable or used for occupation or habitation," and "2: an anomalous, ambiguous, or indefinite area especially of operation, application, or jurisdiction."

Is it no-man's-land because when the phrase was coined, literally all land was no-woman's-land?

The space is most often called a road verge, but sometimes is called a berm, boulevard, curb lawn, parkrow, meridian, sidewalk lawn, or, my favorite, hellstrip.

Webster's has no definition for the phrase *road verge*, but *verge*, as a noun, means "1a: BRINK, THRESHOLD," "1b: something that borders, limits, or bounds: such as (1): an outer margin of an object or structural part, (2): the edge of roof covering (such as tiling) projecting over the gable of a roof, (3) *British:* a paved or planted strip of land at the edge of a road," or "2a (1): a rod or staff carried as an emblem of authority or symbol of office." The obsolete definitions are my favorites and include "2a (2): a stick or wand held by a person being admitted to tenancy while he swears fealty," "2b: the spindle of a watch balance, *especially:* a spindle with pallets in an old vertical escapement," and "2c: the male copulatory organ of any of various invertebrates."

When the woman places the sign on the verge like that, right in front of me, it feels fated—like a literal good sign.

"You're the first one," she says to me through my rolled-down car window. "The fliers are inside. Would you like to come in?"

I nod and park alongside the sign.

I consider the house's paint; I don't know what color to call the house—not quite purple or burgundy or dark brown, but something in the neighborhood of all three. This sounds like a hideous color but is not. The house, with its atypical color, pitched roof, and screened-in front porch, looks friendly, as does the woman, who's still smiling at me.

Inside, we walk through the rooms. This woman and her partner chatter about the work they've put in and the neighborhood and how they're sorry for the mess though it isn't particularly messy.

The house holds original hardwood floors of a lighter color and a built-in buffet with a mirror in the dining room. There's a less-than-excellent galley kitchen, too—really all the features of a period Craftsman.

The remodeled basement holds two bedrooms, and the studio apartment above the garage off the alley holds a checkerboard, black-and-white tile floor. Though I know for now that this space will belong to one of the boys, I imagine myself writing up there someday. There's good light through the windows and the alley is quiet.

We're already talking about the open house, about inspections and timelines, on the walk back from the garage. The partner goes to find a copy of a document for me, and when she returns, the two women huddle in the corner a moment, discussing something in hushed voices.

I think maybe there's already somehow another offer. I think maybe they're going to tell me the disclosure will reveal mold or worse. Instead, they turn their faces away from the huddle and back toward me, and the tall woman says, "We like you, and we hope you get the house. But we need to tell you a few things about the woman next door."

II.

Before the neighborhood becomes Macalester-Groveland, it is part of the Fort Snelling military reserve. A U.S. Army post built between 1820 and 1825, Fort Snelling comes into existence in part because of the fur trade, because of fear that the British would take over the fur trade in Canada and what would become Minnesota. The site, situated at the confluence of the Minnesota and the Mississippi Rivers, is considered by some to be the point of origin for the Dakota people.

A few years before the U.S.-Dakota War of 1862, the land that would become the Macalester-Groveland neighborhood is sold to the new City of Saint Paul. It's sold, of course, despite not ever having been bought, not ever having been rightfully owned.

The fort itself remains and plays a key and devastating role in the war, including confining Dakota men, women, and children who did not take part in the fighting. According to the Minnesota State Historical Society, "The Dakota non-combatants arrived at Fort Snelling on November 13, 1862, and encamped on the bluff of the Minnesota River about a mile west of the fort."

Next, the Dakota were moved by the soldiers to below the fort, to the river bottom. According to the Minnesota State Historical Society, "In December soldiers built a concentration camp, a wooden stockade more than 12 feet high enclosing an area of two or three acres, on the river bottom. More than 1,600 Dakota people were moved inside."

Before the neighborhood becomes Fort Snelling, it is the home of the Dakota and Anishinaabe people. According to research from the Urban Indian Health Institute, as of 2010, the Twin Cities are home to 30,373 Native people, a good many of them Dakota and Anishinaabe. The place still is Dakota and Anishinaabe land, despite war, despite displacement, despite land theft, despite a concentration camp, despite America.

III.

Despite the warning from the sellers, I buy the house and we all move in late that summer. One fall day, I'm talking to the next-door neighbor of the warning. We're talking over the fence as neighbors sometimes do, or at least as neighbors sometimes do on sitcoms. I have never done this before. The fence is a regular brown wood and yet the whole experience seems surreal, as does much of life in my new upper-middle-class neighborhood.

"They only want money," my neighbor says. "They only care about money. I just want to protect my father."

My neighbor, Susan Berkovitz, is reporting, not for the first time, how her family's turned against her. She's in her fifties, with dyed black hair and dramatic gestures. Her voice goes high and whiny on the last part, and she turns her big, dark eyes to me with a mournful headshake.

Since we're not actually in a sitcom, I don't laugh. She's clearly performing, anticipating a response.

"My sister," she says, "is such a bitch. She really only cares about the money."

Susie, as everyone in the neighborhood calls her, lives with her elderly mother and father. In the three months I've lived next door, I've heard a version of this story from her many times. I almost never see her parents, and the other neighbors tell a different story about Susie, but I'm trying to remain neutral. We live next door. It's in my best interest to remain neutral, to try to get along.

It's a beautiful fall day in Minnesota, a respite between summer humidity and winter's cascade of snow and cold. I've been raking leaves, and Jack and Lucy chase and race each other in the postage stamp of our backyard. They're far too big for the yard but are using its space well. Susie, the neighbor, coos to them in her odd falsetto. She speaks in this baby-doll sort of voice much of the time, especially to the dogs.

I've been told the following things about Susie: if you or a visitor park a car in front in her parents' house, she'll yell or slash the tires or kick them; if she's angry with you, she'll fabricate a reason to call the police; if she's angry with you, she'll open the gate and let your dogs out. Two neighbors have warned me of this last part after one family's gate was left wide open, despite how none of the family members were home; their dogs got out and then were hit by a car. It was rumored that Susie had done it, a rumor she didn't deny.

I don't know, of course, how much of this is true or is verifiable. What I know for certain is that we live in a beautiful and stolen neighborhood, which is to say we live in a desirable neighborhood in this, our America. People here walk to parks and restaurants, say hello and know each other's names and families and pets.

In the mornings, the men and I go to work. The wives, who all are as educated as I am or more, mainly stay home with the children. The children seem mostly lovely, and the wives seem mostly on the verge of screaming.

I'm nice to Susie in the same spirit with which I wire shut both the front and back gates nearest her house—precautionary. But it's more than that. There are things I like about her. She's nice to the dogs so far and mainly nice about or indifferent to how strange, how anomalous is our household's makeup.

Jack, in particular, likes her baby-doll voice, and this afternoon pauses his galumphing to stretch against the fence, and Susie reaches out to scratch the wide space between his ears.

She seems to be having a good enough day, and by this I mean she's dressed and put together in a regular way. Her fuchsia lipstick has been drawn in the lines and her shirt is all the way buttoned. Her blackest of black hair is combed down, is not winging out at extreme angles.

"I'm sorry," I say, "about your sister," and nod in a way that is meant to approximate the act we call consoling. She pets some more Jack's soft block head, and he stretches more, toward the top of the fence, to receive her attention.

"She's evil," Susie says. "I don't know what else to call it."

We talk some more about her cousin, who is trying to help, Susie reports, "but I can't be sure," she says, "I can't be sure."

She repeats this several times, which is my cue to end the conversation gently, to feign an inside duty, to shut the door behind me.

During the next year, this cousin, Shelley Joseph-Kordell, will work with Susie's other family members to remove Susie from her childhood home and then to help her parents relocate to a nursing home in California near where the sister lives. Susie will sneak back home several times during the year; she will be especially distraught over being unable to see her father.

Soon after, in the summer of 2003, Susie will go to a gun show, will buy a hundred-year-old .38-caliber Smith & Wesson revolver. Later, she will tell the police that after the purchase she repeatedly takes the revolver to the target range and practices.

That fall day, though, a year or so before, I have no way of knowing she's bought a gun. I have no way of knowing I live next door to someone who's going to become a murderer.

IV.

Before moving to the neighborhood, in Arizona and on the reservation back in South Dakota, I taught English and public speaking classes. I loved the work in both places, the students, my colleagues, the vastness of landscape and sky.

I especially loved the southern South Dakota landscape, the place in the center where it borders Nebraska. The whole area is beautiful, is surrounded by nature preserves and open land. In March each year, about a half a million sandhill cranes migrate through the region, stopping over at the ponds and small lakes of the Valentine National Wildlife Refuge.

I taught four classes each semester while I lived there, yet did not earn a salary above the poverty line. It's what the university had to offer, and I have no complaint with anyone there, only with the overarching system that makes it so. Almost everyone there lived at or below the poverty line; most lived far below it.

Because I was poor, I worked a second job doing public relations of a sort for a nursing home in nearby Valentine, Nebraska, the mostly white town where I lived. It was an easy commute in good weather, the half hour or so north or south on Highway 83, but it was less easy sometimes in the winter. I would rather have lived on the reservation, but there was a housing shortage, a housing crisis. One thing the myth of the vanishing Indian continues to get wrong is that we're disappearing.

All the white people I knew, including members of my family, assumed I left this job because living there was hard in the unquantifiable ways many white people assume it's hard to live and work among people who aren't white. It wasn't.

My motives for leaving were simple—I wanted to hustle less, to work less. I was tired.

This is in the early 2000s, and it amuses me, nearly twenty years later, when people write about the new gig economy, the new second job, the new hustle. There's nothing new, of course, about any of it. What's new is how members of the upper middle class now are part of this experience. Once it's theirs, it's a subject to be studied and written about endlessly. It's a situation, an epidemic, an important cultural shift.

Before this struggle became reality for young people from

the upper middle class, back when working two and three and four part-time jobs was the norm only for those from poverty and the lower middle class, in that time I'll call *since always,* no one noticed. No one studied it because there was no "it" to study. Whether a circumstance is acknowledged openly or formally or whether it's denied, how a situation becomes one worthy of study, is mainly in how it does or does not intersect with or affect the lives of the wealthy. Because it's a commonly held American belief that those from poverty or any version of its neighborhood deserve to suffer, to overwork, to burn out their minds and health and good hearts early. It's a shrug-and-move-on situation if it's a situation at all. It's a Wednesday. It's as regular as bright leaves falling off trees in the fall.

Part of how and why I come to feel sorry for Susie, then, or at least to feel a sort of kinship with her, is through her being poor, being displaced. Even though I learn she's sued almost every member of her family, some multiple times, even though she rants and raves and seemingly has no other work than to make trouble, I feel for how in her middle age, she's both poor and exiled.

V.

That first year in the house next door to Susie's is a back-and-forth year. After we have the fine conversation on the fine fall day, a week or so later, Susie is having a much less good day. She's angry, out in front of our houses, on the road verge, telling one of the boys' friends to move his car.

"Now," she yells. "Right now." She waves her arms around, sticking a finger in his face, even though he's a giant, standing in the middle distance between six and seven feet tall. My brother first attends this college on a baseball scholarship, and many of the other boys and their friends also are athletes.

There are days I want to yell at them, too—not for parking on a public street, but for leaving beer cans everywhere, for leaning back too far in my dining room chairs and reducing them to kindling. So I stand in the front porch, at the window screen, waiting and deciding.

Susie is wearing a soft pink sweater so tight it seems impossible it went over her head. When she turns, I see it rides up a little at the midsection and that her lipstick line today extends upward, close to her nose, and also halfway down her chin. She's wearing one bright red, pointed ballet flat and one that's black and rounded.

I leave the porch and tell the giant boy to move his car, please, and the look I give him is clear. He moves away from and around Susie like she might combust, like she might set all of us on fire.

It takes a minute either for her to recognize me or to acknowledge me, so like the boy who now is moving his car, I keep a distance. After a full minute, she seems to know who I am.

"Oh," she says, "is he at your house?"

I nod.

That's all she says before turning away, before we each go back to our respective houses.

A month or so later, winter having settled all the way in, I'm getting ready for work one morning when a loud knock sounds at the front door. I'm buttoning my shirt, heading down the stairs from my bedroom. It's just before nine A.M., and I need to leave for work.

Two plainclothes policemen stand at the front door, their own dress shirts fully buttoned and pressed. A neighbor, they say, has made a complaint, has said a dog named Jack has been jumping out the window, into the side yard near her property, barking and snarling at her. She's afraid, she says. She's afraid for her life.

"Susie," I say and sigh.

There is frost on the grass in the patches not yet covered with snow. There is frost on the outside of all the windows.

I show them the windows, the dog. He is not always a good dog—he absolutely is capable of snarling and jumping—but only at men. He likes Susie. He has not magically jumped out a closed-tight, frost-covered window.

The older officer nods and smiles when my main rebuttal is "It's winter. Who leaves the windows open?"

He admits there's an ever-growing file at work with my neighbor's name on it. The younger one frowns. He seems more inclined to want to discuss the possibility of the dog jumping out the window.

"Feel free," I say, "to open any of these windows."

And when he tries, of course, he discovers they're mostly frozen shut. The officers stay only a few awkward minutes more.

"Maybe keep your distance," the older one says quietly on the way out, and I nod and hurry off to work, now late.

I'm not fuming or even disgruntled, really, only irritated. I've been prepared by many, of course, for this very visit, for this kind of behavior from Susie. Mainly, though, it's difficult to take such a visit too seriously when the other prior visit from law enforcement had been such a serious one.

A few months earlier, back in the warmer weather, when the police arrive at the front door, it's the middle of the night. I'm upstairs in my bed, asleep, and awake to banging and yelling from below, to shouts of "Get down, hands on your head, don't move, don't you move."

That night I stumble down the stairs as fast as I can without falling. I hear one of the boys' voices saying okay, okay—I hear the tremble in it. When I try to pull open the front door, one of the policemen yells at me, calls me ma'am, and tells me to stay inside.

"They live here," I manage to say through the closed door. "We all live here."

One of the boys does live in the house and the other is familiar to me, is a friend of theirs who spends a lot of time at our house.

Eventually, I hear the police get the boys facedown on the ground in the cramped, enclosed porch. This is no small feat since the friend is an athlete, is well over six feet tall. They have not yet opened the door. They seem to be worried for my safety.

I assure them through the closed door that I know these two—that one of them lives in my house.

When the door opens and the lights come on, the younger officer does not appear to be much older than these boys, is maybe twenty-three or twenty-four years old. He's blond and on the shorter side. He's having trouble holstering his weapon because both his hands are shaking.

"I almost shot you," he says repeatedly to Alex, the one who lives at my house. "Do you understand? I almost shot you."

I don't remember well the second officer, only that he's a little older and is calmer. I watch the younger officer's anguish, how his fear begins to register in the boys' faces.

Alex, who a moment before had been facedown on the cold porch floor, is trying not to cry, is shaking now as well.

I say I know both of them. I say Alex lives here. The officers tell me there have been reports of break-ins in the neighborhood tonight and that when they shined their lights into the front porch, both boys ducked down. The officers thought they were intruders.

The boys clearly are drunk, had been returning home from the bar. One of them says he dropped his keys. The other says he was trying to help him find the keys, there on the porch in the dark.

One of them is carrying a butter knife. There is no good explanation for why. They're drunk and not particularly coherent.

Because he has ID and I can vouch for him, Alex is allowed to stay home, and the other boy without proper ID or anything verifying his address is taken downtown in the police car. He's larger, and I imagine they think he's the bigger threat.

Both boys are white. The one they take downtown has a lawyer for a father, and we call him, and the boy is released soon after, and there is no further trouble for either of them.

They have good friends who've had trouble with the police— other scholarship students, athletes who are not white, who haven't given the police any more probable cause than these boys have, probably less.

We know, all of us, this moment to be a grace note, a rare scare, a good end. The next day, there are two Adirondack chairs in the backyard, alongside a child's Big Wheel and assorted gardening tools.

"You were stealing things," I say to them, so angry now I can barely pull my tone together. "You were the goddamn intruders."

They swear to me they did not break into anyone's home,

but, yes, drunk, stumbling home, they zigzagged through yards and took things left out in the open.

"It's going back," I say. "All of it."

They wait till close to dark to return the Big Wheel and the garden tools, but they don't ever remember where the Adirondack chairs come from.

I tell them they should walk around more. I tell them they should try. In the weeks that follow, they still don't remember. So they sand and peel off most of the chairs' paint and leave them in my backyard, I suppose thinking this destruction will make the chairs less recognizable should I ever have over for a drink or a barbecue the unknown owners.

I know those chairs to be expensive, but no amount of querying makes them remember.

In calling these young men *boys,* I don't mean to suggest I have a "boys will be boys" attitude—I don't. Their lack of responsibility, awareness, care for others or themselves is startling, at times infuriating. I just mean that I feel so much older than they are, that I feel a sense of caretaking. I like to think I would feel this way if they were young women, if they were younger versions of who I was at that age, but I can't say for sure this is the case.

I don't have a younger sister but a brother. I've grown up knowing he's my responsibility. I know part of why my mother is so keen on our living arrangement is because she worries about him. If we're all being honest with ourselves, we're all here together in this house in large part because my mother worries about my brother drinking too much while he's away from home. If we're being honest with ourselves, we're all here together because my mother is worried about my brother turning into any version of my father.

I know how I feel is gendered, is problematic—I'm just reporting the news of my feelings, not defending them. But, also, whether you feel responsible for someone or not, you will carry the sounds of the police at your door in the middle of the night, shouting, "Get down and stay down," and then, their hands shaking, saying to someone you know, "I almost shot you. Do you know how close? I almost shot you." You'll be able forever to conjure up the shaking hands, the officer's voice, the sound of the boy's voice, raised in apology.

This visit—those voices in the night, my flight down those stairs and to the front door—is why I downplay the second visit, the one Susie generates. It's a good part of why I don't perhaps see the danger, why I don't care very much about Susie's attempts toward trouble. Comparatively, the morning visit is nothing, is a mere irritation, is just a Wednesday morning.

VI.

Two years later, on a regular Wednesday afternoon, I'm sitting in my graduate nonfiction workshop in West Texas, waiting for class to start, when my brother sends me a text. After two years of living on Sargent Avenue, I left the Twin Cities for graduate school; living with all those tenants, all those boys, really became, in the end, after all, like another job, another gig, another side hustle.

"Have you seen this?" the text reads. He's sent a picture of a headline and the start of a story. "Holy crap. Is that our neighbor?"

It is.

It's September 2003. That Monday morning, Susie takes her antique revolver to the Hennepin County Government

Center, where a court hearing has been scheduled. Susie is trying to get a restraining order against her cousin Shelley Joseph-
Kordell, who had been helping Susie's parents get legal distance
from their daughter before the father died in July 2002. After,
Susie accuses everyone, including her cousin, of trying to steal
her parents' savings, which were not extensive. A judge already
has denied the restraining order. The Associated Press reports,
"Court documents tell the tale of a power struggle between
Berkovitz and the rest of her family over who should be the con-
servator of her father's estate," which totals $170,000.

That day, having bought the pistol in the summer, having
practiced with it at a shooting range, or so she says, Susie brings
the antique pistol in her purse to the government center building, one of the last such buildings in a major city to not have
metal detectors. Susie follows her cousin Shelley to the restroom.
Shelley knew there were no metal detectors in the building, and
reportedly was afraid of her cousin. So she asked for a guard to
accompany her.

First, Susie shoots and injures Richard Hendrickson, a lawyer
involved with the case. Next, Shelley's guard, who is unarmed,
hears the shots and goes to call the police. They arrive quickly but
also too late. Susie shoots Shelley four times, and she dies from her
injuries. Hendrickson will recover from the gunshot wound to his
neck, in what everyone says is a miraculous recovery.

Though I never met Shelley Joseph-Kordell, she's the victim, and it's important to tell a little of who she was, of who she
might have been. In her 2016 article in *City Pages*, writer Susan
Du threads together stories of Twin Cities residents whose lives
were cut short through loopholes in gun laws or flaws in safety
measures.

Of Shelley Joseph-Kordell, Du writes that her "purpose in

life was to comfort the elderly." Shelley started a business in the 1980s called Rent a Daughter, and Du reports, "It was one of the only geriatric care firms in Minnesota. Shelley kept it contained to a handful of clients, whom she adored. But it would eventually evolve into Pathfinder, a renowned name in senior care."

In her work on behalf of her uncle, Susie's father, Shelley tried to build a bridge between Susie and her home, her family members, and she was killed for her trying, for her kindness.

In an interview with *City Pages*, Shelley's niece Rachael Joseph says Shelley's daughter was pregnant at the time of the trial. "It's just something my family will never get over, having her ripped out of our life like that," Rachael says. "There's a hole where she belongs."

Women, of course, are not the common perpetrators of gun violence; they're far more commonly the casualties. If Shelley is rare for her goodwill, her kindness, Susie, then, is uncommon, is rare in her violence. After her arrest, Susie tells police, "Shelley brought on her own death."

With these and other statements, with a whole life's history of erratic behavior, the conventional wisdom could be that this is a story about mental illness. But Susie resisted diagnosis and then any possibility of treatment. She had the presence of mind and the planning capacity to buy a gun, to train to use it, to conceal it on the day of the crime.

Though many question her mental stability and at times her mental capacity, Susie's statements to law enforcement are clear: "Shelley brought on her own death." Susie was not diagnosed with any particular mental illness, and an insanity defense was not used at trial. In a jury trial, she was found guilty of first-degree premeditated murder and attempted first-degree premeditated murder.

Before Amy Klobuchar becomes a senator and then later a presidential candidate, she's the Hennepin County prosecutor who tries the case against Susie, who gets the conviction.

This election season, before she leaves the race, Klobuchar is my mother's favorite of the presidential candidates. Perhaps the only thing Klobuchar and Susan Berkovitz have in common other than the trial is the tendency of the world to declare them difficult. It's a word used often for both, and I highlight it because its use represents more about how women are viewed than it does about the women toward whom the term is lobbed.

When the former owners of my house next to Susie's told me she was difficult, I was sure I could handle the situation in large part because the word—difficult—is used so carelessly and with such gendered connotation that it has, for me, lost its shape or definition. More often than not, if someone describes a woman to me as difficult, I find that woman to be delightful or unusual or unorthodox. It's a word most often used to censure women who live unconventional lives.

I was wrong to ignore the warnings about Susie—but also everyone was wrong in labeling her only difficult. She was dangerous, and after the murder, neighbor upon neighbor, including the women from whom I'd bought my house, came forward to say they were not surprised. One article in the Minneapolis *Star Tribune* even starts with the line: "If anyone got along with Susan Rae Berkovitz, there's little evidence of it." Yes, she was difficult, and yet I did get along with her for most of the time I lived next door to her.

I'm interested in the narratives we tell about women we've

labeled difficult. The label seems plain enough on the face of it, as most labels do. But I'm suggesting once a woman's labeled difficult, she's put on a shelf, untouchable—and not in the Madonna/whore sort of way. Rather, she's put up on a high shelf, rendered literally untouchable, as in—don't touch, don't speak to, don't vote for—ignore, ignore, ignore at all costs.

I met Susie's sister once, after the parents had moved out and Susie had as well, but before the horror at the court building. Her sister was there, next door on Sargent Avenue, sleeves rolled up, cleaning out the house, throwing into a rented dumpster decades of receipts, papers, old food, and other assorted possessions—the stuff that makes up a life.

We had a conversation about her parents, about her sister. What I remember most from it is how kind her eyes were, how hard she was working. What I remember, too, is the overwhelming feeling of shame, that I'd believed Susie about her, even if only a little bit.

VII.

What does it mean to make a home, to be at home? What does it mean to be made to leave it?

During the years on Sargent Avenue, I have college friends who live nearby, and for the first time in my life, I have only one job and it's a job with regular hours. After five P.M., we go to dinner, to the movies, to the bar, out dancing. I read books and walk the dogs. My friends play in bands or love live music, and I go listen to their bands.

If this seems regular, everyday, not worth commentary, I understand. But it's the one time in my life where I'm not going from one job to the other job, where no one emails after five P.M. to want my work-related time. The two years are bathed in the light of this—of time and regular hours and the ability to participate in leisure.

I walk around lakes, meet friends for shared sandwiches at Como Park, spend weekends browsing book stacks at Native-owned bookstores, drinking coffee at a Native-owned coffee shop. There are Dakota and Anishinaabe and Métis and all manner of other Native people everywhere. There are Native people in everyday urban life, in everyday urban America. I love this more than I can properly explain.

It seems deeply improbable now that anyone, including me, would have thought my living arrangements in that house were a good idea. It seems deeply improbable I would have heard about "the neighbor" and thought fine, no problem, when can we all move in? But I was twenty-nine years old the year I moved there, and I had been working since always.

I had been working for wages since I was ten years old, in jobs including: babysitting (ages 10–14), detasseling corn (ages 15–18), waitressing (ages 16–24), bartending (ages 22–24), newspaper reporting and editing (ages 18–23), telemarketing (age 20), public relations (ages 28–29), technical writing (ages 29–31), and teaching (ages 21–29; 31–present day). At sixteen with the waitressing job, then, I began the two-job hustle. It's no surprise I have nostalgia for the two years I set the hustle down.

I was so swayed by the idea of less work, of leisure, of comfort. I was swayed by the built-in drawers in the dining room, the shine of the wood. I wanted, even if only for a brief moment, to have what was considered good in regular, middle-class, everyday America.

In particular, in that first year in the Cities, though, I had one job and one job only. I recreated. I leisured. And I lived next door to a woman who would very shortly become a murderer.

But this is America. Everywhere we live, our neighbors may commit gun violence. Everywhere we live, the police may commit gun violence on us or on our neighbors. To think otherwise is to participate in a dangerous sort of nostalgia that leaves us too comfortable in an imaginary past place, in an imaginary past time.

I felt at home, in part, on Sargent Avenue, because and not in spite of Susie's presence next door. Everyone in the neighborhood loathed her. Everyone avoided her. I have to consider that my belonging happened partly because Susie did not belong. My house, then, even overstuffed with boys, even filled with our parties and noise, with the occasional police presence at our door, was not ever going to be the house most hated, most vilified.

I don't have nostalgia for my hometown or my home state or my country. But I have a complicated nostalgia for those two years in the Cities, for the two years I lived next door to a woman who was plotting a murder.

VIII.

If it's true I see those years through the lens of nostalgia, I also think of that time as anomalous or as the in-between years. The years I lived in Minnesota are the only non-teaching years in my adult life, the only ones spent pushing against the schedule of semesters, of fall meaning back to school and spring meaning graduation. They are then also the only years free from summer meaning working two and three jobs, so there's enough money for the next year, so the cycle can start all over again.

There are times I grow nostalgic for the moments of leisure but am also glad to be back in familiar rhythms.

I never saw the Minnesota state bird, the common loon, though I heard many people imitate its cry and argue over whose imitation was best. From loon.org's "Loon Behavior Fact Sheet," I learn, "If you approach too near a nesting loon or a loon with chicks it might give a 'tremolo' alarm call that sounds like crazy laughter. If the loon is very agitated it may rear up and thrash about in the water. If you are close to a loon that is calling or displaying, please move away!" Also, I learn that loons "use mud, grass, moss, pine needles and/or clumps of mud and vegetation collected from the lake bottom to build a nest."

The seriousness of the language is of course also comic, but there's something to be said for sounding the alarm bell through something that sounds like crazy laughter, there's something to be said for building a home from the bottom up, from what's already there in the first place.

IX.

That fall of 2003, just after the news of the shooting, I go for the first time to Muleshoe National Wildlife Refuge outside Muleshoe, Texas, to see the arrival of the sandhill cranes who winter there. About seventy thousand of them arrive in the early fall and stay through March on the saline lakes that pepper the 6,440 acres of the refuge's short-grass prairie.

Though the landscape may seem barren at first glance, a virtual no-man's-land, the cranes share their wintering ground with Swainson's hawks and other raptors, with black-tailed prairie dogs, badgers, and rattlesnakes.

I bring with me that day two bottles of water, a few granola bars, and an overpowering feeling both of déjà vu and of unease and uncertainty about leaving Minnesota, about being absent during a time of turmoil and grief. I suppose it's odd to have survivor's guilt, but that is probably the closest to what I feel or the closest to what I know how to name.

When the sandhill cranes take flight or when they come in en masse to land, the sound of their wings is thunderous. Before they draw close enough, though, when they're still high in the sky, they trill to each other, a lovely sound that clearly is meant as communication from one crane to the next.

According to ecologist Christine Hass, "Sandhill Cranes use at least 20 different vocalizations, including soft purring sounds for maintaining contact among family groups, loud squawking flight calls for coordinating groups in flight and on the ground, and trumpeting alarm and unison calls (and many variations of each type)."

This fall day, the purring gives way to squawking and then settles back into purring once they've landed. They seem to tiptoe on their stilt legs along the sandy soil, their long, slender necks stretched up, still alert. Their elegant heads swivel so that the red patches around their eyes seem on display.

I fall into the rhythm of watching them, of listening to their language. It's clear after a little while has passed that they're familiar with the place, that this for them is one version of home.

Late that night, back in Lubbock, back in town, I read a little more about the cranes. I learn the small pools of water I saw at the refuge outside Muleshoe are shallow saline lakes attractive to the same cranes that migrate through the Sandhills of Nebraska near where I lived in Valentine.

Webster's secondary definition for *verge* is the verb definition: "1a *of the sun:* to move or tend toward the horizon: SINK, 1b: to move or extend in some direction or toward some condition, 2: to be in transition or change."

In other words, like the birds, in many ways, I've come a long way to see a place much like one I already know—I've come a long way to find another version of home.

NINE

The Worry Line

I.

When my daughter is born, I make the nurse say it twice—"Girl, it's a girl." We had not wanted to know the gender, or more precisely, my mother had not wanted to know. My boyfriend mostly agreed with her on the not knowing. He and I had known each other for three years but had been dating only five months when we learned I was pregnant. On the baby's gender, I didn't really care about either of their opinions, which were much stronger than my own. I didn't care either way because I was certain I already knew. Though I hedged all bets, said repeatedly there was no way to be sure, I had been. I was certain I was carrying a boy.

It's the winter of 2006, and boys are being shot all over America. Pittsburgh, where we live, provides ample illustration. We're years before the mass shooting at the Tree of Life synagogue, well before Pittsburghers will take to the streets to protest police officer Michael Rosfeld's fatal shooting of unarmed teenager Antwon Rose II.

Still, in 2006, fifty-six people are murdered in Pittsburgh and 1,593 assaulted. Men and boys are shooting and being shot, and they're leaving behind grandmothers and sisters, wives and mothers.

Overall, today, as I write in 2020, though crime is lower than it was when we lived there, Pittsburgh's violent crime rate is 109 percent higher than the average for Pennsylvania and is 71 percent higher than the national average.

The rate alarms. Still, having helped raise my little brother, I was sure I could raise a boy. Given what boys are encouraged to become in this, our America, I was not sure about raising a girl.

If you have a room full of women and a separate room full of men, all but one of the women not only will know what I mean by the phrase "arrange her face," but also, as the words are spoken, she will execute the maneuver. In the room of men, only one or maybe two men will have any idea what I mean, and perhaps one will move the muscles of his face accordingly, and perhaps not. When I say I thought I was carrying a boy, what I mean to say is that I wanted for the child I carried a life where the life—down to the facial muscles—remained theirs.

My daughter is born a daughter in the early morning hours on December 21, 2006. It's the shortest day of the year and this year also one of the coldest. As we headed to the hospital the day before, Pittsburgh seemed hushed by the cold, perhaps, or by how little sun breaks through the winter gloom this time of year. Even the birds were quiet in the trees, huddled together, their wings tucked into themselves.

We arrive at Magee Hospital on the twentieth, and in the

late afternoon that day, as I labor in my room, as my daughter resists being born, a teenager is shot and killed four miles away in Homewood. His name is James Stubbs. He's seventeen. He's just left school for the day when he's shot through the neck and dies. He's holding his cellphone.

Soon another teen, Joseph Hall, will be accused of his murder. The evidence is thin, is based on no forensic evidence and on testimony that is changed and changed again and then recanted. Still, Joseph Hall is convicted of third-degree murder, is sentenced to seventeen and a half to thirty-five years in prison.

I am leery here of calling these two *boys* or *men* and so am settling on *teens* or *teenagers*. They are Black, and I know the disrespect, the connotation *boy* so often holds when it's lobbed toward Black teenagers, Black men. I am a middle-aged woman, and if I wrote the word *boy*, I would only be meaning that I see these seventeen-year-olds as not yet grown. I am meaning I see them with a mother's eyes. I am meaning I'm old enough to be their mothers, and I know they were and are loved. But I know the connotations and power of language. So they are teenagers.

Because I know, I am even more leery of making these two *men* before they are. I am more leery of what happens when we call a Black teen, a Latino teen, a Native teen, *grown* or *man* before he is. The leap from *man* to *thug* to *criminal* to "of course he deserved it" to "of course, he did it" is in this, our America, an everyday leap. I am tired of the semantics of this leaping. I want to be still. If white boys get to be boys through their thirties, and sometimes indefinitely, sometimes into perpetuity, then these two get to be teens a moment longer. Except, of course, in life, they don't.

James Stubbs's cousin Lawrence Godfrey told the *Pittsburgh Post-Gazette* his cousin liked to play basketball, and that "he was never into gang-banging or street stuff. I don't know how this could have happened."

I want Stubbs and Hall both to be seen as not yet grown, as children still, as somebody's children, the way my girl, the next day, is seen as baby, as infant, as someone's child, as belonging to a particular someone. They are statistics, yes, and also they are teens—are goofy and basketball-loving and particular. They are loved by their people, their families, their uncles and aunties, their mothers.

II.

It's dark, and the hill is steep, and the flashing lights go on behind me as I reach my house. It is two months before I give birth. I am still having a boy. I pull my car into its spot out front and park. He's been following for about two miles, his car drawing closer and closer as I draw closer to home. Even when he makes the move, it's just lights, no sound. He's probably worried about who lives in the house, about who might come out from nearby houses or the apartments across the street, about who I am. His is a logical worry.

Webster's primary definition of the verb *worry* is the British one: "1 *dialectal British:* CHOKE, STRANGLE." The other definitions include:

2a: to harass by tearing, biting, or snapping especially at the throat
b: to shake or pull at with the teeth // a terrier *worrying* a rat
c: to touch or disturb something repeatedly
d: to change the position of or adjust by repeated pushing or hauling

3a: to assail with rough or aggressive attack or treatment: TORMENT

b: to subject to persistent or nagging attention or effort

4: to afflict with mental distress or agitation: make anxious

The police officer behind me is experiencing worry in the most American of senses. He's worrying over the neighborhood, that he's crossed the line into a place where he's much more likely to be shot.

Webster's definition of the phrase *worry line* is "a crease or wrinkle on the forehead or between the eyebrows," with its first known use in 1972. Most Americans would recognize the way I'm using it here, though—as a marker between neighborhoods or blocks. Turn left, walk two blocks, and you've crossed the worry line. Did James Stubbs have his phone out to call for help? Did he know by leaving the school he had crossed the line? Sometimes, of course, the front door of a school does not in fact act as a line of safety. All of which is to say, in this, our America, the worry line is redefined daily. It is in constant motion.

The British, of course, also have worry lines, but they don't have gun crime like we do. In London in 2018, fifteen people were murdered by gunshot, and the same year, forty people were murdered by gunshot in Pittsburgh. A *Guardian* headline on crime in London indicates worry: "London killings in 2018: how homicides in the capital rose to a decade high," while a *Pittsburgh Post-Gazette*'s headline about their citizens' deaths the same year reads, "Pittsburgh gun violence dips in 2018 as police clear more homicide cases." In 2018, London holds 8.136 million people; Pittsburgh has 302,500 people in the city proper, with a greater metropolitan area of 2.36 million people. Though they may have similar worry lines, London's worry over gun crimes seems lovely to me, decent and civilized.

Without leaving my car that night, I have no way to convey to this officer that his worries are unfounded, that I'm not a threat. There's also no way to leave the car without becoming perceived as a threat. So I sit, seven months pregnant, the baby pushing and kicking into my bladder, and I wait, and I worry.

The street is dark. Hip-hop blasts from the apartments, filtered by the TV laugh track from the house next door. A nice old man and his wife live there, and the sound is up because the man is hard of hearing. The kids in the apartments across the street play their music, one sound layering over the next, over the even louder next, like an auditory game of chicken.

I don't hear the dogs inside my house, but they are part and parcel of why we live here. I brought two large dogs into the relationship, into the move, my boyfriend, a third. Combined, we bring to Pittsburgh about 220 pounds of furry black dog. It's hard to get anyone sensible, anyone in the neighborhoods surrounding campus, to rent to us—given the dogs, given that my boyfriend works part-time, seasonal work, temporary.

Chatham College, which later that year becomes Chatham University, sits in tony Squirrel Hill, which borders the equally posh Shadyside. In addition to how no one will rent to us, we also can't afford to live there. The architecture in those neighborhoods is similar to where we live—tall, two-story brick buildings—but the yards are a little wider, the lawns slightly more lush.

When I think now of that time, I remember most the voice of an older woman, a landlady who owned one of the very few rentals we could maybe afford within walking distance to campus. On the phone, I told her I'd be teaching creative writing in the new MFA program at Chatham, and when she asked about my boyfriend's job and I told her—archaeologist—she said, "But what does he do?" When I explained in my loudest, clearest voice what a field archaeologist does, she said again, this time with less patience, "But what does he *do*?"

It became clear this was a neighborhood for doctors and lawyers and perhaps a stray accountant. She had sighed a little when I'd told her I was beginning a job teaching at the college. "Oh," she said—the small sigh, followed by a larger one— "you're a teacher."

Where we live, where we rent a house in Pittsburgh's South Hills, the buildings mostly are brick, two or three stories, built in the 1920s and '30s. Pittsburghers know one another by neighborhood, and yet ours is hard to define. We're one block off Allentown, two blocks from Beltzhoover, at the southernmost part of what some might try to pass off as Mount Washington.

Put another way, Mount Washington is a solid lower-middle-class to middle-class neighborhood, known mainly for its steep hills that afford the city's best views of its other neighborhoods, its downtown and stadium lights, its rivers and bridges. People take the Incline, a cable car from the late 1800s, to a stop near Emerald View Park. People go there in the early morning to watch birds or hike, to watch the sun rise.

Nearby Allentown is known for being situated near other things—the Mount Washington views and the Southside neighborhood's bars, the Beltzhoover crime.

Beltzhoover, when we move there in 2006, is known by outsiders mainly as the territory of the ZHoove Crips, who have been at war with the gang from St. Clair Village. The shooting death of sixteen-year-old Keith Watts, Jr., in 2005 is at the center of that fight, but bad relationships between the two gangs go back to the eighties.

Many are killed the summer we move to our neighborhood, the closest to our house the shooting death of nineteen-year-old William Roberson IV. Roberson has no gang affiliation, has no ties to either neighborhood. He's shot as he waits for a bus at a stop in Beltzhoover, less than a mile from our house.

I don't know any of this yet. I know Allentown is where I go to get the best takeout pizza, and Beltzhoover has the best Italian food. It's still early days, early October, and it's unseasonably warm, the last gasp of summer-like weather, the dog days interrupting fall.

When the officer exits his car, he keeps one hand on his gun, the other on a small flashlight, which he shines into my eyes and all around the car, once, twice, three times. It becomes clear he is not thinking of Italian food or pizza takeout. It becomes clear he's both nervous and displeased about being in our neighborhood.

It has already been a long day, which has turned into a long night, and I would very much like to climb the stairs to the house and then climb more stairs to the second floor, to the bedroom, to the bed, more precisely, to fall into the bed and into sleeping like tomorrow, perhaps, will be better.

I have taught two classes, met with four thesis students, attended a faculty meeting after which I learned I would not be receiving any maternity leave. I'm seven months pregnant. It's legal in this, our America, for any workplace to deny paid maternity leave if the woman is in the first year of her job. I have been told I can take unpaid leave, but no one is sure how this taking might affect my health insurance benefits, and I am, of course, quite sure unpaid leave will leave us homeless.

My boyfriend, the father of this child, is out of town

working at his "but what does he *do*" job, which pays about twelve dollars an hour.

This job is my first tenure-track job, after graduating with my PhD, though I have been teaching undergraduates for almost a decade. It takes the college almost four months to reimburse me for our moving expenses from West Texas to Pittsburgh. It takes almost two months to get a first paycheck. We rent the house, a two-and-a-half-story Victorian, because the property manager drives us through the nicest part of Mount Washington, the nicest nearby neighborhood, to get there. We rent the house because of the dogs, because we're poor and because it's beautiful—tan bricks, a wide front porch, hardwood floors, stained glass in some windows.

Our house sits right off Beltzhoover and Warrington Avenues. The crime rate in Mount Washington is average for Pittsburgh, which is to say, about 37 percent higher than average for the rest of the country. The crime rate in Allentown is 176 percent higher than is average for the rest of the country, and Beltzhoover is higher still. When I check the current statistics near our old address recently, in 2019, there have been seven arrests, four assaults, one burglary, one theft, and one case of vandalism.

Our house sits right in front of a bus stop, and the city buses provide a steady commotion as they jerk to a stop out front, as their doors whir open and hiss shut.

The Council of Three Rivers American Indian Center buses pass by, too, taking kids to Head Start or elders to local senior centers.

For the first few weeks, my head swiveled every time one passed. Were there other Native people in Pittsburgh? And if so, where were they? The idea for the Council Center had been first proposed in the late sixties when "members of two Native

American families in Pittsburgh sought to overcome the feeling of 'floating' in the mainstream," or so say the Center's promotional materials. The actual Center had first been housed near me, in Homewood, but had been moved in the seventies to a suburb, Dorseyville, a half hour's drive in good traffic.

I was the only full-time fiction writer and teacher in my new job. There were dozens of fiction students and only one of me. There also was this baby I carried. They hired me because they liked me. They hired me because I'm Métis, though no one there in that year learned to pronounce Métis. They hired me because my face is one that is read over and over as lovely, as nice, as compliant. I think often that I should not be held responsible for other people's misreadings. My face is a very clear face. But in order to read it, you have to be willing to look. You have to be willing to read a woman's face as something other than compliant.

I had been hired, in part, because I was Métis, yes, and though no one said this aloud, all my invitations to faculty or donor events were occasions for people to query me about my Indianness, to query me about social or racial issues about which they felt a real, true Indian would have opinions. It was part of what was making me tired already.

In the 1700s, there had been more of us—Mohawk, Onondaga, Cayuga, Iroquois, Seneca, Lenape, Shawnee, Wyandot, Mohican. The 2010 census revealed Pittsburgh's population to be 0.2 percent American Indian or Alaska Native.

The census also reveals Pittsburgh to be almost 67 percent white and 23 percent Black. My neighborhood balance is closer to the inverse. So this statistic startles me.

In 2016, the *Public Source* reported, "Eighty-five percent of Pittsburgh homicides have had a black victim," and added, "Police attribute violence to very few individuals. In other words, these aren't neighborhoods brimming with violent criminals. Residents often feel helpless."

Before being accused of and then convicted of third-degree murder, Joseph Hall was a literal choirboy. He sang in the Afro-American Music Institute, which was founded by his grandparents. By all accounts, he and his mother are good members of their community, are good neighbors.

James Stubbs's uncle was Ken Stubbs, who called his nephew a good kid and told a local TV reporter after his murder, "It's just what's happening now." Eight years later, Ken Stubbs also was shot and killed in Pittsburgh. Stubbs had owned businesses in Homewood on Hamilton Avenue. Another neighborhood business owner, William Baker, told Heather Abraham of CBS local news, "He's always been a gentleman to me. He's always treated me with utmost respect. It is a shame. I'm sorry to hear that. I mean that sincerely."

What does it mean to show respect in life and in memorial? What does it mean to show up for each other—for your wife, your neighbor, your co-worker, your community, your daughter or son?

While we live in this house in our Pittsburgh neighborhood, the nice retired man next door will have his front door gang-tagged because he yells at the kids selling drugs in the alley. My boyfriend and I will feel helpless, as will the nice retired man's wife, as will his son, who is a state trooper, and still nothing is done. He is at the hospital having chemotherapy when the kids tag his house. The tag reads, "Die, old man, die," without the direct address commas I've added because the old man is a lovely man, is deserving of both proper punctuation and some dignity.

He doesn't die, though, at least not while we live there. He throws leftover food on paper plates over the chain-link fence into our yard and makes friends with the dogs through pasta, pizza, bits of ham sandwich. It takes me a very long time to consider his lack of appetite, to connect it with these paper plates. Once I see it, I marvel at how much he loves his wife, at the love it must take to get out of your sickbed, to make the walk to the yard, to throw the food where she won't see it, where it will be consumed, where there are three waiting mouths.

On good days, the neighbor continues to patrol his backyard fence along the alley. He hangs on.

Our house was once the neighborhood dealer's house or at least the grower's, though I don't know this at the start. The delivery kid still deals and distributes directly behind our house, his moped revving all hours in the alley, the city buses shuddering and hissing to a stop all hours out front.

The policeman brings all this knowledge to the traffic stop. After I hand him my license and registration, he says, "What is your business here?"

"I live here," I say.

"You have Texas plates," he says.

"They're not expired," I say, losing my patience. I know better than to give any cop any back talk. If one-third of stranger killings are committed by police, how many of those are the deaths of women like me—alone on a street in the dark, exhausted and afraid and saying the wrong thing because of this awful combination? But this is how tired I am. This is the state of me.

He asks then for me to step out of the car, and I expect when he sees how pregnant I am, this will end shortly. It doesn't.

Instead, he seems yet more suspicious, and later, I will wonder if he thinks I'm one of those women who run drugs, who pretend to be pregnant as cover.

That night, when I tell him I'm coming home from work, when I name the fancy college across the bridges and tunnels of this city, he squints his dark eyes at me, clearly in doubt.

I say that I haven't bought Pennsylvania plates because we might not stay. I say, "It's a one-year appointment." I say, "I'll get it taken care of, though. I will."

His hand doesn't leave his gun, and his eyes never stop moving.

None of what I say is true, or none of it is yet known to be true, but as I say it, I realize I want nothing more than for the lie to be made truth. I am seven months pregnant and so very, very tired. How am I going to have this baby and go straight back to work? How are the two or three days of maternity leave I've been offered going to be enough?

The policeman keeps his hand on his gun while I tell him my lies, and he writes nothing down. In this behavior, in my lying and making him afraid, I'm like almost everyone else in our neighborhood ever to be pulled over or followed home.

This man is dark-eyed, with dark hair and olive skin, and his surname suggests he's Latino or Chicano. This is a Black and white neighborhood, with the nearby neighborhoods being predominantly Black. He's the one with the gun, and yet he's clearly scared to be here, clearly made uneasy by a white-facing, white-passing pregnant woman with nothing in her bags but books.

How I would like to tell him I know where we live—though I don't yet, not entirely. I have not yet received the many-months-past-due water bill for $1,132, a bill that explains why the sunporch off the kitchen was converted into a "greenhouse room," a bill that explains why the former tenants moved out in such a hurry.

As I stand there, in front of the concrete stairs up the steep hill to the front door, I would like to tell him I know what he thinks. I would like to tell him that the kid who runs the drugs behind our house is a white kid. I would like for him to understand that where a person lives isn't always an indication of what he or she does, of his or her heart. But I know it sometimes is or, with time and necessity, is made to be. I know there are limitations we find ourselves unable to breach. I know sometimes we drown in the stagnant water of where we're from.

There is so much I'd like to convey, including this feeling—that I'm so close to drowning. But he keeps his hand on his gun, and I talk and talk—I use my most soothing of teacher voices—and he eventually seems to grow tired of my talking. Eventually, my white face earns me free passage. I get to climb the stairs. I get to go inside.

III.

When we moved to Pittsburgh from Texas, my boyfriend sold his guns. We were poor—the kind of poor where you have a garage sale to raise cash to move across the country.

They had been family guns, handed down. He made sure I knew this. It's fine, he said repeatedly. It's fine.

We had known each other about four years at this point, but we'd only been dating a few months. He had recently dropped out of graduate school, but still, our grad-school friend groups overlapped. When I expressed an interest in him to one of the women in the group, one of his close friends, she tilted her head and said only, "He's a project. It would be a lot of work."

We'd been dating about five months when I learned I was pregnant, when I received the job offer. We'd already decided he would move with me, wherever the job. We'd already discussed having children but not, of course, this soon.

One afternoon, in my rental house in Texas, he gives me a ring and asks me to marry him. I say I'll think about it. I say thank you, which is, of course, not quite the right thing.

I wear the engagement ring and also refuse all inquiries as to a wedding date with a polite smile and a "We're so busy." I haven't said yes, though, not exactly. It's too soon. I'm certain about the baby, but I'm waiting to see on this idea of marriage.

My boyfriend sometimes works in geographic information systems, GIS, and as a field archaeologist, traveling around the region. Archaeology in Pennsylvania and many other parts of the country mostly entails digging holes called shovel tests, to make sure there are no artifacts in the way of the many pipeline and natural gas projects taking over the region. Field-workers without graduate degrees in 2006 make between $12 and $20 per hour, but the wage is usually closer to $12 an hour. They most often work far from home, ten days on with either two or four days off.

Though it would mean working in Pittsburgh or even from home, my boyfriend does not apply for any GIS jobs. He has some contacts in archaeology in the region and takes fieldwork jobs, one of which is local, and most of which are far-flung—all corners of the state, over into West Virginia, even back south to Louisiana. I had known when we started dating that he preferred the outdoor work, despite its lower pay. I had known how much he loved the bro culture of archaeologists—the long days of hard physical work in the outdoors, followed by long nights of pool playing and drinking beer.

It hadn't mattered much then, but now it very much does. He is mostly always gone—when the police officer pulls me over in front of our house, when I learn the kid on the moped deals drugs, when the first of the neighborhood kids throws a rock at our dogs, when it's fireworks they throw, when it's another rock then more fireworks—like that on repeat.

He is not there one rare, bright-skied Saturday when I head down Carson Street to the SouthSide Works shopping area, to the grocery store.

I don't remember everything I had on the conveyor belt that day—apples, for sure, chicken and ice cream—but I know what I ate when I was pregnant and before regular paychecks started coming in. It's one of academia's dirty secrets—how you leave a job having received a half paycheck for May and you often aren't paid again until September. If I had to guess, the conveyor belt that day held hummus, ice cream, apples, bananas, bread, bell peppers, canned tuna, and one package of chicken thighs, the smallest kind that holds four, skin on.

The first weeks of the semester at Chatham feature parties with a lot of Brie I can't eat and wine I can't drink. The views are nice, though. The campus is set against impossibly green hills, manicured gardens of bright but not too bright flowers, each building a stone cottage or mini-mansion featuring the names of those synonymous with Pittsburgh's oil- and steel-town roots—Mellon and Rea, Laughlin and Falk.

Chatham's campus sits about two miles from where James Stubbs is shot and killed in Homewood. But the worlds could not be further apart.

Sometimes, when I went to campus, I'd bring along Jack,

the biggest of our dogs, and we'd walk the paths, and students would pet his giant, square head and coo over his long, dark mane. I liked how beautiful it was there, how genteel, how quiet.

At home, Jack had decided he hated Luna, my boyfriend's dog. Lucy, the smartest of the three, had tried to intervene, had tried to correct Jack many times, as had I, but nothing was working. I was able to keep the warring dogs separated during the day because the old house still had one room with sliding pocket doors.

On campus, though, Jack had good manners. He only ever barked at the rogue turkey who chased us sometimes, who chased co-eds, too, until it was relocated.

The woman who ran the program brought her little dog with her every day, and so no one seemed to mind Jack or at least no one questioned me.

That day at the grocery store, I am grateful for how we still have a bag of dog food at home. First, the nice woman behind the counter has to tell me my bank card's been declined. It's the kind of store where you bag your own groceries, so it takes me a minute to stop putting apples in a sack, to find my other card. Next, of course, it's the other card, the credit card, declined.

The cashier is white, late-middle-aged, and has glasses that cover most of her face. She looks tired in her shifting side to side a little, or perhaps it's time for her break, or perhaps she's embarrassed for me.

Sometimes, my boyfriend mails home to me from his job a little of his leftover per diem cash. This is not one of those weeks.

I tell her thank you, which is not quite right, so then I say I'm sorry. I try to hold my back straight as I walk toward the doors, but I'm undone a little by how the chicken thighs and ice cream sit, huddled together at the end of the conveyor belt.

It's hard to explain properly how tired and low you feel sometimes when you're pregnant and poor and employed by a place where everyone else seems to have enough, to have so much more than enough. I've worked all manner of physically hard jobs—waitressing, bartending, babysitting, cleaning hotel rooms, detasseling corn, helping tear down a half-burned house—but I have never before or since been as tired as I was when I lived in Pittsburgh.

That day, I had thought I might drive over to the Babies "R" Us in the suburbs later, at least to window-shop. Instead, I go home, and there's peanut butter, and some pasta and a few other odds and ends, and it is, of course, enough. The dogs greet me with wagging and licking and only the smart one, Lucy, seems to understand anything's wrong. She sits at my feet, and I scratch the back of her head like she likes and then the wide, husky ruff and under her collar, and we sit like that a long time.

When my boyfriend calls, I tell him we're out of money until I'm paid, but I don't tell him about the specifics of this day because what is the point in spreading the humiliation? I've learned already in our short time together that he reacts poorly to humiliation, to any insinuation that what he's contributing is not enough, to any insinuation of insufficiency.

And there also is how he's trying, at least after a fashion. We're still in a world where I think he's doing the best he can. He's sending home some of his per diem in cards decorated with his drawings or funny stories. It's hard for me to parse sometimes, whether this sentiment is for me or for the baby.

It shouldn't matter, perhaps, but it does. Am I enough without this baby? Am I enough without the sentimentality of motherhood attaching itself like an anchor around my already swollen ankles?

At least every other night, when he calls, his voice is thick with beer. Hanging out with the guys and drinking beer is what field archaeologists do, but I'm here alone, my chicken thighs conveying and conveying, and I'm not even able to drink the Chatham wine, to eat the Chatham Brie. I'm feeling sorry for myself, which is something I'm good at, which is something I hate. This is how both the dog days and fall pass, me hating my boyfriend more than a little for his part in how I'm hating myself.

IV.

Our daughter is born on that bitter cold December morning, on the winter solstice, the shortest day of the year. She's eleven days past her due date and most welcome.

Here, throughout my pregnancy, no one shifts on a bus, even as I grow larger and larger. In Pittsburgh, people will cross an icy sidewalk to yell at a pregnant woman that she has no business being out when it's so slick, but no one will offer an arm. This happens to me twice in the Southside when I go to deliver our rent checks and once on our own street. No one else offers to shovel the sidewalk. I am glad for this baby I carry inside me to be arriving.

Because she's so many days tardy and seems content never to arrive, the doctors induce labor. I labor for twenty-two hours, and my boyfriend's family arrives, descending on the hospital with their loud Texas voices, their swagger, their holiday cheer. They had planned to arrive a suitable amount of time after the birth, yet they are thrilled with the timing.

My boyfriend's father spends the most amount of time in the room with me, reading aloud from a book and then from the newspaper while I labor. I've met the parents twice, and there isn't anyone I want in the room, except the nurse or perhaps the doctor. Really, I'd like to do this myself. Really, I'd like to do this unaccompanied by recitations from the *Pittsburgh Post-Gazette*'s news and sports sections.

The one person I can imagine wanting is my grandmother if she were still living, and so I think of her, I focus on her—her calm and strength, the way she'd rock my brother and sing to him when he was small, the way her voice and body reflected peacefulness. I mimic it the best I can.

I have read three books on birth and early parenting, yet I am unprepared for a late baby. I have had many conversations with my mother and my sister, too, but both of them report they loved being pregnant. They report it so many times with so little variation that I begin to question both their veracity and my sanity. I have spent the last months swollen and over-warm, a baby's foot kicking my ribs and bladder. I have spent the last few weeks working and then lying on my left side, on repeat. My blood pressure is not yet too high but is higher than normal. I have not experienced the bliss of my mother and sister. I do not glow.

My mother and my sister and my grandmothers all gave birth to many early babies, and a few were perfectly on time. It never occurred to me to study this late-birth scenario. I studied premature babies, premature labor, uterine prolapse, and breech births since they run in the family.

I'd thought the most about the breech—the way the baby has to be turned and redirected seemed so dramatic, so unnatural. This type of breech is Webster's second definition: "a: the hind end of the body: BUTTOCKS" and "b *medical:* BREECH PRESENTATION, *also:* a fetus that is presented with the buttocks first." Its first definition is plural, dealing with short pants, breeches. Its third is "the part of a firearm at the rear of the barrel."

There are shotgun weddings in my family history, but no C-sections. Still, when after all those hours of labor the operation becomes necessary, becomes urgent, I agree.

No one tells you when you have a C-section, they strap you down. It's important you don't move. They draw a white curtain across at the midsection, so it's like the theater except for how you can't watch.

My boyfriend watches. He's wearing white scrubs and a mask over his dark skin, only bits of his dark hair poking out, his large, brown eyes made more giant with fear. His fear irritates me. He is not the one who labored, who's drugged, who's strapped down. The very least he could do while wearing a literal mask is to mask his fear.

Before my daughter is born, this will be the dominant emotion I remember—irritation at her father. I should have known then that we were not to last. A part of me probably did.

But then she's born, and the nurse says, "They never do that—look right at you. I almost dropped her," before saying, "Girl, it's a girl," and handing her off to me. And she looks right at me, too, and I don't let go.

A few months later, the day before my birthday, on Valentine's Day, a daughter is born to Joseph Hall and his girlfriend. He's still in jail, awaiting trial. His mother gets to meet his daughter before he does. According to his interview with *City Paper* reporter Bill O'Driscoll, Hall has never seen his daughter outside of jail or prison. The visitor Joseph Hall sees the most during these years is his mother.

V.

Why I don't expect my own mother or bring myself to want her there for my daughter's birth can be traced back to my own childhood, perhaps, but certainly the year before is an easy dot on the line of the why.

Back in Texas, the year before, in my rental house in Lubbock, I awoke one night with a headache of intense, singular focus, and my grandmother's voice narrating to me the steps of what I should do. It wasn't a dream, and I pulled from my head one lone hair as she told me, and I followed the rest of the steps, her instructions for this ritual, and I fell back into dreams, despite the headache, and when I awoke in the morning, fevered, my vision blurred and narrowed as if I were in a tunnel, I felt ill, very ill, and also very calm. I called my friend Gail to drive me to the urgent care and then the hospital, after.

I was so calm at the urgent care center that the doctor, Jack Dubose, hesitated before sending me to the hospital. "I have a high pain threshold," I told him, and he nodded, his glasses slipping down his nose. I didn't elaborate, didn't explain my childhood, didn't debate nature versus nurture. I was lucky enough not to need to have this conversation. My simple sentence was enough. He listened.

It is such a rare thing for an older, male doctor to listen to a woman. Factor in West Texas. Factor in how this is the year Lubbock is named the second most conservative city in the nation. Factor in that I'm Métis. Dr. Jack Dubose, then, is a miracle. At the hospital, Gail and I learn I have meningitis, probably viral, perhaps bacterial.

To be clear, to be transparent, I am withholding the details of the nighttime ritual because they are ritual or ceremony and are, therefore, not for public consumption. I am naming these doctors here because they all paid attention; they all offered good care; they all seemed to me to be miraculous. It is not an exaggeration to say that if not for their attention and good care, for the miracle of each of them, I would have died. I still almost did.

At the hospital in Lubbock, I have my first spinal tap, am given pain medication and then released with orders to stay home from work for a few days, to rest.

Nearly two days go by, and I don't feel worse. I'm taking half the prescribed amount of Vicodin, am watching television through the tunnel of my vision and am cooking meals. I'm cleaning out my sweater drawer when the hospital calls. The culture they took has grown bacteria. They should not have released me. It's urgent that I come back. It's urgent. The woman's voice on the phone is trying for calm and is failing.

Later, I will realize she's thinking of a lawsuit. Later, I will learn this delay in treatment often results in a lifetime of serious health consequences ranging from seizures to hydrocephalus to worse. Later, I will learn that the odds of survival for people with delayed treatment are 14 to 1, that according to the National Center for Biotechnology Information, "up to 50% of survivors of bacterial meningitis suffer from disabling neuropsychological deficits," and that a delay in treatment makes that number rise and rise and rise.

Back at the hospital, I meet Dr. Lawrence Martinelli, who begins my treatment and tells me about my bacteria, about the difference between viral meningitis and bacterial. The viral kind is contagious and clears up on its own, usually in about a week; it's not deadly. The bacterial kind requires intravenous antibiotics, a hospital stay of at least a week, and then outpatient IV treatment for several more weeks if all goes well. I don't ask what happens if all goes poorly.

My bacteria is called *Serratia marcescens*. Despite how it can be deadly, it is beautiful under the microscope. A cluster of these bacilli looks like someone spilled a box of Hot Tamales—they're similar in shape and shade, except the bacteria are even brighter, the shade of red leaning more toward coral.

Dr. Martinelli explains some of the bacteria's storied history. Because of its bright color, *Serratia marcescens* was used as a tracer agent, to track the movement of other bacteria. Before science knew what it was, the bacteria was the cause of a "miracle" when communion bread in a Catholic church turned red. Much later, from the 1950s through the '70s, the bacteria was used by the U.S. Army to test biological weapons.

When I go into the hospital, I have just moved back into the city, into Lubbock, from a house at the edge of a cotton farm. I won't think of it till much later, but while at the farmhouse, I had one day gone outside barefoot and stepped onto a spent spine from a cactus. It had gone more than an inch into my right foot, my driving foot. I had pulled it out by myself, then, bit by bit. It went something like this: pull, wince and shudder and wait, and then pull some more. It healed fine. I didn't think about it much, after. I don't think about it when Dr. Martinelli asks about puncture wounds, but later it occurs to me this may have been the source.

I like Dr. Martinelli straightaway for how he explains the history, how he makes it into a compelling narrative for me, how he seems to understand this will help me stay calm. He's funny and smart. He says repeatedly, "You don't seem that sick," and I agree. I say again, "I have a strange high tolerance for pain." I say, "It's not always helpful," and he agrees.

We never do figure out for certain how the bacteria entered my bloodstream.

I spend the first day in the hospital making calls to my family, my friends, and my department. My classes are covered easily and well, and because of the double vision, I spend the rest of the time watching television with one eye shut and then alternating. I have a steady stream of visitors—fellow graduate students and friends—who bring me balloons and candy, who walk my dogs and clean my house.

As the days pass, the antibiotics do their work, so my fever abates and my vision begins to be less tilty, but then I'm awakened one early morning by someone turning my left arm this way and that, by hushed and then raised voices. My fever has spiked in the night, and a nurse—the one I think of as the "good nurse"—tells me she needs to change my IV.

I can't hear all of what's being said, but I do hear the last phrase: "If you're trying to kill her, you could have done worse."

When Dr. Martinelli returns from the hall, he says only that I gave them a scare, that my fever had spiked, that the other nurse—the one I'd come to think of as "the mean one"—had installed my IV incorrectly, and a new infection had bloomed bright and colorful along my left forearm.

Dr. Martinelli has paged the nurse, and I hear him—we all hear him—dress her down in the hallway outside. I never see her again.

I also never see my family during this time. On that first day in the hospital, when I call to tell my parents about my bacteria, about my hospitalization, each wants to know if I called the other first.

My mother wants me to decide whether it's serious enough for her to come. She wants me to tell my father to quit being an asshole. My father wants me to apologize for how long my mother seems to have known I was in the hospital before he did. He wants me to explain myself.

I never do any of those things. Instead, I practice being grateful—to the nurses for their care, to Dr. Martinelli for his good humor and good care, to Dr. Dubose for his good care and for the advice he gives after.

"It'll take your body a full year to recover," he says, "at least."

I nod like I understand, but I don't—not really.

"Try not to put it under unnecessary strain. Maybe don't get pregnant," he says, "for example."

I nod again.

In my last days at the hospital, I'm grateful for my friends who bring me peanut brittle, who wheel me around until they get kicked out because we're too loud. I'm grateful for how they check on me, too, once I'm home with my central IV line, with my new equipment. I give myself IV antibiotics for a few weeks, and I'm grateful to my brain for remembering the instructions. I'm grateful to my body for beginning to heal.

It's hard work, practicing gratitude, when you also are experiencing both the temporary loss of your health and the loss of your family. It's a breach, a rupture. I entered the hospital with a family, even if damaged, and I left without. It felt a lot like a puncture wound I couldn't quite explain. It also felt a lot like being born.

VI.

In Pittsburgh, after my daughter's birth, my blood pressure rises and rises, and my daughter's weight drops and drops. She is born a healthy weight—and all newborns lose some weight before beginning to gain—but she's shrinking and she's quiet, so quiet. First the nurse and then the doctor says "failure to thrive," which is, of course, terrifying in a way few phrases are.

We stay in the hospital longer than is usual, then, and they also say "postpartum preeclampsia," but I pay less attention to this, given the other phrase. Much later, I'll google and learn postpartum preeclampsia is when blood pressure rises dramatically after the birth. It's uncommon. I have none of the known risk factors—obesity, family history, diabetes. The possible outcomes include stroke and pulmonary edema.

We have to stay until her weight begins to stabilize, until my blood pressure begins to drop, and they're sure I'm not developing postpartum eclampsia, which is like the condition I already have, except with the addition of seizures and possibly permanent damage to my brain, eyes, liver, and kidneys.

I listen to the doctors and begin taking blood pressure medication. We begin mixing formula with breast milk to feed my daughter. We wait. My boyfriend stays in the room with us for most of these days, and there's a chair that folds out into a makeshift bed. The nurses are nice—all of them. I like and trust both my doctors. There is a menu from which we order our food, even, and it tastes good. I focus on these things because it's necessary to focus on the good if my blood pressure is to fall, if we're going to be home before Christmas. It seems urgent to me, for some reason, that we be home for Christmas. And I trust my impulse toward this urgency.

When I had meningitis, I learned to respect this sense of urgency when it arrived, to trust it. At the Lubbock hospital, I also learned that in order to be released on a weekend, you have to advocate for yourself; you have to make repeated noise.

When my Pittsburgh doctors insist that we stay longer, I use the skills I'd practiced. If they released us Christmas Eve, I would agree to bring my daughter back for daily weight checks. I would agree to take my blood pressure medication for one month. I would agree to accept a pain medication prescription, a narcotics prescription, with the understanding that I wouldn't fill it.

"Stop saying that!" my doctor says over and over. "You have to take it."

I smile back at him with my best calm smile. In this, our America, once they've strapped you down and cut you open for your C-section, they will not release you until you agree to take a prescription for narcotics. Never mind that you're feeding a baby from your body. Never mind that pain medication filters directly into breast milk. Never mind that the narcotics also will make you feel better than you really do or than your body really does—that you might rip your new incision, strain muscles already overstrained from labor.

"Give it here," I say to my doctor. By now, nine months in, he's learned to read my face. He sighs.

"You don't have to fill it," he says, shaking his head.

"Oh," I say, "I know. Whatever you think is best."

We both laugh a little at that, and he still shakes his head, but he signs the release paperwork, and my daughter and I make it home for Christmas, where my boyfriend's family has made the house smell like good food and floor polish and cookies.

The day after Christmas, in nearby Penn Hills, Joseph Hall's mother, Cecilia Coleman, says goodbye to her son. She sends him to Indianapolis, to stay with her brother, after learning the police are looking for him. She reports to Bill O'Driscoll that she's afraid for her son's life, that the police have reported him as "armed and dangerous." Later, Joseph Hall will say he's never shot a gun other than a paintball or BB gun.

Back at our home, in the South Hills, the Texans stay after Christmas only a few more days, but they fill the house with food and laughter and enough presents for at least four children. The gifts they give our daughter are beautiful and plentiful—row after row of tiny, improbable onesies and colorful T-shirts, plush-footed pajamas and a snowsuit with matching mittens and hat. They had to be instructed repeatedly and with considerable force not to buy for our daughter one or more of those giant stuffed animals. This was made easier because they had been arguing, apparently, over giant panda versus giant giraffe.

In the days after giving birth, I began to understand, then, that this man, my boyfriend, the father of this daughter, was one of those people who had been cared for, who had people who would care for him. And I suppose, looking back, I began to resent the withholding of that care.

It's a fast-moving thought, though, as all thoughts are in the first days when a baby is new. Most thoughts are only for her. She is still too quiet, is still not gaining weight at a good rate. The only time she cries is when the relatives dress her in a Christmas outfit for yet more photographs. One of the sisters has cleaned the house, has been taking care of the dogs, has made the most delicious food—enough that we'll be eating it for weeks. I am grateful.

On one of the trips to the doctor for a weigh-in, we're out front the same time as the next-door neighbors.

"A girl," the wife says.

"I told you," says the nice old man. He pats our daughter on the head with care.

The Texans leave soon after, and my blood pressure goes

down and my daughter begins to gain weight. At home, in her room, I fold onesie after onesie, line her dresser with two rows of stuffed animals.

My family sent a few presents, what I would consider to be a regular amount, and I'm not sure what to make of all the rest. I have the impulse to sort, to give away. It's Christmastime, after all, and there are other babies without.

"It's too much," I say.

"I had to talk them out of one of those giant giraffes," my boyfriend says. "I had to threaten them that I'd throw it away."

I don't know what to make of this, either—that they would have bought one, that he would have thrown it out. It's such a wasteful impulse, but his face is all righteousness, all indignation.

I sort and fold and sort.

"I'm surprised your sisters were able to come," I say, in a quiet voice.

"What?" he says.

"The tickets?" I say. "The time off?"

They're both in their twenties or early thirties, are just out of school, are not yet gainfully employed.

"My parents," he says. He shrugs at the look I am probably giving him. "It's Christmas."

And just like that, I move toward almost understanding. The casualness of his delivery, the ease with which it's delivered, this feels like the other sort of breach—a line, a divide.

I come from lace-curtain Irish married into Métis. I come from the land of pretending we have enough, of faces scrubbed clean with rough cloth, of generic cereal boxes pushed down deep in the trash, their contents having been poured into the one lone Cheerios box.

But it's Christmas, a time when many people overspend,

and we've been so poor the last year, I have a hard time putting together the pieces. I will have been with this man for several years before I learn he grew up with servants. He won't call them that, but that's what they were—women who were paid to come into his childhood home on the Mexican border near Brownsville, Mexican women who crossed the border to cook and clean, to mind the children.

I don't yet know this. When he delivers the information later, it's in much the same shrugging way as he delivers the tale of the oversized giraffe.

It still makes me furious in my body. I see the chicken thighs conveying and conveying. But maybe I'm not explaining this right. It makes my breathing change, my mouth set to the side, my eyes narrow, my arms tingle like they do in illness. It makes my body so furious it wants to do something to someone. It's what I imagine people mean when they say "cold fury."

Because this man comes from enough, but he believes it's important to withhold it from me—both the enough and the knowledge of the enough. He's been too prideful to ask his parents for help they certainly would have given. He's been withholding this certainty perhaps because he understands I come from less, as did most of our graduate school friends.

I would never have entered into this relationship had I understood he came from safety, from financial, material safety and denied it to me while I worked and worked, while I carried and carried and carried our child. I would never have hooked my life to any man who came from safety and pretended otherwise. There is no greater betrayal than this pretending. I came from the opposite sort of pretending. I knew in my body its cost. There is no worse life than a pretending life. There is no worse house than a pretending house.

VII.

The night the neighborhood kids set our tree on fire, my boy-friend takes his baseball bat out to the front porch. The sky shifts from gold to navy. It's just past the start of the new year, and from a further distance, the way the tree is lit against the shifting sky might look festive. The grackles squawk as they flap away from the sparking branches, and the song sparrows spin and dive but keep quiet, as is their way in winter.

Our daughter is sleeping upstairs, and this is what I say first to her father when he's still inside, looking for the bat: "Stop stomping around. She's asleep." Next, I say, "Come inside," but he stands there with the bat, staring across the yard to where the kids laugh and run back and forth along the chain-link fence.

Only a few tree limbs spark now. Both the tree and the kids seem to be working toward wearing themselves out.

"Come inside," I say again.

One of the boys sees the bat, the stare, and he stops the run-ning of the other two. They stand still and face our porch, their shoulders wide now, their faces backlit by the last of the sun. There had been a fourth kid before, a larger one, and I'm hop-ing he's not gone home for reinforcements of any kind.

My daughter's father has called the police, though I had said not to. This is his version of waiting.

"I'm going to go brush my teeth," I say, "and if you're still outside when I'm done, I'm locking the door."

The worry line, then, has come inside, has been pulled inside the house. Or more accurately, I've brought it inside.

By the time I'm done brushing my teeth, the policeman has arrived. He's nicer than the last one and seems smarter, too, or at least seems to understand his job as promoting safety and calm.

"Go inside," he tells my boyfriend. "Listen to your wife."

No one corrects him, least of all me. I'm happy in this moment to be the wronged wife. I'm happy in this moment to be the one he's supposed to listen to.

After this night, I say it sometimes to my not-yet-husband—"Listen to your wife"—and it sometimes shifts the look on my boyfriend's face, and it sometimes shifts the look for the better.

If he'd had his gun that night, if he'd brought more than a bat to the front porch, he would have been shot, or he would have gone to prison. The policeman tells him this, too, and ends with "think about your family."

Cecilia Coleman was thinking about her family, about her son Joseph Hall, when she sent him to Indianapolis to stay with her brother. The police find him there in early January, around the same time the policeman comes to our house and offers his advice. After, Joseph Hall is held in the Allegheny County Jail. He speaks with his mother nearly every day, but he does not come home.

Later that night, the birds come home to roost in the burned-out tree—the noisy grackles and silent songbirds, the most everyday of birds, too, in the sparrows. A grouping of sparrows can be called a variety of names, including a host, crew, flutter, meiny, quarrel, or tribe. According to Webster's, the primary and oldest definition for *meiny* is "company" or "retinue." Both words conjure soldiers, their togetherness, their close proximity, one to the next to the next. Tonight both words conjure lack.

I go to bed first, our daughter still asleep in her bassinet beside me. I lie awake, thinking about the policeman as a strange ally, as unlikely company. It is strange indeed to have this policeman as my main or primary company. I have never before considered such a possibility, such a loneliness that would engender such a feeling. Outside, the birds are tucked together in their meiny. Because even the birds, after they've flown, know the comfort, the importance of being able to head back home.

VIII.

We stay through the spring. I apply and then interview for one other job, and the offer is made the same time as my boyfriend receives a job offer back in Lubbock. It seems like the best thing, like going home. Though many of my friends there, my company, already have left, it seems like the right choice still. I feel the weight beginning to lift as we plan and plot. We consider our options. There is nothing as good, perhaps, after a long year of feeling stuck, as having options.

My boyfriend walks the dogs and takes care of our daughter while I'm at work. He's teaching himself how to cook delicious meals. We're settling into being parents. I am not then thinking so often of the oversized giraffe, of how late my boyfriend came to bed that night once he put the bat down. I am thinking less and less of burning trees and the way the birds looked against the night sky.

We come to Pittsburgh with three dogs and leave with two. Jack has a series of strokes and passes away that spring. One of my last days as a Pittsburgher, I argue with people from Animal Control over the phone. Someone had reported our dogs for barking, saying they were left out all night, which was never true, not once.

The man on the phone wants me to license our dogs, all three, and when I say we're leaving and when I say there are now only two dogs, he asks me to prove it. I tell him to feel free to drive to our neighborhood to count the dogs himself. I tell him to feel free to drive to our house in a few days' time to see that we are, in fact, gone.

We're on the phone more than an hour. I'm transferred and transferred to a series of increasingly angry men, and I grow angrier and angrier as man after man asks me to prove my dog is dead. I offer to send them a copy of the transaction from the veterinarian's office, but they say that can be forged. That can be faked. It's such a bizarre exchange that I expect someone to break out into laughter, to say, "I'm kidding," to apologize. Not one of them apologizes. Not one is willing to come to our house to verify only two dogs remain. After learning our address, not one of them is willing to cross the line into our neighborhood.

Eventually, I outlast all the angry men. The last one, a mid-level manager, ends our conversation by saying he'll delete all the tickets from the system if I'll just stop talking. He ends our conversation by saying, "Don't come back to Pittsburgh. You're not welcome here."

The last day, with the car packed, our daughter in her car seat, the dogs in the far back, my boyfriend rinses out the dog dishes in the yard. The car is running, and we had been all set to go when he remembers the dishes.

The sky is starting to turn—we're leaving later than planned—and I'm trying to focus on small details like this instead of thinking about how I've just quit my first tenure-track job, about how happy this makes me but also how afraid.

I reach into the back to check on my daughter, and when I turn around, a group of teenage boys makes its way up the hill toward our house. It's a nice spring day. Neighbors have been out on their porches or steps. Some are finishing up the last of the day's yard work. One by one, as they, too, notice the group, they turn and head back into their houses and apartments. The doors shutter one by one by one like dominos falling.

It is taking my boyfriend a very long time.

The teens each wear a black bandanna tied around an arm, and they're dressed in all black, except for their jeans.

I debate yelling at my boyfriend, but it seems unwise to call attention. The last of the neighbors are inside their homes. Some now are faces in their windows. Everyone but my boyfriend seems to know something is about to happen.

He finally makes his way to the car, taking his time putting the dog dishes away in the car.

"Drive," I say.

"What?" he says.

"Just drive," I say again with more force.

He makes a huffing noise with which I'm familiar. It's meant to tell me I'm being ridiculous or a bitch or some combination of those two things.

The group is at the intersection by our house, is a few feet away, when my boyfriend stops huffing and puts the car into drive.

"Didn't you see that?" I say.

"What?" he says again.

As we drive through and then away from Pittsburgh, I explain the neighbors, the shutting doors, the faces in the window.

He looks over at me and shakes his head like I'm crazy.

Later, back in Texas, any time someone asks about Pittsburgh, I will say what it was like, and he will say, "It was not that bad." It will take years before it occurs to me that perhaps he really believes this—that he experienced a different year than I did.

In the weeks and months after our daughter was born, I went back to work full-time. He stayed home with our daughter. I'm not meaning to suggest this was or is an easy task—to the contrary. But while he watched, some of the birds, the migratory winter birds, began to take their leave, and the trees turned from brown to green, and the first yellow and blue spring flowers began to bud. He chatted with neighbors about their yards and lives. He and our daughter went to museums and restaurants. He strapped her to his back in an elaborate pack, a gift from his aunt, and walked the dogs and our girl up the steep hill to the overlook park. His body was being made stronger.

Mine did not have a chance toward recovery and would not for the next few years. Dr. Dubose had been correct—it was hard on my body, having a pregnancy and then a child so soon after meningitis. It was exponentially more difficult because of the going straight back to work, the lack of maternity leave, the lack of rest. It would take almost three years before I felt back in my body, back in myself.

My boyfriend experienced a different Pittsburgh because he spent less time there but also because he spent the time in a healthy body, with a brain that worked fully.

Still, I think about that day often, how he shook his head at me after huffing. How he was calm and slow-moving and displeased at what my face was doing. We had barely begun our life together, and I could feel the rift forming already, the separation. I could feel it in how ready I was to climb into the driver's seat, to roll up the windows and drive myself on home without him.

There are so many ways to be under strain, under stress, in a place like Pittsburgh. My daughter lives, and so do I. When my mother comes to meet her granddaughter, she stays less than twenty-four hours. But she's there, in our home, meeting her granddaughter.

Across town, James Stubbs's mother visits her son's grave. Across town, Joseph Hall's mother visits her son through glass. There's no touching. She doesn't get to hold him. Neither mother gets to take home her son.

Later, I will learn that as we were leaving town that spring, three teens were convicted of the killing of teenager Keith Watts, Jr., not far from our house.

Watts's grandmother, Wendy Watts, in the *Post-Gazette*, after the trial, said, "I don't blame the parents, we raise our kids as best we can and then we put them out there. They have their own judgment, their own will."

I don't feel any fear or its cousin anger thinking about those teens on the hill that day, who must have been then right around the same age my daughter is now or just a little older. I wonder about their lives, I wonder about their mothers, about their mothers' worry.

Pittsburgh is often called a "most livable" city—it made those lists then and makes them now. That spring, as we left, violence increased in our neighborhood and in nearby neighborhoods as retribution began both for Watts's killing and for the sentencing of teens from a rival gang who shot him.

The birds in the trees as we leave that day are the kind called resident birds—ones that overwinter or that winter at home.

We spent a winter in Pittsburgh only to leave for the heat of a West Texas summer. We were not residents. We were not welcome back. But my daughter was born there, and she likes to tell me how wonderful it is, this place not really fixed in her memory.

"You were born there," I say, "and that is a wonderful thing."

TEN

Fracture and Song

I.

Of the nearly two hundred Arapaho and Cheyenne killed at the Sand Creek Massacre, two-thirds were women and children. I use the preposition "at," not "in," because those women and children were not "in" battle—they were at home; they were invaded at home. I say "at," not "in," because location matters. This location—Sand Creek—has become a contested space. Its history is as contested as it is important. To memorialize correctly, language matters. To remember lineage, both of people and of place, language and image matter. To place Sand Creek in a line of people and space that connects to today's people, today's spaces, and to work toward survivance, language and image together must matter.

The Sand Creek massacre occurred at the edge of the geologic formation now best known as the Niobrara Shale Play. At the time of the massacre, November 29, 1864, the Niobrara

Shale was between 82 and 87 million years old. The formation sometimes also is called the Niobrara Chalk.

The most familiar image of the Sand Creek Massacre is not chalk but oil on canvas, Robert Lindneux's 1936 *History Colorado*. The image is displayed in *The Wall Street Journal*'s article on Sand Creek and on the National Park Service website, for example. The latter is where the *New York Times* article on the 150th anniversary leads readers for more information on the massacre.

Lindneux's painting offers a landscape that stuns: panoramic, row on row of teepees in taupe and tan against the brown of the ground, with the light blue water of the creek winding through the scene like ribbons, the clouding sky above a mix of both palettes. The details, though, the people. Soldiers in blue ride roans and chestnuts. The soldiers have their guns drawn, long, thin barrels out front—this seems like how it might have been. But they're shooting, most often, at men. At Arapaho and Cheyenne men. Some hold guns pointed back at the soldiers, some lie fallen to the ground by the teepees or in the creek, facedown. Image and language—they matter.

II.

Two-thirds of the Arapaho and Cheyenne killed that day were women and children. In the painting, the women and children are few, not many, and they are standing or walking. They hold their children's hands or carry them on their backs. It is easy to find them; they wear green and so are bright among the tans and blues.

Green is the color of growth, of spring, of hope. Two-thirds of the Arapaho and Cheyenne killed that day were women and children. Words matter. Images matter.

The women and children that day—wearing green, wearing brown, wearing blue, wearing all the colors—were not left to stand, were not left to play or work or see the beauty of their homes, their panoramic vistas, their land.

III.

A "shale play" is a formation of fine-grained sedimentary rock that also contains a notable amount of natural gas. In oil and gas terms, the Niobrara Shale Play is most often called "an emerging play" or "an exciting, new play" or "a young play." It is an active play, producing natural gas through hydraulic fracturing or fracking. Water and sand and chemicals, millions of gallons, are forced down into the shale, the rock, to break it apart, to release the gas, which is then taken.

In October 1865, the Treaty of the Little Arkansas acknowledged the government's blame for the Sand Creek Massacre. But the treaty also took Cheyenne and Arapaho rights to land titles in the state of Colorado. The language matters, and the actions do not speak, they shout.

IV.

What has happened since fracking began in June 1998 in the Barnett Shale of Texas, what is happening today across the country, is this continued shouting. The degradation and exploitation of Indigenous women and children continue through the force and power of history, through the force and power of this fracking industry.

Indigenous women and children are sold for sex to fracking camp workers; they are exchanged, they are bartered, they are trafficked; they are supply meeting demand. They are made to be goods on the land their families once inhabited, their own lands.

The taking by force of our land always has been twinned with the taking by force of our bodies, of our most vulnerable bodies—our women, our children.

In the Bakken Shale Play in the Dakotas, there has been a 30 percent increase of sex trafficking cases filed in the last three years. In April 2015, a coalition of Indigenous women filed a formal request for the United Nations to intercede on behalf of Indigenous women who are being trafficked for sex near fracking sites across the Great Plains.

The taking by force of our land always has been twinned with the taking by force of our bodies.

In rural northern Pennsylvania, along the New York State border, sex trafficking around Marcellus Shale sites has grown so great, a local YWCA received a $500,000 federal grant to provide help to trafficked women and children, many of whom come from nearby reservations in New York. The organization Sing Our Rivers Red has taken its art exhibit to New York and to North Dakota and to most states across the country. They collect single earrings and display them on red backdrops to memorialize the missing and murdered Indigenous women.

The taking by force of our land always has been twinned with the taking by force of our bodies.

V.

History is lived, in our lands and in our bodies. In this country, we bear the repetition of the words—the times "battle" is chosen over "massacre"—and the images, those women in green still whole, still standing. We repeat them whether they are true or false. We spin them until we are dizzy, until we fall to the ground.

But the ground receives us. Always. We practice survivance through language and image and memory. We protest, we draft petitions, we make art, we memorialize.

The taking by force of our land always has been twinned with the taking by force of our bodies. Images matter. Words matter. These lives matter. We understand that alongside every creek, every rock formation, every piece of land that was once and still is ours, there is crying, yes, there is blood on the bright green of the women's dresses, but there also are our images, our words, ringing out like song.

ELEVEN

How to Make a Trafficked Girl

I.

When the girl, the niece, is twelve, tell her she has a too-much body. She sweeps the floor, she does the dishes, she watches her younger siblings. To say "she watches," to say, "siblings"—both are complications. Her father has many children with many women. To say "she watches" means she watches her father watching the girl children. She watches the boy children go to the movies with her father. She watches the door shutting behind them. She is invited to watch the children. She is not invited to watch the movie.

Give her a body. Just one. Tell her at twelve she got this body too early. Tell her at twelve her body is too much. Tell her at twelve her body is not enough.

Give her a father. Make him a musician almost twice the age of her mother. Have him father at least a dozen children whose ages range from five years old to fifty-two. Don't call him a minor cult leader, of course, but his beliefs include the separation of his many families from their original families. His beliefs include how he should make all decisions. Make the girl move house to house, city to town to city. Make sure there are strangers invited to live in each house, each city, each town. Hang sheets in the windows and have the father say he thinks better in the dark. He makes better music in the dark.

Make the strangers into family. One of the strangers will be a woman, young, attractive, soon to be pregnant with this man's child. All the women will beg on the street corners of the towns and cities for food, for money, for luck. Make them all have long hair and pleasing faces. Avoid having a neighbor of the original family spot the pretty women begging prettily. Avoid having it reported back. If this happens, when this happens, move, move, move. Another town, another house, no new phone number, no way to reach in or out, no way for anyone from an original family to make contact.

One of the women will help with "the business." The other will stay home. Make the girl's mother the one who stays home. She is in charge of spiritual guidance. She keeps the candles lit. She keeps the crystals crystalling on the windowsills, on the corner altar, in between the spoons and forks in the utensil drawer.

Have the mother ask her original family for help, ask for money, on repeat. After the help is sent, have the mother cut off all contact. Provide no forwarding address or number. Have this happen at least twice yearly for more than a decade.

Ask the girl's auntie to drive cross-country through a snowstorm to help pack for one of the moves. Make the girl still small, the brother not yet born but living still inside the mother, who is about to give birth. But never mind—there is packing to do. There is always packing.

The auntie drives a rear-wheel-drive car, a small car, a Chevy Chevette, which is reliable for how its engine will always start but perhaps is not the best car for winter roads. In the snowstorm, she drives fifteen to twenty-five miles per hour through most of the eastern part of Colorado, through the flatlands that once belonged to the Arapaho and the Jicarilla Apache. Mostly, now, the land belongs to white ranchers, who've filled it with cows and more cows. The snow falls onto the cows, onto their black-and-white backs, their broad heads and noses. The snow falls on car after truck after car lining the road's narrow shoulder.

On the two-lane, a large SUV passes the auntie with his lights on bright, cutting so sharp through the thick, wet-falling snow. When she comes up over the next hill, the SUV has wrecked itself off the left side, off the sharp edge of the road. The SUV dangles, roadside, two wheels on, two off. There is no way to stop her car without it also becoming a dangling thing. She is sorry. She keeps driving.

The siren's wail behind her shakes the snow-quiet, and she wonders the next twenty or so miles if help got there in time. She wonders about her sister, about the imminent baby's arrival. She wonders if she will get there in time.

The auntie's arms want to tighten and shake, but she won't allow it. She holds her back and arms so straight, and she drives and drives. She does not press on the brake, only taps the accelerator light, so light, so that the car will go slowly and will remain on the road. The exit to Sterling, Colorado, is a steep rise and then a fall, but she takes it and slows and slows until she comes to a stop at a Comfort Inn.

She has prayed the whole way in a quiet way, in a way that focuses on her grandmother's voice, on her body, on her breathing. At the Comfort Inn, there is one room left, one home-made muffin remaining in the basket with its red-and-white checkered cloth. She takes both, and in this last room, she falls into a long, deep sleep, muffin crumbs littering the bedsheets like a trail to her sleeping mouth.

The next day brings a bright, clear sky—it's Colorado, after all, where the weather sweeps in and back out as if its main function is to provide surprise. Her arms are sore from being held so stiff, but she eats another muffin and shakes out the stiffness, and she drives and drives.

At the house, upon arrival, she is not too late. The baby is not yet arrived, and she helps with the packing. She cooks meals. She plays with the girl, who is clever and darling, though no one else ever tells her she is clever and darling. The baby does not yet arrive.

Time runs out. There is the teaching job for which to return. When she says this, the household laughs. It is not a household for jobs.

The auntie opens the living room curtains, and when she comes back from the store, the curtains again are closed. Open and shut, shut and open, their fabric thick like a velvet cape tied tight around a neck.

There is talk of who might be watching. There is talk of leaving as soon as possible.

When the auntie is the first to leave, she does not take the girl, though this will be her impulse, then and always. When she leaves, she waves and smiles and waves, and she has to focus to calm her breathing.

After, she will be told to stop calling. She will have said something, she will have somewhere crossed a line she was not meant to breach. She will perhaps have not closed or opened the velvet curtains at exactly the right angle. She will not hear any word, any darling words from the clever girl. She will not be allowed any contact. She will not see the girl for several more years.

Later, back in contact, she will be told to mind her own business. If she has questions, she will be told she has no right, she has no right, she has no right. She will be told she has had such an easy life. She will be told she has no idea—no *idea*. She will be left with so much anger she will have to work and work to find a large enough container.

II.

Make the brother born. Make him grow up noisy and encouraged to be louder still, except when the father wants to make music or sleep or think. Make the girl the brother's keeper. Take the brother to the movies. Take the brother to The Shopping Mall—you know the one—where the father first met the mother.

Make the mother have grown up so small-town. Make, then, a shopping mall such a rarity in the mother's childhood that pretty much anyone she meets in one still seems like a miracle. Make Webster's third definition the relevant one: "3a: an urban shopping area featuring a variety of shops surrounding a usually open-air concourse reserved for pedestrian traffic, 3b: a usually large suburban building or group of buildings containing various shops with associated passageways."

It will be the one where the mother, not yet a mother, only twenty years old, wanders the stores, the hallways, the associated passageways, her head burning with fever. In a fever dream, the father takes home the woman who becomes the mother. Make her have had a childhood that did not feature caretaking. Make her have had a childhood of illness during which she was made to feel like a burden rather than a darling child.

When she is sick in this childhood, in winter, the sister, who is not yet the auntie, will roller-skate in the basement. With eighties pop as the soundtrack, the sister practices figure eights and limbo moves with one leg kicked out at a sharp angle. What must it have sounded like from upstairs, from a sickbed?

Make their childhood front yard hold a maple tree with leaves bigger than waving hands. When the tree is cut down, make the baby squirrels who've lost their home come inside the house to be fed at regular intervals from an eyedropper. There are neighborhood hawks, so the baby squirrels live inside, in the basement.

Everyone feeds the baby squirrels—the sister who becomes the mother, the not-yet auntie, their mother, their father. No one hits the baby squirrels or yells or whispers about how they should just get up already. Isn't it about time? Isn't it? Baby squirrels are called kits or kittens. A litter of kittens is a dray or scurry.

The baby squirrels grow up to be regular, everyday squirrels, named Chipper and Charlie. One later day, they are released from the basement into the wilds of the front yard. Chipper scurries away; Charlie lives in the front yard's last remaining tree. The sturdy sister, the auntie, plays with Charlie and also with the neighbor girl a game called "high seas."

The auntie sails the ship of an old mattress in the basement or a wide expanse of front-yard grass. She map-reads. She plots exit upon exit upon exit. When there are Barbies, they are busy Barbies, off to work, to the beach, to dinner, to the movies—off, off, off.

When the sister who is not yet the mother leaves her sickbed, she likes to play baby doll. She likes to play kitchen. Her baby dolls are well dressed, their hair brushed flat and sleek to their shoulders. When the auntie plays baby doll, she dunks the dolls upside down in the bathroom sink she's pre-filled. They have troll hair thereafter. She is not allowed to touch the sister's dolls.

Sailing the high seas only involves learning to sail. Driving the highways of America only involves learning to drive. But the sickbed sister who is not yet a mother never plays high seas. She never does learn to drive.

The sickbed sister who becomes the mother never does like to play in the childhood basement. Later, years later, the sickbed sister says, "Don't you remember that time when Mom was so mad at you, and she took you down into the basement, and you were gone so long—you were down there so long—and I was sure you were never coming back up?"

"No," the sister/auntie replies. But she can well imagine the choices. She broke something, said something, her face did or did not do something, her mouth would not stop saying something, her mouth would not stop.

The sister who is not yet the mother reports hovering near the basement stairs, convinced the mother was killing the auntie. That's what she remembers, what she says: "I thought she was going to kill you. I thought she was killing you."

The childhood house in which they grew was a metaphor-drought of a house, was metaphor-poor. So when the sister who is not yet a mother says, "I thought she was killing you," she means exactly what she says.

III.

Make the man at The Shopping Mall, who is certainly not a minor cult leader, become the father twice over. At The Shopping Mall and just after, make him offer his care until the fever breaks. His hold will not break for better than a decade.

In Walnut Creek, California, as reported in *The Washington Post*, another shopping mall, after a renovation, is overcome with pigeons. Remmy, a Harris's hawk, is hired to solve the pigeon problem. He swoops over Nordstrom and Neiman Marcus and seems to particularly enjoy the pigeons who lurk near the Lush cosmetics store.

The Shopping Mall where the mother meets the father offers no pigeons or hawks, but the food court offers ice cream. Give the brother an ice cream big enough he will not have finished it by the time he arrives back home. Never think about the sister and whether she will notice or whether she likes ice cream or whether she is growing up to be a pigeon or a hawk or another sort of bird no one yet has ever seen or invented.

At home and in the yard or the park or everywhere, encourage the brother to take the world as his territory. He plays sword fighting. His first words are "en garde." Enjoy with total joy his high-pitched squeals. Never hear the mother say stop or shush or sit down, goddamnit, sit down and be quiet. The girl grows to know those words only in reference to *her* voice, *her* body.

The brother grows tall and is praised. All limbs and territory. The sister owns no territory, not even her body, not even her own growing limbs. If her body is a too-much body, why should she want it? If it's been claimed as belonging in the land of the too-much, is it really even hers, anyway?

IV.

Tell the girl this body is not only a too-early body but a too-far body. Mark the edges of her body like we are carving up territory. How many steps past territory and timelines do we have to go before we're making a commodity? How many steps back does this too-much body have to make before it is again hers?

At twelve, give her a first period. Give her pain. Have her report her pain to the mother, who at first receives these reports with *shush*. Have the girl escalate. Have her perform the act called doubled over. Have her say she can't walk or move. Have no one consider the potential other sources of pelvic pain in a twelve-year-old girl, in a twelve-year-old girl who looks as if she might be sixteen or seventeen. Have no one ask any of the right questions.

Have a lone doctor visit end with an OxyContin prescription. Have the mother fill and deliver it. Have no one question whether narcotics for a twelve-year-old are a good idea. Have no one question why it might be seen as a good idea to shush and drug a twelve-year-old.

If generous, report how tired is the mother, how loud the younger brother. If generous, mention the move after move, city after town after city. If generous, forget to mention how many times the prescription is filled and filled and filled before somebody asks a question. If generous, report how the incidences of begging and smiling and saying thank you at street corners increase during this time. If generous, report how during this time, it is winter.

If generous, report how many people fill such prescriptions. If generous or if stingy, if at all interested in accuracy, report how the father during this time escalates his violence against the mother to a breaking point.

V.

Make the hospital visits complex and frequent. Make the girl overdose so many times it is not possible to keep count. Make there be so many drugs. Make there always be Oxy. Make there always be paperwork.

Make the girl turn into a woman. Make her learn the ways of the methadone clinic. She will eat bag after bag after bag of Snickers and Reese's, drink Pepsi after Coke after Pepsi. Make her too-much body turn large. Then, hallelujah of all hallelujahs, make the methadone work.

VI.

Make the girl, who's now a woman, give birth to a child who's mostly clean. The woman/girl will have been mostly clean, so the child will be born, too, in this liminal state. Make the girl go through more rehab. Make the child be born into weeks of detox before the hospital release, the blanket swaddling, the taking home. The mother now is a grandmother and also she is again or still the mother.

VII.

Make the auntie the one with the narrative of the too-much mouth rather than the too-much body. Both of them, all of them, all of us, know this really is one common narrative: she should have learned, she wouldn't learn, she should have.

The girl posts online she's forty-eight days sober. Despite a flurry of calls, no one in the original family knows exactly what this means, only that there has been more relapse, more recovery, more repeat, repeat, repeat. Except this time, they learn, it's booze, not pills—it's drinking, not snorting or smoking or shooting up. This time, the girl joins most of the rest of the family with a drink in her hand.

She is different, though, in how she's working toward sobriety. She is different only in the tenacity, the accountability, the reporting of the exact number—forty-eight days.

VIII.

In the repeating cycle of the girl's childhood, not all the strangers who come to live in the houses are women, made to smile and beg, to mind the children. In the childhood, the stranger men visit; they to and fro. They have access to everything. Everything is theirs.

When the auntie visits this time, she is writing about trafficking, about fracklands and water protectors, about the endless sea of parking lots filled with trucks, hotel after hotel after hotel. When the mother leaves the room to make more tea, the girl leans forward from her perch on the sofa, says, "I know those hotels."

The mother appears with the tea, and what is there to say, upon her return? The girl's face shutters, and the auntie has so many questions that will go unanswered: What is the state of the girl's mind, of her sobriety? Is she clouded by Oxy, by other pills, or through drinking? Is she clear in what she says, and why does she say it? Is she wanting only a connection with her auntie? Or if she does know the hotels, what sort of knowledge is this—through rumor or through worse, the kind of knowledge that lives in the body, the kind we call firsthand? The auntie's hand shakes as she sets down her tea and prepares for her departure.

It is once again winter, or perhaps it is perpetual winter. The auntie no longer owns an ice scraper, so upon her departure, she clears her windshield with her coat sleeve and a credit card long past its expiration date.

IX.

Meanwhile, the brother grows and grows. For his nightmares, no one prescribes Oxy. For his nightmares, he is given books and a cat to pet and a turtle that he turns his back on, one time so very briefly, at a park, and then it is gone. He searches and searches. In the last place, it is perhaps surprising how fast a turtle can make an escape, or in the first place, it is surprising how long the turtle lasted inside the house.

The brother has no Oxy for his nightmares, no rest from how his mind wheels and wheels, no rest from what he saw when he was small and freshly back from the movies.

There is college for him while the girl works the liquor store, the big box store, the grocery store, the online knife store. She practices her online knife store pitch for her auntie, who offers praise but does not buy a single knife. She does not trust herself with knives that sharp.

The brother plays music like the father but is in no other way like the father. He misses the turtle. He pets the kitty. Hawks, of course, can't be trusted around kitties or baby turtles, but no one here has hired a hawk. The brother's wheeling mind becomes all spokes, becomes all splintering spokes. He can't unsee or forget. He begins wearing a surgical mask and telling people not to get too close—he's worried about germs. Back off, he tells them, please, just back off.

In childhood, the brother remembers how the girl was supposed to behave, and how, for him, there was no supposed to. He remembers the sword fights, the high-pitched squealing fun. He remembers the mall. He remembers the movies. He remembers what he sees upon return from the movies, what he was not supposed to have seen in the first place. He replays his rememberings like movie stills, scene after scene after scene, till his mind fragments.

X.

The girl's child is raised by the grandmother/mother, but for a time, they all live together in something approximating a family. The girl for a time holds down a job. She brings home a boyfriend, and they all live together until the night he tries to choke her to death and almost succeeds but not quite.

Unlike the father, who goes to Chicago and Philadelphia and California, who goes and fathers and goes, the boyfriend goes to prison. The father, this past Mother's Day, posts online, "Hey my people, today is a day of honor, to the mothers who bared our children who gave them life and nurtured them and most of the time have to protect them. To all the fathers who are men!, stand up for the day of motherhood; and give thanks to the Queens who brought forth life, Bears the pain and Joy of childbirth, it's always nice to take a few minutes out and say thank you from the bottom of my heart, mother of my children, happy Mother's Day! happy Mother's Day! happy Mother's Day, peace out."

The father's latest child, in the picture, looks to be four or perhaps five years old, though the father by now must be in the ballpark of seventy. As far as she knows, the auntie is the only one googling. The auntie is the only one maintaining contact, if you can call online surveillance contact. The auntie is the only one calling a school that one time, asking about the father, saying, "It appears from your website this man is working with children, with teenage girls." The auntie is the only one suggesting various spellings and iterations of the father's last name.

The boyfriend will be released soon from prison. The boyfriend from prison passes along how he remembers where they live, how he remembers the name of the store where the mother works at the shopping mall in a nearby town.

The phrase *shopping mall* is descended from "pall-mall," which Webster's describes as "a 17th century game in which each player attempts to drive a wooden ball with a mallet down an alley and through a raised ring in as few strokes as possible" and "*also:* the alley in which it is played."

The mother and the girl and the girl's child and the auntie all are Métis, all are descended from trappers and traders and strong women, original women. The mother and the girl and the girl's child all come from the Road Allowance people—from Métis women who lived through Alberta winters in shacks, roadside, after being kicked off their land, and they also come from the men who did the kicking and sometimes worse.

The mother and the girl and the girl's child and the auntie are waiting in the alley for the mallet to come down. Or they're walking The Shopping Mall halls or the road's edge or the bottom of the ditch. Maybe they're watching for the hawk, waiting for it to stop its pigeon feast. Maybe they're in charge of themselves now at long last or at least in charge of this narrative. Maybe at long last the curtains are flung wide, and the sun is shining into the house, into all of the houses. Maybe at long last, the story is being told from the inside out—even if the snow is coming back tomorrow, even if the snow arrives the next day and the next and the next. Maybe they're sailing the high seas or driving safe down a lone highway, nowhere near the edge, nowhere near the hawk or its catch, the view in the rearview only the brightest of skies.

TWELVE

City Beautiful

I.

Our first year in Orlando, we live in a rental house in what's considered a good part of Orlando, College Park, bordering Winter Park, but we live in the under-the-freeway part. Our house is constructed of concrete blocks, is low-slung and small, with a long, narrow backyard that features lush grass, flowers that bloom year-round, and traffic noise that revs and blooms and belches.

This day, we're out looking at houses, at other neighborhoods. I teach at the University of Central Florida, and we're trying to find a neighborhood in which to buy a house, perhaps, or at least, one to rent where the backyard air is not filled with the exhaust of car upon car upon car.

The traffic stop, at first, seems ordinary, seems everyday, though all we've done is turn left across a double yellow stripe into a McDonald's parking lot. Our daughter wanted ice cream.

The officer is young, Latina, and she speaks first to my then-husband in Spanish. He replies in kind, and it's then I notice her hands, how they shake a little, how one of them never leaves the gun at her hip.

My then-husband is a self-identified white man, a gringo, who grew up in Olmito, Texas, close to Brownsville. He's dark-skinned and dark-eyed with straight black hair. In Pennsylvania, everyone assumed he was Italian. In Texas, Mexican. Here, in Florida, in Orlando, he's Cuban. He enjoys speaking Spanish back to the telemarketers and evangels of varied faiths before shutting the door of our rental house in their faces.

My then-husband's family for years were self-identified Cherokee, and his family does feature surnames that are known in Cherokee country, that are featured on the Dawes Rolls, which the National Archives defines as "the lists of individuals who were accepted as eligible for tribal membership in the 'Five Civilized Tribes': Cherokees, Creeks, Choctaws, Chickasaws, and Seminoles. (It does not include those whose applications were stricken, rejected or judged as doubtful.)" His family members identify less and less as Cherokee as the years pass, as one family member takes a through-the-mail DNA test and becomes discouraged, after.

My then-husband, then, is one of the men America considers brown, foreign, other in some circumstances, and in other circumstances, he's a gringo. He's white adjacent. Urban Dictionary defines *white adjacent* as follows: "A person who is technically a minority, but has access to, utilizes and sometimes benefits from white privilege. This is usually accomplished by said person distancing themselves from the socio-political problems their ethnic group commonly faces." I'm reduced to Urban Dictionary because Webster's is mute on the subject.

I understand my idea of the term is an Urban Dictionary reversal. I'm suggesting another way to be white adjacent is to be white ethnically and be considered non-white visually by those around you. I'm suggesting our categories for whiteness are contradictory, backward, easily turned inside out, easily seen for what they are, if one bothers to do the looking. I'm suggesting they serve no one other than their creators, other than their enforcers.

Today, the enforcer is a young Latina officer. Our world is equal parts complicated and strange.

In the back seat, my daughter cries and fusses a little. She can see the golden arches, and where is her ice cream? She may be thinking this or she may be simply reading in the air the tension.

The young police officer is having trouble with the registration, has called in backup. She's put my then-husband in the position, arms and legs spread, arms on the car's hood, and she's checked his pockets with the one free hand. She's instructed me to stay in the car and to be quiet.

We've been in Orlando less than a year, have been married only a little longer. The previous fall, back in Texas, we exchanged vows at the courthouse gazebo in Lubbock. It was Halloween. I wore a wedding dress like the costume it was. The judge who married us wore a witch's hat and threw down firecrackers at the end, startling our daughter.

This day, as we wait and I work to stay quiet, our daughter cries a little more and kicks at nothing in her car seat in the back. I understand the sentiment.

If the young officer would let me speak, she would learn this car is registered to me, that my then-husband and I have different last names.

Her body posture tells me she's both inexperienced and

afraid of my then-husband. She holds her shoulders rigid, but her head and eyes swivel almost continuously.

It's possible, of course, that she's reading him as white—that as a brown woman, she's afraid of a white man. But white men are not often treated this way at routine traffic stops. It's equally or more possible, from the statistics, that she's afraid of him because she reads him as brown, as Cuban or Mexican or from who knows where.

Later, after the older, white male cop shows up, lets me speak, releases us to ice cream and an expensive ticket, I wonder over the young officer's fear. What or who in her life developed this in her—an uncle, a teacher, a father, a brother, a first or last boyfriend? Or some terrible mix of most or all? In addition to wonder, I hold my own fear. If one-third of all stranger homicides are committed by police, how many of those officers also were afraid? How many were driven to shoot by their own fear? There are few things as frightening as the fear of an armed officer.

Even later, when I ask my then-husband about his recollection of that day, he'll say she wasn't that bad, he wasn't in the position that long. She was just green. He may be right, of course. But while he was facedown, I was face-to-face with her, with the fear and anger in her eyes. He dismisses my observations and says I'm just still mad about how much the ticket cost.

There's an expense absolutely to this day—on this we agree. He may have forgotten or tried to, but I also remember that his hands shook when he assumed the position, that he kept his head down a moment or two after she released him.

II.

Eight years later, as we argue over the Latina officer, I'm waiting for the list of names. It's June 2016, and forty-nine people have been shot and killed and fifty-three more wounded at the Pulse nightclub in Orlando, in our former city, one of the few in this country I love. In Spanish, Orlando means "famous land." Now in this moment, Orlando is famous for all the wrong reasons.

When we lived there, in our under-the-freeway house, my creative writing students and some of my colleagues, too, went to Pulse on a regular basis. UCF is the kind of school where students, of course, come from all over the country and world, but a good many of mine were from the Orlando area or had good jobs there and have stayed.

During this time, in summer 2016, I'm not sleeping well. All spring and into the summer, I awaken each morning either at 3:14 A.M. or 4:14 A.M., and then I'm awake for three or four hours before falling back to sleep for a few brief hours in the regular morning time when everyone else is waking up, going to work, or, say, driving a daughter to school.

I'm exhausted from the interrupted sleep but also from the eeriness of the timing—the exact nature of when I wake—if not one hour, then the next, down to the minute, exact and strange in equal measure.

The house where we live together as a family in the Arkansas countryside is a remodeled and expanded log cabin, whose original rooms were built in 1846. It's one of the oldest homes still standing in the county. It sits on an acreage that includes a pond, walking trails around the pond, an overgrown blackberry thicket, a plethora of hummingbirds, sparrows, wrens, and ravens, one fat groundhog my daughter names Sir Num Nums, and many, many ticks.

We bought this house together and moved into it as a family, but I'm not there long before I know my marriage is ending. Part of me certainly has known this for some time—my body with its eerie waking certainly is trying to convey something.

When I learn about the shooting in Orlando, I'm in my office, a small, rectangular room just off our bedroom. I like its cozy size, its shape, which holds just enough room for my small desk and long mid-century couch. The space holds knotty pine walls and painted concrete floors that stay cool to the touch in the humid-thick of Arkansas summers.

The window next to my desk features a good view of the old barn and the connecting sheds, one of which has been tunneled under and claimed by Sir Num Nums. The first time I see him, I'm certain my then-husband and my daughter have put out a statue and forgotten to tell me. Standing on his hind legs, stretched to his full capacity, he sits with his front paws tucked in front, a doofy look on his face. After some time, when he unfolds himself and shifts back to ground, I startle and let out a small scream.

This day, the bedroom TV is the bearer of the bad news from Orlando. I hear it through my office door and then come out and turn up the volume. My then-husband has been attempting to fix the broken ceiling fan. This is a task I've been asking him to do for weeks, maybe months.

When I hear the news, when I see the first images from this city I know well, he turns to me and asks what I think Hillary and Trump will have to say. It seems so long ago now—so impossibly long and far since we were back in this time. Trump has been the presumptive Republican nominee for about a month, this day, and with about five months left till the election, many of us still believe a Trump presidency to be impossible.

I hate crying in front of other people, and even though we've been together at this point for more than a decade, my then-husband has almost never seen me cry. But between not sleeping well and now, with the news, I feel spinny, like the world is moving under me or like somehow I'm drunk despite how it's early morning, despite how I've not been drinking.

When he asks again what political points I think Hillary and Trump will make of this news, I can't arrange my face. I tell myself, Do not pick a fight with your husband when he says he can't fix the ceiling fan and begins a conversation about the shooter, about the ramifications for the election, how and what each presidential candidate might say. I work to summon my best self from wherever she is hiding.

I know myself well enough to know I usually do love conversations about all things geopolitical. I tell myself he can't be expected to know today is not the day. I still, of course, do expect him to know, but I tell myself anyway.

Anger is good for pushing me past the impulse to cry, at least for the moment.

"I can't talk to you," I say, "with all that fan shit in your hair—I can't." I go back into my office and both shut and lock the door.

Later, I will work to forgive myself for my tone, for that thing I know my mouth is doing that is not smiling.

I would have been up for a conversation about nostalgia. I would have been happy to have talked about the Cuban restaurant, Numero Uno, our favorite, which sits four blocks from Pulse. I would have been happy to have talked about the piano player there and how he opened the door for our daughter and bowed to her that time and how she curtsied back, even though neither of us knew she knew how to do that particular maneuver.

We could have talked about this while we waited for the list of names.

We could have talked about my students, about Ashley, who is not answering her phone or marking herself safe on Facebook—how she's just moved back to town, to Orlando, how she has posted so recently about looking forward to going to Pulse.

We could have talked about Curtis, who meets his spoken word friends at Pulse, or Pedro, who sometimes shows up there in drag or for other people's drag shows.

This is a truncated list, but I worry over my longer list while I wait for the TV newspeople to deliver theirs.

While I wait, I find I have nothing to say to my then-husband, at least nothing nice. Probably the last time he saw me cry was when we drove away from Florida, leaving for yet another job, in yet another place. That last year in Florida, we lived out at Cocoa Beach, and when my daughter and I, on our last day, drive to the strip mall where we return our cable TV equipment, we park the car close to the water, to a public access point. When we return to the car, we go past it, to the water's edge, and there at the edge are three manatees, their whiskered snouts poking out, their faces set in what appear to be perpetual smiles.

That night as we drive off, our daughter waves to the neighborhood and cries a little and then falls asleep. In the front, in the passenger seat, I try to cry quietly but I probably don't manage it.

This day, as the TV grows too loud but still offers no new

information, I take my grimace/smile to the park. My grief is still there from the last time when I'd run around and around, when, halfway through the second lap, I knew I couldn't stay in this marriage any longer.

This late afternoon, the grief meets me on the sprint up the hill. No one knows the difference between sweating and crying, anyway, and besides, look, it's starting to rain. And now I'm laughing at myself a little on the downhill, the kind of laughter that's close to hysteria, that could turn into practically anything.

III.

When their list comes, none of my names are on it, and I am sorry for those, including people I love, who've lost dear ones. I watch with the rest of America as family members and doctors rush in and out of hospitals, as family members exit, some of them collapsing in grief against the trunks of palm trees out front or onto the soft and waiting grass, that thick-stemmed Florida grass that is lush and prickly all at the same time.

I come to realize one of the hospitals where the wounded are being treated, and, yes, where the dead are being collected or counted, also houses a wing that used to include my doctor's office. I rarely like a doctor. Perhaps this feeling is a byproduct of our treat-and-street healthcare system in this, our America. Perhaps this feeling goes back further, to childhood. Doctors are people to whom you could tell some truths but not others. Doctors, like policemen, could separate a family, could make an already bad situation worse.

But I like very much my doctor at this clinic in Orlando. He's young, the second-generation son of Chinese immigrant parents, and his father is refusing to take his thyroid medication. I take the same medication, and he's asking me how I remember.

"I just get up every day and take it," I say.

"That's what I tell him," he says. "He's too busy, he says to me," reports the doctor. "He says he forgets."

"It's important, though," I say.

"I'll have him talk to you," he says. "I'll put it on the schedule," and we both laugh.

Pulse sits on the same block as this hospital, with its doctors' office wing, where they took some of those who were shot. It is a tall brick building but is not modern, is the seventies style you see in so much of Orlando—outdated and square, not notable—but with palm warblers strutting under the two palm trees out front that flank the sidewalk like sentinels.

My doctor has black hair that looks as if he's received a static shock. We talk several times about our fathers, and I imagine his has the same hair as his son.

On the day he takes my medical history, he asks a question no other doctor has asked before, at what age had I grown to my full height, and I say twenty-two. He pauses and says, "Do you mean twelve?" and I say, "No, twenty-two. I was just over five feet tall from twelve till twenty-two, and then that year, I grew almost four inches."

"Eating disorder?" he says.

"No," I say.

"Sexual abuse?" he says.

"No," I say.

"The other, then," he says in a clear but soft voice. "Physical abuse."

When I do not say no, when I look at the wall instead, he explains to me, quietly and well, that sometimes a body will shut down this way, and once it's out of the bad situation, the body will remember itself—will literally allow itself to resume growth, but only after it feels itself safe.

At twenty-two, I'd been out of my parents' home for almost four years. It took my body four years to be sure it wouldn't have to go back.

When I get the news about Orlando, then, I am thinking of my students, their beautiful bodies. I am checking my phone, refreshing my newsfeed, crying as each one marks him- or herself as safe. But I know, of course, they are not. Not really. They are alive, yes—we all are. And I am grateful for this fact. I am. But their world is changed. They are not safe, not exactly.

I think of my doctor, who is most likely there at the hospital, with the victims' families, with the living.

That past day when he records my history, I must have a look on my face—a trying-not-to-cry look. On the way out, he stops me.

"Are you using your nose spray?" he asks.

"What?" I say.

"Your allergy spray?" he asks. "Every day?"

"Not every day," I say.

"Every day!" he says in a voice that is almost a shout. "You breathe every goddamn day. Use your nose spray every day." He grins at me, that hair standing on end.

"Okay," I say, throwing my hand into the air. "Fine."

"Okay," he says, throwing his hands into the air, mirroring my gesture.

It was the perfect thing to do and to say, a regular and profane thing to get me to my car without falling apart, to get me all the way home.

I want to think he was there that night and into the next day, holding space for the families of the grieving. I want him to have been there with those families in the building that houses the only written record of my family's imprint on my body—the only written record till now.

Later when he is home with his own family, I hope someone says just the right thing to him to make him wave his hands around in the air, to make him laugh/cry, instead of crying only.

IV.

That summer, as the news confirms the name and some history about the shooter, I am planning a trip to Standing Rock, to the Dakota Access pipeline protest, to the water protector camps.

Omar Mateen, who shot and killed forty-nine people in Orlando and hurt so many others, once was employed by G4S, the private security firm that begins providing security forces for Dakota Access that summer. They will be the ones who bring the attack dogs to Standing Rock. Mateen was employed by G4S in 2007 and spent time each year of employment going through their weapons training.

On June 12, 2016, as peaceful water protectors were making camp at Standing Rock, Omar Mateen took his training, took his body, took his guns into Pulse nightclub in Orlando and shot and killed forty-nine people and wounded fifty-three others. I keep repeating the numbers because they stagger me. Orlando is sometimes called the City Beautiful, and I sometimes have called it my city. Pulse is the nightclub where my students went to drink, to dance, where they converged after workshop.

On Saturday, May 30, 2020, the Pulse memorial site also becomes the site of Orlando's largest protest over George Floyd's death in Minneapolis. Another protest takes place that weekend in Windermere, an Orlando suburb, in front of a home owned by Minneapolis police officer Derek Chauvin, charged with second-degree murder in Floyd's death. The protest at Chauvin's home ends with the arrest of two women for throwing paint at the house. The protest downtown that began at the Pulse memorial ends with police using tear gas against unarmed protestors.

I don't know where to put these connections—I don't know where to put my grief and my rage sometimes in this, our America.

Sometimes I think of the rage and grief like a road through traffic and there's nowhere to turn off and there's nowhere to park.

In the days after the shooting in Orlando, I can't stop thinking about the neighborhood that houses Pulse—how it is mostly a driving neighborhood, not a walking one, meaning most of those there that night would have driven their cars. Meaning, it's possible nearly a hundred family members and friends had to drive there in the days following the shooting to collect the cars of the dead and the wounded.

How do you enter that car? How do you collect yourself for that drive home? How do you make your knees fold like they're meant to or your hands hold the key?

What I want for everyone there is to have the will to do this everyday, regular act under these terrible, irregular circumstances. What I want is for everyone all across this, our America, to say no more, to say this will be the last time anyone will have to make a drive like this, to say this will be the last time anyone will have to feel the weight of holding those keys.

V.

After the list of names, my students are doing what they are so good at—making art and making themselves useful.

Curtis makes himself busy organizing, as is his way. When the parishioners from Westboro Baptist, an organization best known for hate speech, show up to the funerals, Curtis puts his body between the mourners at the funerals and the intruders. Before the funerals start, he instructs his peers on the etiquette of that task, reminding them that though this is to some extent a counterprotest, what it is first and foremost is someone's funeral. He instructs his friends to show up in dress shirts, offers that, if need be, he will teach them how to knot their ties.

Pedro offers up his poems and pictures of himself in drag, alongside makeup tips too complex for anyone but him ever to master.

Ashley offers the work of other queer writers, posting them online, using her position as an editor to showcase work of newer queer and Latinx writers from Orlando.

This is another way to make a list. This is another way to get to grief and through it, to get through mourning.

VI.

By a few months later, in the time I spend going to Standing Rock and returning, there are so many additional mass shootings I lose count. My then-husband and I have not found a way to talk about the Orlando shooting or my time at Standing Rock or the election; we won't find a way.

On election night, we're with our daughter at a party at the home of acquaintances—the parents of one of our daughter's friends. As the results roll in, state by state, and some of the children begin crying, I begin to drink too much. Most of the adults at the party are beginning to drink too much or are already long since drunk or going outside to smoke weed or some combination of all.

The children's faces, especially the girl children, are hard to look at straight on. Many of the girls are wearing pantsuits, and someone's brought blue eye shadow, which they've been applying to all—grown-ups, male and female alike, babies and toddlers, et al.

The blue-shadowed eyes by the end of the night are a grotesquerie. Webster's says this word dates back to 1666, and its synonyms include "monster, monstrosity, ogre."

Technically, it's a school night, and before we can be a hundred percent certain of the results, of the outcome, my then-husband starts telling me it's time to go home. Our daughter lobbies to stay a little longer. She and I both want to see this to the end or to something closer to it.

I drink in front of my daughter, but this night is the first and last time I ever drink too much in front of her. Later, she'll say it was fine—that I was hilarious—and her face will show no trace of any other meaning, and for this, I will be glad.

That night, eventually, we do go home, and I awake in the morning early and with the kind of headache most often described as splitting. My then-husband is surprised to see me up so early and says he thought last night he was going to have to leave me there, and when I say, "Ha, ha," the look he gives me makes it clear he does not mean this in a ha-ha sort of way.

When I say leaving me there would have been unacceptable, terrible, that it also would have been scary and strange for our daughter, he says, "Well, it was a school night, and you didn't want to go home."

I get dressed then and wake our daughter for school. I realize I've slept through both 3:14 and 4:14 A.M. for the first time in a very long time. On the drive to school, I sing along with my daughter to a song she likes, and we laugh together a little, and I start to feel like though the world is falling apart on the macro level, though my head and other parts of me feel split wide open, perhaps at the level of the micro, starting this moment, I will begin to put my world back together and to make it once again mine.

THIRTEEN

Chicken

I.

The news vans swarm the neighborhood. Women with micro-
phones and over-sprayed hair huddle with cameramen, considering angles. I approach from the park, which sits at the bottom
of a tall hill. We're having an over-warm day for October, with
lush green leaves from the tall trees giving way to gold and red,
the damp-wet of their fall underfoot. The air holds no crisp,
only the still and humid-thick of autumn in Arkansas.

The house, two-story, white, is maybe a mansion, depending
on your definition. It's older construction, a foursquare with a
wide front porch that sits atop the hill. From the porch, I imagine, you could sip coffee, look down at the dog walkers and jog-
gers circling Wilson Park. Instead, since Carla Tyson's moved
into the house, the maybe-mansion, a wrought-iron fence rings
the property. Carla is the daughter of Don Tyson, who founded

the Tyson Chicken and then Tyson Foods empire, which in 2018 had a net worth of just over $40 billion.

Carla to and fros exclusively through the garage, which is tastefully tucked off to the side. Her standard poodles are the only life I've seen in the yard today or most days—they're curious and fast, one well-behaved, the other down for mischief.

In this, our second year in Arkansas, my family and I rent the last affordable place in the neighborhood, a light blue ranch-style house with good hardwood floors and total wrecks for bathrooms and kitchen. The neighborhood features proximity to the park, to campus, to downtown. When we move out later that year, the landlord will raise the rent by about half. Someone will pay it and then another someone and so on.

It's also the sort of neighborhood to have block parties and ice cream socials, semi-regular gatherings around holidays and long weekends. Children run the streets in small packs. People have backyard chickens and walk their dogs and wave.

As I make my way up the hill toward the news vans and lights, a neighbor greets me and answers my question with "Haven't you heard? It's all over the news and the Facebook group."

I've been at work on campus all day. I didn't know we had a neighborhood Facebook group.

"She pulled a gun," the neighbor says, "a shotgun—on the kids who live next door."

"Who?" I say.

"The chicken princess," she says, smiling.

II.

The first day I arrive in Fayetteville, my first in the neighborhood, I meet Carla Tyson at an ice cream social two doors down. From visiting campus to interview for my job, I already know the three big names in Arkansas are Tyson, Walton, and Hunt— of chicken, Walmart, and shipping fame, respectively. Campus buildings hold their names on shiny placards; our graduate students compete to be Walton Fellows, to have the relative luxury of a year off from teaching while still receiving their stipends.

That first day, the moving truck parked out front, taking over the street, we're unloading our last box when two children arrive at our door.

"A girl! A girl! It's true, you're a girl!" the older one says to my daughter.

Her feet are bare and so are her sister's. The older girl bounces up and down as if on springs, her brown hair flapping up and down with her arms.

She quickly informs us there are only boy children in the neighborhood—and tonight, there's ice cream. She hands over the flyer and bounces homeward.

I have not had homemade ice cream since I was about my daughter's age. My grandmother would make it sometimes in the summer when my cousins came over, and I remember the big spoons, the churning and churning. I have never been to an ice cream social and am having a hard time believing they exist outside very small towns, outside the 1950s.

That night, at the social, Carla Tyson is recovering from knee surgery and we make pleasantries about a colleague of mine she knows. I figure out she's from those Tysons when the bouncing girl calls her Miss Tyson and ma'am when all the other grown-ups have first names only.

Carla has the kind of eyes that never stop moving. She traces the flow of people from living room to kitchen to the backyard where children swing and grown-ups congregate near the chicken coop.

Carla and I seem to be rare in our disinterest in the backyard chickens. Though this hobby becomes popular in the mid-2000s and its popularity escalates through the present day, I don't understand the desire for backyard chickens. The eggs the chicken produce, no doubt, are superior to factory-raised eggs. But in order to get the eggs, you have to give over your backyard space to strutting, pooping, squawking creatures.

Too, before the millennium, backyard chickens were largely the province of the poor or some combination of the rural and poor. Both sides of my family had small family farms; both my parents grew up cleaning chicken coops, plucking feathers, collecting eggs, or wringing necks.

According to Webster's, the word *chicken* is defined first as "a: the common domestic fowl (*Gallus gallus*) especially when young, b: any of various birds or their young," secondarily as "a young woman," third as "a coward," fourth, "[short for *chickenshit*] *slang:* petty details," and fifth, "*slang:* a young male homosexual."

As an adjective, Webster's defines *chicken* as "scared, timid, cowardly," and "insistent on petty details of duty or discipline." I had no idea *chicken* could be verbed, but Webster's lists *chickened* and *chickening* as meaning "to lose one's nerve," usually combined with the word *out,* as in "chickened out."

I grew up with my mother's constant refrain that chickens were dirty, and my father's that chickens were both stupid and mean. My mother, as a child, was expected to catch and pluck, my father, to catch and wring. Living in town meant an escape from chicken labor, a shift into a slightly higher economic class.

That upper-class and wealthy people want backyard chickens is too far a bridge for me to cross. My reaction always is visceral—recoil and head shake and more recoil.

The people who host the party, the parents of the bouncing child, will become our good friends. My daughter and I once will chicken-sit. One of the chickens will not want to return to its coop, and we will chase it with a stick, laughing and swearing and laughing some more. We will not know till later that our friends have a chicken cam. We are not asked to chicken-sit again.

III.

The land that houses Wilson Park's nearly twenty-three acres was once used as hunting grounds by the Osage and was inhabited after by the Cherokee.

Wilson Park becomes the first official park in Fayetteville in 1944 and before that is owned by a private citizen, A. L. Trent, who maintained it as a private park starting in 1906. A part of the park's history and a favorite of mine is the hundred-year-old Osage orange tree. Given a plaque as one of town's "Amazing Trees," the structure and stature of it stuns. Its branches tower over all the other trees and some nearby houses, its gnarly roots twist and turn like something out of one of the darker fairy tales.

Technically called *Maclura pomifera* or Bois d'Arc, this tree and others like it are more commonly known as Osage orange trees. The Parks Department reports it's one of the most photographed trees in the city, and that it's considered a "Witness

Tree" for all it has seen: the tourist camps that used to be a part of the park through the 1920s, A. L. Trent's swimming hole, which became a formal swimming pool years later, the Great Depression, the tenure of seventeen U.S. presidents.

According to the Parks Department site, "the name *Bois d'Arc* or 'bow-wood' was given to this tree by French explorers because the Native Americans used its extremely hard, durable wood in crafting their bows. The tree's green, pebbly fruit (which grows only on the female trees) resembles an orange, but is hard and inedible by humans, though horses and squirrels do eat it. The fruit has also been used as a traditional pest management remedy: placed around a home's foundation, the fruit is said to repel bugs."

History books and a quick survey of my Osage friends confirm the Parks Department account. Osage people did and do use the wood from the tall trees to make bows, clubs, and other things, and the wood is prized for both its strength and flexibility.

I like the neighborhood when we live there, for proximity to the park and its tall trees, for the mix of back-to-the-landers who moved to the neighborhood in the 1960s and '70s and the newcomers, mostly university professors, lawyers, and doctors now that the neighborhood's homes have increased sharply in price. Also, to avoid the narrative of past-ness, the fallacy of past-ness, while I live there, I have both Chickasaw and Cherokee neighbors, which is likely to be true in most neighborhoods here. I like this mix of people and am sorry when we begin to get priced out, when the balance begins to shift in favor of the wealthy.

IV.

That later fall day, Carla Tyson's weapon of choice is a sixteen-gauge double-barreled shotgun. When the young couple, age twenty-one and twenty-two years old, parks in front of Tyson's house on Cleburn Street, one block from Wilson Park and its tall trees, Carla taps their car window with the shotgun and reportedly says, "You need to move or else." The house they live in is a few doors down. It's a public street. She reportedly tells them they're on private property before backing away from their car, before telling them they're scaring her.

The couple later reports being afraid, but they have the presence of mind to leave the window up, to stay in the vehicle, to call the police. When she learns they're calling the police, in a sort of odd game of chicken, she calls the police, too.

When the officers arrive, Tyson reportedly tells them she's "worth a billion dollars" and "was afraid of being kidnapped." She's charged with two counts each of terroristic threatening and aggravated assault, all of which are felonies. She's released on a $2,500 bond.

It might not seem odd or unusual to outsiders for an Arkansan to pull a gun on a neighbor. I know, from the outside, many view the state as full of poverty and backwoods characters. Poverty does exist in the state, of course—we rank forty-sixth on the poverty index—and there are many woods and even some real pockets of wilderness left, and people who live there in those pockets out of choice or necessity.

But our corner, the northwest corner, holds more wealth than any other part of the state. If the stereotype of the state doesn't quite hold in our corner, though, we still do meet a statistical probability for high gun ownership: despite how most people think of rednecks or hill people toting shotguns, statistically speaking, all across the country, those at higher income levels have a much higher gun ownership rate than do the poor.

A recent study through the National Opinion Research Center at the University of Chicago on "Trends in Gun Ownership in the United States, 1972–2018" found "Household gun ownership was greater among respondents in households with higher incomes. . . . It rose from 18.4% for households with income below $25,000 to 45.8% for those with ($90,000+)." The same study found that "in 2010–18, household firearms ownership was higher among households with white respondents (39.3%) than among those with black respondents (18.8%). Similarly, it was greater among non-Hispanics (36.4%) than among Hispanics (16.2%)."

Put more simply, our national gun problem includes the wealthy and white to a degree our narratives don't accommodate. It's then no surprise Carla Tyson owns a shotgun.

After the threats, the posting bond, Carla pleads no contest to reduced charges at a hearing that June. She's found guilty of misdemeanor first-degree assault and is sentenced to a one-year suspended sentence and to pay a $1,000 fine and $170 in court costs.

In Arkansas, pleading no contest to misdemeanor charges for a first offense means you can petition to have the charges expunged from your record after some time has passed. In Arkansas, pleading no contest to misdemeanor charges means you can still legally own a gun.

Back in the fall, after Carla pulls the shotgun on her neighbors, she begins the moving-out process. When I walk to and from the park, her yard remains poodle-less, and no one sees her or her driver coming and going.

The incident occurs the week before Halloween, and on Halloween night, we trick-or-treat as usual in a gaggle—kids sugared and costumed up—racing house to house, receiving mini Snickers and Skittles, homemade popcorn balls and Rice Krispie treats at one house. At the corner of Cleburn and Vandeventer, Carla's tall house stays dark.

Parents talk low about how we wouldn't have stopped there, anyway. There is a whisper-chorus of "so crazy." No one calls her Miss Tyson.

That night, as we circle around the park, I can't help but think of my other encounter with Carla. In between the ice cream social and the shotgun incident, one weekend morning, I'm running at Wilson Park, and Carla and her driver approach me. Carla's in tears, her gray hair wild and uncombed.

The driver hands me a flyer, and I learn her poodles both are missing. They'd been in her yard one minute and then, the next, gone. It's raining, and I'm about to head home, but I tell her I'll keep an eye out.

I know when I get home, my daughter will conscript me into walking the neighborhood with her, calling the names of the dogs, which are printed on the flyer. I know we'll carry empty leashes, certain of her ability to call them to her. She has an ability for this, for dog finding. It's a little spooky how often she encounters a dog who's either run off or been taken from its owner and how often we're able to return the dog to its home.

My daughter's eight, and by now, this find-and-return cycle has happened at least ten times, probably more. My favorite is the time in a northern Houston suburb, at her aunt and uncle's house, when we encounter a purebred bull terrier, which then follows us back to the relatives' home. I know the breed is expensive and this one is well-mannered and very friendly. She's been well cared for, too, so we begin our search with hope that her owner is just around the corner.

We convince the relatives to let us keep the dog in their backyard while we try to track down the owner. Our small dog likes this terrier, and the two of them chase each other around the fenced-in yard while we post things on Facebook neighborhood groups and google vet clinics.

The next day, at a nearby vet clinic, we learn the terrier's name is Skittles, and she's been missing from a suburb on the other side of the Houston metroplex, about an hour's drive from where we found her. The dog's been missing for over a year. Her owner cries and cries, and she calls us later that day from the vet clinic to ask questions to which we have few answers and to thank us.

So when Carla's poodles go missing, my daughter and I do indeed walk the neighborhood in the rain, calling their names, holding onto extra, just-in-case leashes.

We go to bed that night having had no luck, and at bedtime, my daughter is quiet and a little sad. "They're out there," she says, "in the rain and the dark."

I know she's thinking she's failed or that her ability has failed her, though neither of us would be comfortable naming it or saying so. I tell her we'll look some in the morning and to try to get some sleep.

We awake the next morning to barking in the back, in the yard next to our backyard. No one lives in that yard's house at the time, yet there are Carla's poodles, crying and barking in the middle of the yard. It's rained and they're muddy, and the chain-link fence is tight. We call Carla, and between her and my daughter, they get the chain-link bent back and my daughter squiggles through, and Carla's face is wet, either from the rain or from crying or both.

After, I joke with my then-husband that maybe Carla will donate money to the writing program now. The signs had mentioned a reward, but none is mentioned as we wave goodbye to the poodles.

V.

Three years after Carla Tyson pulls a gun on her neighbors, a man in Kentucky takes his gun to a Tyson Foods plant in Henderson, a town south and west of Louisville. In April 2018, Christopher Hancock learns of allegations that his wife is having an affair with another Tyson Foods employee. According to reporting by Beth Smith in the Henderson *Gleaner*, Hancock drives his wife and two small children to the Tyson Foods building, and he takes with him a 9-mm pistol, a .22, a .410, and a 20-gauge shotgun.

His wife manages to contact her sister, who contacts the police, who meet the car at the Tyson Foods building. When Hancock tries to swerve around the police vehicle, he is headed off by a sheriff's deputy. Hancock has told his wife, whose alleged lover is Black, that since he doesn't know what the man looks like, he'll wait and kill all Black men leaving the building—except instead of saying "Black men," he uses a racist epithet.

Hancock leaves his car when he's met by the deputy and tells the deputy he has a gun and where it is on his body. He has a legal permit for the gun as well, a concealed carry permit, which gives him the right to carry the gun. What he doesn't have, of course, is a good story or excuse for any of his behavior, which is indefensible. What he doesn't have is a father whose last name is Tyson.

Though Hancock is armed, he doesn't ever point a weapon at anyone. Though he's made threats on Facebook, he doesn't threaten anyone in person or at gunpoint.

It's not difficult to understand, of course, that he's convicted. According to the Henderson *Gleaner,* "The one-day trial of Christopher Hancock, 42, . . . came down to just 15 minutes of jury deliberation before the panel came back with a guilty verdict," and the jury took less than half that time to decide a sentence, recommending Hancock spend ten years in prison.

He's serving his time at Blackburn Correctional Complex in Lexington, not far from Harrodsburg, Kentucky, where another historic Osage orange tree stands on the old Fort Harrod site.

Fort Harrod was the first permanent settlement by colonists in the state of Kentucky. Osage orange trees are not native to Kentucky, but there were prominent tribes whose citizens travelled back and forth to Kentucky through the territory that encompasses what is now Arkansas and Tennessee—including the Chickasaw, Shawnee, and Cherokee.

The Osage orange at Fort Harrod is circa the late eighteenth century and, according to the Historical Marker Database, is technically the largest in the nation—76 feet tall at its crown, 88 feet tall at its full height, with a circumference of 12 feet 4 inches. Because it has a split trunk, though, apparently it can't be crowned the tallest.

Registered consulting arborist Jud Scott writes, "Was this tree brought to Fort Harrod in the late 1700–1800's by a pioneer, did Lewis and Clark bring it back during their travels or was it planted by Indians because of its good bow making properties? No one seems to know who planted this tree but it is a sight to be seen if you are in the Harrodsburg area."

Carla Tyson left the Wilson Park neighborhood and its Osage orange tree shortly after her arrest. Christopher Hancock can see the one at Fort Harrod in ten years—or less, of course, if he earns a good behavior early release.

By telling these stories, I'm not arguing against Hancock's verdict or his sentence—both are well earned and just. I am wanting only to put his story in proximity to Carla Tyson's. In this, our America, the collective narrative readily embraces a story like Hancock's as one typical of gun ownership, of gun violence. But what of Carla Tyson's story? If more wealthy Americans own guns than do those living in poverty, why do we have such difficulty fitting this fact into our collective gun narrative?

Because when wealth and whiteness are combined, the narrative shifts most times toward plenty, toward goodness instead of lack or deformity. We're unwilling to acknowledge abhorrent behavior from an heiress but expect it from a working-class man. We're willing to sentence him and to give her a pass.

VI.

After we leave the Wilson Park neighborhood for South Fayette-ville, one day my daughter is playing with her friend who lives around the corner, whose grandparents have a farm in the country. They call to say they're going out to butcher chickens and my daughter wants to go along, and is this okay with me? Also, when they're out there, they shoot guns—shotguns or BB guns—at cans. If this makes me uncomfortable, they understand. They want to know what to tell her if my daughter wants to shoot a gun.

I've known them now for years; they're good friends who've seen us both through many things, including my recent divorce from my daughter's father.

"It's fine," I say. "I trust you."

And I do, implicitly. My daughter at this point is eleven years old. I have talked to her about guns and gun safety many times. I ask the parents of her friend to put her on the phone, and I tell her to listen to them. I tell her if she wants to shoot the gun, that's fine with me, but she has to watch first and to listen and to follow every instruction. She agrees.

After I hang up, I think I'll stop thinking about it, but I don't stop thinking about it. In particular, I think of a high school friend whose father is killed in a hunting accident, in a trip and fall with him out in front of the other hunters, the trip and fall and then the shot coming from behind him.

I text my daughter to tell her to stay behind other people if they're out walking with guns. She texts back, "Mom I know o my god." Apparently, as she'll tell me later, this is something I've told her at least a dozen times.

She's eleven years old, and that day, she learns both how to shoot a gun and how to skin a chicken. The report later is that she's good at both—a good shot and less squeamish than her friend about skinning the chicken.

I'm proud of her and then sheepish about this pride. In other words, I don't know what to feel or how to feel. I'm an American, perhaps, after all, complicit and conflicted and worried.

Chicken, by its primary definition, originates as a word pre–twelfth century, according to Webster's, and *sheepish* dates to the thirteenth century. *Chickenshit* by its secondary definition—as in weak, as in afraid—must be a newer concept, since the word is not first used even in its primary sense, referring to petty details, until 1943.

I am interested both in the naming of things and in the quantifying of them. I am interested in how contrary are our natures, mine included.

When she arrives home both safe and happy, I ask my daughter if she wrung a neck or plucked a chicken, in addition to the other tasks. She cheerfully reports she did not.

"Your grandma hated the plucking," I say, "and your grandpa hated the neck wringing."

"The chicken stuff was fine," she says, "and the shooting was fun." She smiles her wide smile at me, her enormous hazel eyes, so much like my grandmother's, held wide and bright. "I liked it," she says. "I'm good at it."

FOURTEEN

Pass

I.

After the last of her classmates say their goodbyes, she tells me. The room for my graduate seminar is nearly windowless, cinder-block, small. This is our final class of the spring semester, 2019, and we sit near the corner, in our ridiculous desk-chair combos. She's leaving the university, she says. One of her undergraduate students has accused her of showing up to teach her class drunk. She can't take any more. She can't. It's a last-straw sort of situation.

This woman, I'll call her Marie, is one of the few students of color in the MFA program where I teach at the University of Arkansas. She's a talented writer, a steady, intelligent presence in her classes.

As a graduate teaching assistant, she's been bullied by some undergraduates in one previous class. They accused her of being incompetent. Though none were particularly specific, though none came forward to speak to her directly or to levy any direct, specific charge, the department began a file. There were meetings. There was no conversation about race, about the confluence of race and gender, unless the student was the one talking.

In the class, this semester, though, the one containing the drunk-talk student, all has been well. We're in the last week of the semester when the complaint arrives alongside the spring rain. The department will add this to her file. She may have to go on probation.

"Is everyone passing the class?" I ask.

She shakes her head.

"Did they ask you that?"

Another headshake.

No one outside this small, nearly windowless, cinder-block room is talking about the accuser's potential motivations. No one is talking about how Marie doesn't drink. No one is talking about where we live—Arkansas, which some say is where the Midwest meets the South. I would say we're Midwestern in how we don't, as a culture, as a practice, talk straight, if we talk at all. I would say we're Southern in how the last thing we're good at is holding meaningful conversations about race.

When I say, repeatedly, "You don't even drink," Marie laughs the kind of laugh that is a last laugh, an all-finished laugh.

"It's so insulting," she says.

I say to my student that I both know what she's going through and that I don't. "You can pass," she says, nodding.

From my slumped position in my desk-chair combo, my head swivels, and then I nod. It's true. I'm Métis, I'm Native, but I absolutely can pass.

The kind of passing to which we're referring just barely makes Webster's top ten definitions for verb variations:

a: to serve as a medium of exchange

b: to be accepted or regarded // drivel that *passes* for literature

c: to identify oneself or be identified as something one is not // tried to *pass* as an adult // Mom could *pass* as my sister

Webster's doesn't account for what some now call white-coded, which is meant to define those of us who pass but perhaps aren't actively trying. What does it mean to try to pass? What does it mean to pass without trying? With this act, how do we measure intent? With this act, this action, how much does intent matter?

There isn't much to say, after. Outside, in the dark and damp, we hug and shake off some of the seriousness, and we laugh a little because, what else? I watch her turn right, and I turn left, toward my car, and the rain shifts from hard, straight, and steady to intermittent, to the kind that comes toward you at all angles. A cloud of blackbirds alights in the tree next to the parking garage, and as I approach, they begin the dive and swoop they do after spring storms, which is called a murmuration.

I drive down MLK Jr. Boulevard toward home. The historic marker two blocks from my house will let you know where you are if, before, you didn't. It's good sometimes to be reminded you are driving down the Trail of Tears, even if the reminder leaves you holding in your breath a beat too long. It's good sometimes to have the impulse toward forgetting and then to be reminded of the literal—where you are—with the past made present, with it carried and lived as you drive on home.

II.

When I was a graduate student in Texas, the first time I brought a story into workshop, a fellow student told me if I was going to "write about Indians," I would need to separate my writing more from that of Louise Erdrich. Then this man misquoted from the beginning of Erdrich's novel *Tracks*, ostensibly to show how similar it was to my story. At the end of workshop when it was my turn to speak, I corrected his misquotation and suggested in my most polite voice that perhaps to him "Indians" writing about snow all seemed the same. I assured him we were not. I assured him though we might both have written about snow, neither of us was "writing about Indians."

There were so many things that afternoon I did not say. I did not tell this man how it felt, in my first weeks on campus, to have my favorite book mistreated this way. I didn't trust my voice for that. I did not explain how "Erdrich" rhymes with brick, not witch. I did not trust my voice for that either.

Her books were sent to me by a friend when I was young and lived in Wales for nearly a year, so far from home I thought I might float from my skin, I might shift shape, I might no longer be who or what I was. Her stories were the first fiction I read to contain the word *Métis*. I kept that part very quiet. There was no part of me that wanted to hear this word mangled and spit from this man's mouth.

I did make two friends that day in workshop, a Black woman and the white, Republican son of a wealthy Texas oil family. I learned fast that I would be surprised in this place by who would be good company. The class held mostly white, female faces, and not one of those women looked me in the eye or spoke to me, then or any time soon after.

Later, more company arrived—queer writers and Latino and Chicano writers and another Native writer—so I had far more company than did Marie, far more voices pushing alongside mine.

We needed each other. The next semester another white, male student wrote as his comment on one of my poems, "Stop writing the in for the moment but sure not to last Indian poems." What I was writing, it seemed, was considered a fad, temporary, "sure not to last." I was writing my life, as had so many generations of Métis before. So then I was, we were, temporary, a fad, "sure not to last." How can you stay in a place if your very existence is "sure not to last"? If not for my company, I might not have stayed. If not for my company, it could have been a last-straw moment.

The next year, yet another white, male student in workshop started writing hate stories using all of us in the class as recognizable characters. He put only the thinnest of veils around all the terrible things he thought about each of us, yet mine was the only character he killed off over and over and over again.

The second-to-last time, the character was run over by a Ford Escort. The Ford Escort then backed up and ran over the character that was me but was not me, of course, of course. It backed up and ran over again and again and again. At the bar, after class, every time my company called me by my name, I shook my head and said, "I now only answer to the name Ford Escort." I drank plenty that night, despite not having bought a single drink.

In the weeks after, they called me "Ford Escort" in the halls. They maybe said it too loud because the next story from this writer was a different sort of story, a domestic violence sort of story, featuring my character tied to a chair, a man holding to her head a gun.

The land on which that university sits was for so many years land lived on and fought over by Apache and Comanche people, who still live there, of course, just not in such numbers. We were all of us visitors. We were all of us invaders—though some more than others.

"Why—" my friend Marcus asked in that workshop, "why do you think you can do that to her?" He clipped the ends of his words, so that it sounded like someone snapping a towel. I admired how he could do this—make spoken language sound dangerous. I admired the level of control.

"It's a character," said another white man.

Marcus let out a sound like a hiss, like a deflating balloon or a coiled snake, and the writer began to laugh.

The writer's laugh was not believable as humor or comedy, and it went on much too long. I felt such anger but also a little sorry for him, for how long everyone held the silence, after.

It was in that same workshop where I learned how to shut down these men. When we arrived to class one day, the same white man who told me to stop writing my "sure not to last" poems had written a story set in Mexico City, in the garbage dumps. Locally, the people there sometimes are called Garbage Dump Dwellers, so they are known by location and also for their ingenuity—for making homes and a meager living through recycling everyone else's garbage. In this man's story, the people who lived there ate with bare hands after sorting through garbage, their faces were filthy, and their movements were described like those of animals.

It is not that difficult to see more variety in the people if you are looking. A quick Google search, for example, provides images of men wearing gloves and cowboy hats, children who work and also play, mothers who make meals from what they find.

One friend in the class, the only Mexican American person in the class, was so angry his voice shook when he told the writer, "They're like animals. You've made them like animals."

"I've been there," the writer said, "with my church group. This is how they live."

His words were answered with a chorus of "They" and "Who are you calling—" and each voice shouting over the next.

There are so many ways this place, this South, was and is bad for me, but this day also—like you're supposed to in graduate school—I learned.

"What if the kid," I said. To be heard, I had to pause a moment, to wave my arms around like I was perhaps trying to fly. "What if the kid had a toy?"

Everyone looked at me like I was a crazy person. The thought was clear in all their eyes, their expressions. Why was I talking about toys when, clearly, we had a racist among us, or why was I talking about toys when we had an accusation of racism hanging above us, beneath us, in between us?

But then everyone quieted.

"If the kid had a toy," I said, "we'd see him playing with it. He's a person then, doing person things."

A few people nodded, but most still looked doubtful.

"People throw out toys all the time," I said. "It's plausible."

"What if the mother had a flower," I said, "just one flower—plastic or cloth or whatever—just one beautiful thing?"

My friend looked at me now like maybe I wasn't crazy. The writer still shook his head, but he had stopped talking.

"Stereotypes are bad because they're lazy writing," I said. "I don't believe this story because I don't believe the characters. I don't believe the characters because there's no teddy bear, no flower, nothing beautiful."

"It's a little boring," I said, "when everything's so ugly in a predictable way."

The writer, of course, looked like he wanted his friend to resurrect the Ford Escort, but the writer also was not arguing. The professor agreed with me, and we moved on to the next story.

After, I was shaky but also not sorry. I had gone into that class thinking I already was a teacher, but I left knowing I hadn't been one before. You can't teach racists to be less racist by calling them what they are. They remain unbothered by insinuation or even direct accusations of racism, but they are not fine with being told their writing is bad.

The commonality in workshop, then, sometimes is not common humanity—it's a desire to write better. In the South, I decided thereafter I would foreground every workshop I led with talk of how stereotypes are harmful, yes—and also how they're indicators of bad writing. I would shut down these men and, yes, sometimes also women, before they had a chance to begin, before they could begin to harm.

That day is the how and why of earning Marie's trust. That day is the how and why I don't quit.

My friend, that semester in Texas, the lone Mexican American student in the class, would not come back to workshop, after. He finishes the class as an independent study with the professor. I imagine everyone in that class passed, as per Webster's definition number four: "to give approval or a passing grade to." My friend goes on to finish his degree, to publish another book, to teach writing at a university. He doesn't quit, either, and I respect his choices, but that semester, I greatly missed his company as cost to his passing.

III.

That first year, my first rental house in Lubbock had been rented before me by a man who dealt drugs. It was a small, tidy one-bedroom house, a neat square built on a slab in the middle of a neighborhood everyone I met said I should leave.

It was and remains true that this neighborhood has one of the highest crime rates in Lubbock, which has one of the highest crime rates, per capita, in the nation. The crime rate there, over-all, is 69 percent higher than the national average. Only 9 percent of cities in the country are considered less safe.

In that neighborhood, when I walked the dogs, I spent our time avoiding needles on the ground and eye contact in general. It was good practice, perhaps, learning to look clear-eyed into the middle distance. I grew more and more practiced, more and more comfortable. I didn't want to leave—the tidy house or the cheap rent, the neighbors who got my mail when I travelled, whose children called me by name and petted my dogs and laughed loud in their backyards.

Judging by the customers who knocked on my door after dark, after the neighbors' lights had gone out, I would guess the previous tenant dealt pot, mostly, but also crank or meth or speed. The men who wanted crank made me the most grateful for my dogs—for Jack, whose giant Chow/Newfoundland head held crazy eyes; for Lucy, who watched and waited with a husky's patience.

Huskies generally pass for polite or curious or well-mannered around those who don't understand dogs. Our neighborhood was all pit bulls and Chihuahuas. Lubbock is all chain link, dirt yard, Chihuahua and pit bull. Even the tweakers seemed cowed by the surprise—nearly 150 pounds of long, black fur between the two dogs. No one came knocking twice.

I never had much hassle from the men who came to the door. Still, I cited them when I explained my move to the house in the country. I cited them or the night at the bar after workshop when a familiar house came on the TV, on the local news. It was a meth lab. It had blown up. It had sat a block and a half from my house.

Really, though, I could have moved anywhere in town, but I chose the country. Those boys in workshop—the ones I've been calling men—they had as much to do with the move to the country as did the ones who showed up late at night, shaking and glassy-eyed, asking if I knew what had happened to Brett. They called me ma'am sometimes, the younger ones. They said they were sorry to have bothered me.

Though I had earned some grudging respect with my writing and my thoughts on their writing, none of the workshop boys ever said they were sorry to have bothered me. They were calculated in their bothering. They were not sorry. They wanted me to evacuate the house of workshop like I did the one-bedroom.

The country house sat on an acreage, a cotton farm, an hour's drive east of campus, of town, and it seemed most days almost far enough. Out the kitchen window, I had a view of Blanco Canyon, which sits at the edge of the Llano Estacado, a region of stark cliff faces and rolling slopes in all shades of red and brown, dotted with the green of yucca and tall grass. West Texas, as it turned out, was not entirely brown and flat.

Locals often told stories of how their families came to live in the region in early years—how their people were just passing through but decided to stay because of the wind, the sandstorms, tornadoes. This version of history, of course, ignores how many people already lived there. Webster's third definition for *pass* is

"3a: to go across, over, or through: CROSS" or "b: to live through (something, such as an experience or peril): UNDERGO."

I crossed out of Lubbock and into the house at the canyon and into happiness. The house came complete with a giant red-headed woodpecker, who pecked just outside my office window, and an elderly landlady who drove out from Lubbock after church on Sundays to tend the trees she'd planted, dozen upon dozen upon dozen.

She brought pizza or fried chicken. Either came with those wedge potatoes that never are cooked all the way through. She brought her granddaughter and sometimes her daughter or husband. I ate the potatoes and drank the Pepsi. I learned about the region, about how hard it was to farm there with so little rain. We planted a garden together that first spring—cherry tomatoes and all manner of peppers and row upon row of okra.

In this way, I made a life there in my first attempt at the South. I had my company out for hikes and dinners, an occasional party. I wrote the draft of my first book while the woodpecker worked alongside me, providing rhythm and an example.

In the end, then, because the workshop boys ran me out of town, I was able to stay. I drove the hour to workshop grateful to be going and grateful to be returning. In between, I passed a historical marker that bragged about "the eradication of the Indian menace" in the region. It became part of the day-to-day, passing that sign, thinking, *not quite*. That's how I stayed—good company and *not quite*, fried chicken and overgrown okra, Blanco Canyon and the way the sun set into it. It's the dust in West Texas that makes the sunsets so stunning—how it never leaves the air entirely, how the rain doesn't come to wash it away, how it lasts.

IV.

I've been a student or a teacher for so many years in this region we call the South. I've worked so hard to make the four walls of my classroom a place where all the Maries are welcome, where all the Marcuses know they can ask the question, where all conversations are possible, where everyone knows where we are—the limitations of it, alongside the possibilities.

In my neighborhood, just off the Trail of Tears, the day after the last day of class, I'm writing at my desk when I see a familiar motion in the yard. The backyard woodpecker on the fence post out the window is so much smaller than the one in Texas that, to make sure, I have to crack the window, to listen for the sound it makes while it works. Since I'm already on a break, I walk the dogs around the block to see if we're flooding, to see whose yards or houses have taken on water. That's how I think of it now, this place—a *we* rather than an *it*. I've acclimated far enough to feel a measure of belonging.

But how much of that is on account of my ability to pass? How much grace is it possible to give others when you move through the world with more than a small measure of safety—when this is safety you own but have not bought?

Where my family is from, where some Métis are from, on the southern prairies of Canada, we were once known as Road Allowance People. Between 1885 and 1945, Métis got this name after the Canadian government decided to dissolve our land base, to sell 160 acres for $160 through scrip certificates, which were easy enough to forge or transfer, which were often forged or transferred through impersonation. If Métis sometimes could pass for white, whites could sometimes pass for Métis. They could sometimes steal our land through this passing.

Without a land base, some Métis became squatters on our own land, became Road Allowance People. We lived in shacks made from logs or leftover lumber, covered rough with tar paper, not much different than the homes of the Garbage Dump Dwellers. We lived like this through prairie winters.

Back in my neighborhood in Arkansas, the water has flooded the street and the sidewalk as the dogs and I round the corner. This walking route also sometimes becomes the driving route when the main street is blocked by the police, when the mentally ill son of a neighbor threatens his father with a gun.

Across the field a crow pecks at a full, intact pineapple washed up through the drainage system and landed here at the intersection. A neighbor pushes mud from her sidewalk with a wide broom across the street and into the drainage opening by my yard. "There's mud on the sidewalk," she says, shaking her head, but no word on the pineapple lying a few yards behind her.

I know the South is not the only place capable of irony, capable of rough treatment, of racism and threatened violence and worse. I know I have spent so much time considering the safety of my students within my classroom walls, but I have not considered enough the limitations of this place, of this South, of this history, outside my classroom walls, outside my own defining of it.

I know my own passing to be a complicated crossing.

FIFTEEN

Contagion

I.

The Walmart shelves stand emptied of all paper towels and toilet paper, all canned goods, save for six lone cans of cannellini beans. It's March 2020 in Arkansas, and this Friday, my last day before I begin social distancing, I go to one Walmart, my fiancé to another across town. He reports there's no toilet paper there either, but the gun section holds a cluster of men, waiting for the cashier to return.

According to Webster's, *cluster* can mean many things, including "to collect into a cluster," "an aggregation of stars or galaxies that appear close together in the sky and are gravitationally associated," and "a larger than expected number of cases of disease (such as leukemia) occurring in a particular locality, group of people, or period of time."

After Walmart, I go to my hair appointment. My hairdresser makes a string of what she thinks are funny jokes about how no one's eating at Meiji, which is a Japanese restaurant in town. It's my favorite restaurant in town. She clarifies several times that she hasn't, you know, really been in the mood for Chinese food lately.

It's possible, then, the cannellini beans are left on the shelf because cannellini is an Italian word, because people here and everywhere in this, our America really are that terrible, really are this odd mix of dismissive toward and terrified of this newest contagion, coronavirus or COVID-19.

My hairdresser keeps saying, "You know," and I keep giving her my blank face, and she keeps saying, "No one wants Chinese food right now," and I feel unprepared for this conversation, for explaining how Japanese and Chinese are not actually the same, for explaining racism right now. I'm so rarely surprised into silence, but I am. I've known her two years but apparently have not, not really. I'm also unprepared for walking out with chemicals on my head, with foil strips and color mid-process. I'm so rarely quiet, but I don't say anything, not one word, and she finally grows quiet, our soundtrack thereafter becoming the metallic click of foil meeting foil.

Before this coronavirus contagion, we were, a good many of us, talking about the contagion of gun violence. Now, too, after George Floyd's death and the subsequent uprisings across the country, police gun violence more and more is part of the day-to-day conversation. Even before the coronavirus or the uprisings across America, though, members of the media began, in summer 2019, to talk about gun violence as potentially contagious.

On June 1, 2019, the *Today* show declares the mass shooting in Virginia Beach the 150th mass shooting of the year. Kathy

Park does the reporting, and she presents a slew of statistics that should alarm—how many shootings already in 2019, how many mass shootings—but somehow, for many, these numbers don't seem to be ringing the alarm bell.

The next day on his Sunday morning show, George Stephanopoulos announces he's not going to announce the shooter's name. He fumbles a little and looks uncomfortable trying to explain contagion theory, trying to explain what he's clearly been told to say is supposed to be the new media norm. He ends with something along the lines of now that they know better, they're going to do better.

Contagion theory as a concept started getting attention in the 1890s when French doctor and theorist Gustave Le Bon said he believed individuals become less rational when part of a crowd. He proposes, "by the mere fact that he forms part of an organized crowd, a man descends several rungs on the ladder of civilization."

In recent years, those who study gun violence have utilized contagion theory as one way of understanding how mass shootings occur, as one way of understanding human behavior—the how and why we don't seem to feel responsible for each other any longer in this cultural moment.

Researchers at Arizona State University are led by Sherry Towers, who according to an article on npr.org, previously "had spent most of her career modeling the spread of infectious diseases—like Ebola, influenza and sexually transmitted diseases. She wanted to know whether cases of mass violence spread contagiously, like in a disease outbreak."

Towers's research begins with plugging mass shooting data into a mathematical model. Her findings suggest some elements of contagion in how mass shootings occur, though her model is predicated on timeliness—one shooting, say, on a Wednesday having a correlation to a shooting that Friday. This element—the timeliness—doesn't necessarily always mean contagion. In relation to disease or virus spread, of course, proximity and timeliness matter. But with mass shootings, if for example, four family members are killed at a birthday party in Kentucky on a Wednesday, and on that Friday, five acquaintances are killed after bringing guns to a drunken argument outside a bar in New York, is that evidence of contagion or is that just a regular, everyday week in this, our America?

Most, though not all, researchers and data gatherers consider four dead by gunfire to be a mass shooting. There's no one set standard. Still, in the broader public, many if not most people think of the shootings at Newtown, Columbine, Las Vegas, or Pulse nightclub when they think of mass shootings. But in the majority of mass shootings, as in the majority of all gun violence, the shooter and the victims know one another. In the majority of mass shootings, because we have so much everyday American violence, a shooting like the ones I mentioned above—at a birthday party, outside a bar—doesn't make the local headlines for long and doesn't make the national headlines at all. How then is the contagion spread?

Certainly, there is validity in the idea of copycat killings, and in the research that goes into their examination, as detailed thoroughly and well in the 2015 series in *Mother Jones* by Mark Follman and Becca Andrews. Their research and reportage found that the shooting at Columbine in 1999 "has since inspired at least 74 plots or attacks across 30 states."

But contagion is different than copycat behavior in its

purported timeliness, and the media standards for publishing details about the shooters have also shifted since Columbine, though not perhaps as far as they could or as far as many would like.

There is an interesting, less publicized conclusion of the work on mass shootings and contagion, which all the researchers seem to note as a side fact. As Towers and her co-authors put it, "state prevalence of firearm ownership is significantly associated with the state incidence of mass killings with firearms, school shootings, and mass shootings." So having more guns in a state is linked to a state having more incidences of all these types of gun violence, including mass shootings.

In particular, though, I'm interested in the research on mass shootings by Jillian Peterson and James Densley. In a project funded by the National Institute of Justice, Peterson and Densley have spent two years researching the lives and histories of mass shooters. Their findings, published in a series of articles for the *Los Angeles Times*, indicate four commonalities among the perpetrators of nearly all the mass shootings they studied. In their study, the "vast majority of mass shooters" reported experiencing "early childhood trauma and exposure to violence at a young age." In addition, the authors note, "practically every mass shooter we studied had reached an identifiable crisis point in the weeks or months leading up to the shooting. They often had become angry and despondent because of a specific grievance."

Peterson and Densley's third finding centers around their idea that mass shootings "come in clusters" and are "socially contagious." Their definition differs slightly from Towers's since it relies less on timeliness. They found that "most of the shooters had studied the actions of other shooters and sought validation for their motives. People in crisis have always existed. But in the age of 24-hour rolling news and social media, there are scripts to follow that promise notoriety in death."

And last, they found, "the shooters all had the means to carry out their plans."

So though they differ slightly in how they're defining and quantifying what they mean by "contagion," they agree on means, on access—that mass shootings happen most often where and when there's the most access to guns.

It's startling to find this assertion so minimized, rendered so secondary. In this, our America, where everything, including gun control studies, requires funding, I wonder about this reduction. If we've ceded the idea that we can limit access to guns—because we don't think we can or because no one will fund a primary study on its effectiveness—then it makes sense to be focusing mainly on an idea like contagion.

But contagion can exist without mass shooting as an end result. It's becoming both anecdotally and statistically more and more clear that free and unfettered American access to weapons can't exist, that it won't exist, without mass shootings as an end result.

II.

When DeWayne Craddock kills twelve people and injures four more in the mass workplace shooting at the Virginia Beach Municipal Center, CNN reports not only the shooter's name but also the most minute and chilling detail—that he brushed his teeth in the workplace bathroom and exchanged pleasantries right before the shootings.

The same week that George Stephanopoulos and other journalists make the proclamation—no more naming of mass shooters—*The New York Times, The Washington Post,* the *New York Post, USA Today,* and the Associated Press all include the shooter's name in headlines and cite it multiple times each per story. In addition, reportage from ABC affiliates out of Houston, Chicago, and other cities, ABC's Twitter feed, and Stephanopoulos's own ABC staple show, *Good Morning America,* all name the shooter. *GMA* not only names the shooter on June 1 but also reports details of his life and reactions to the crime from interviews with his neighbors.

Too, a quick Google search, then and now, produces a good photo of the shooter, wearing a nice, proud-of-himself smile, a nice jacket and tie. He looks sharp and everyday, both.

It's not just the Virginia Beach shooting, either, of course.

Two months after the Virginia Beach shooting, when a man enters an El Paso Walmart and begins shooting, he kills twenty-two people and wounds twenty-four others. *The Wall Street Journal,* the Associated Press, the *El Paso Times,* and *The Independent* all use the shooter's name in headlines.

Six months after the Virginia Beach shooting, when a Saudi national shoots dead three people and wounds eight at the Naval Air Station in Pensacola, Florida, *The Washington Post,* the BBC, *USA Today,* NBC News, and Fox News all name the shooter quickly, either in the headline or the first line of the story. According to reportage in *USA Today,* at a press conference, Florida governor Ron DeSantis says, "Obviously, the government of Saudi Arabia needs to make things better for these victims. They're going to owe a debt here."

When Trayvon Martin was killed in Sanford, Florida, no one, including George Zimmerman, was made to pay a debt to Martin or his family. In fact, Zimmerman, who shot Martin dead, now is suing Martin's family.

If Saudi Arabia owes these victims for its citizen's action, then what of the rest of us, here in America? Does DeSantis, for example, as Florida's governor, then owe Martin's family a debt? Does Donald Trump, as president?

Who owes all of us and what is owed and where do I get in line to collect and when? If there is contagion in all of this, it's in our unearned self-congratulations. We're not doing much better in our media coverage, so there's no way to test or make valid our ideas about contagion theory.

Most of our ideas about coverage of mass shootings stem from the No Notoriety movement. Started by Tom and Caren Teves after their son Alex was killed in the Aurora movie theater shooting, the movement's basic tenets include a shift toward the journalistic equivalent of "do no harm." Some of the specific ways suggested for enacting this principle include not mentioning shooters' names in headlines, not publishing their names at the starts of articles, and only mentioning their names one time per article.

These protocols—whether they'll stop contagion or not—are good as a courtesy to families of victims, and this courtesy or decency, of course, has value. I'm not trying to devalue it.

But when we confuse courtesy with meaningful change, with meaningful action, we do no one, including the families of victims, any service. Patting ourselves on our collective backs—thinking we're somehow now part of the solution instead of very much part of the problem—is the most American of gestures. Journalists and newsrooms proclaim they're going to follow these protocols, but even a cursory glance shows in most cases, they aren't.

Too, when the vast majority of mass shooters are men and the majority are white men, by obfuscating the names of these shooters, we're obfuscating white male killers while publicizing each day the names and faces of Black and brown men who commit lesser crimes. In Virginia Beach and Pensacola, both shooters were men of color whose faces and names were directly publicized over and over and over. It's hard to see this variant as anything but purposeful when mass shooters of color are so rare, when we claim to be moving away from publicizing faces and names and yet there theirs are.

We have to look straight on at who commits mass violence, at who commits all violence, to understand the social, familial, and policy-related changes needed to shift the country toward change. We're all in this. To withhold the names, profiles, and white faces of the majority of mass killers is to pretend otherwise.

III.

I end up having a third-hand connection to one of the Virginia Beach shooting victims, as she's the dear friend of a former girlfriend of my current fiancé. My fiancé is a war veteran, has written extensively about his PTS from his time in the infantry in Afghanistan. He's lost family members, too, some to gun violence, and is someone often called upon when friends, acquaintances, quasi-strangers need to know how to cope after violence, tragedy, loss. His former girlfriend has lost a close friend in the Virginia Beach shooting. She's struggling with sense making, with meaning finding, with loss.

When she reaches out to my fiancé, I'm glad, and he offers her comfort and advice, and she reports both help her, and I'm yet more glad. "Reach out to your friend's family again in six weeks," he tells her, "when everyone has forgotten."

Another side to my reaction, though, is an irrational fear. Week by week, month by month, as I read research by those analyzing gun violence, as I write about my experiences with gun violence, I have, increasingly, more and more personal intersections with this violence: a former student writes of his time in lockdown in Savannah at the college where he teaches; a friend waits in the hallway at STEM Highlands school outside Denver till his son comes out to him unharmed; a local acquaintance, gone too soon from suicide; yet another relative of my fiancé, a young relative, also lost to suicide by gun.

I know I am not responsible for any of this—I know. But it's hard, perhaps, to study contagion theory and not begin to consider your own part in it.

I'll admit, though, it takes longer than it should for me to consider how if I'm three degrees of separation from a victim in the Virginia Beach shooting, then I'm four degrees from the shooter who was her colleague. This is, of course, an uncomfortable thought.

But it's a thought I want for all of us, for all Americans, this lack of comfort. I want us to consider our fourth-hand connections, our tears for the shooters if they come. I want us to be uncomfortable in our complicity.

I also want us to consider how much attention—money, media coverage, energy, fear—we put toward mass shootings when more than 99 percent of gun deaths in this, our America are from shootings other than mass shootings.

IV.

It's becoming more and more common today to say everyone knows someone who's affected by, who's a victim of, gun violence.

Gun violence is rarely random. If it's true we know victims, then we also know perpetrators. Let's talk about that. Let's not allow ourselves the over-fixation on mass shootings, which represent less than one percent of the gun violence in America. Let's not allow ourselves to feel as if withholding those names means we're doing something about gun violence.

As long as we distance ourselves from the perpetrators, we're part of this, our American problem. I'm going to argue it's important for Americans to become less comfortable with these shootings. It's important for Americans to begin to see these men as our neighbors, our co-workers, our sons—because they are. Before they act, they are often considered the good guy with the gun. We do ourselves no favors by pretending otherwise.

We have to know who the perpetrators are—their faces, their names—if we are to know how to stop making them. We have to acknowledge their humanity, that we all make them, that they are made culturally even though, yes, they act individually.

As I wrote these essays, over the past years, more and more people I knew, more and more people I loved were in lockdown or had loved ones in lockdown or were shot. I wish this book could be more of an accounting of their lives—though that is what it is, in part. I wish this book could be more of a reckoning.

It began to feel like I was part of it, the contagion, but that's paranoia, of course, and self-aggrandizement—neither of which are useful to anyone.

This winter 2019, as I began to consider contagion theory in reference to gun violence, there's a shooting in my town, downtown on the square where we have each year before Christmas what's called Lights of the Ozarks. According to a Fayetteville website, "Each year Fayetteville Parks and Recreation workers spend over 3,300 hours decorating the Downtown Square with over 400,000 lights." It's a spectacle, sometimes complete with camel rides—and with or without the camels, it's something to see.

The news is coming in through Twitter. The Fayetteville Police Department website remains unchanged, the Facebook page thanking everyone for coming out to an event earlier in the day called "Dodgeball for Doggies." This is the sort of town in which I live.

People are reporting a coroner on scene and that both a suspect and an officer have been killed. There's nothing to do but wait for more information.

The next morning, at the press conference, it's announced that officer Stephen Carr has been shot and killed, executed at point-blank range by a man we'll later learn has a conviction for domestic violence in Florida in 2012. Another strong indicator for who commits gun violence is who has first committed domestic violence.

The gun used to shoot Stephen Carr is a 9-mm Taurus pistol, which a quick search tells me is in stock at Academy Sports, Cabela's, Sportsman's Outdoor Superstore, and Bud's Gun Shop. Internet gun reviews report, "There's nothing wrong with cheap and cheerful, which is exactly what this Taurus is about."

From blog.cheaperthandirt.com, I learn Taurus guns are from Brazil and had a rough start in the U.S. market, due to perceived quality control issues, but now are extremely popular— due to the improvement of quality and the low price point.

I live now in the kind of town where everyone, including me, knows someone on the police force, where police presence, as in so many places, is considered regular, normal, everyday America.

The night before, as I wrote about contagion, Stephen Carr is shot and killed execution-style while he sits in his parked police car behind the precinct, waiting for his partner to come outside, waiting for his shift to start. The suspect is pursued and then shot and killed by two other officers who heard the initial shots and left the precinct at a run.

I did not know officer Stephen Carr—or the man who killed him, for that matter—but once his name and picture are released, I realize I've seen him around town. He was once a bicycle cop downtown on Dickson Street, and he seemed too large to be comfortable on his bicycle, a little overstuffed in his summer shorts. He was twenty-seven years old, from Texas, his face still somewhat of a baby face, and though it's perhaps trite to say, he was, of course, someone's baby, and it's hard not to know that, not to see it, especially in a face like his—broad, wide-eyed, a little round.

The shooting happened off the downtown square where a lighting ceremony was occurring for the annual Christmas light extravaganza.

This isn't about me, except for how it happens in the town in which I live. This isn't about me except for how I'm home, writing about contagion theory. This isn't about me, except for how my new colleague and friend is having a birthday celebration only a few blocks away from where the shooting happens. This isn't about me, except for how my daughter sends me a video on Instagram, telling me she's okay. She's at her father's this week, and we check in regularly through Instagram, and I had opened the app to check on her since I know she's at a sleepover. She and her girlfriends are fine, she reports. They were at the lighting ceremony, were walking around the square, and left about five minutes before the shooting.

We got a little bored, she reports, and I have never been more grateful for how easily thirteen-year-olds shift into boredom. But, again, this is not about me or my daughter or her easily bored friends.

This is about Stephen Carr, about an assault on a police officer, and perhaps also about the man who shot and killed Carr.

I report these details like they matter, much in the way some proponents of contagion theory report more mass shootings seem to happen after a mass shooting. We are, all of us, trying to contribute to the narrative, trying to make the narrative matter.

What's true is that I did not start this life, this year, or even this essay thinking I would become one of those people who finds the answer to this violence is simpler than we are trying to make it. But it is. People who kill other people with guns have to have access to the guns. The more access, the more violence. We have in our country almost entirely unfettered access.

We can study and report and study some more, but increasingly, I think studies and reports and even narratives should be the province of civilized nations that might respond to the studies, the reports, the narratives with subsequent, substantive action. We are no longer a civilized nation if ever we were.

The day after the shooting, my ex-husband texts about returning my daughter and her things later this afternoon. She's going to spend time around the corner from my house at a friend's first, and we arrange logistics, and so soon he'll drive north on Highway 71 or the interstate beside it. He'll head west on MLK Jr. Boulevard, that Trail of Tears.

I don't know of any greater reminder that our country is in crisis than how when the information started rolling in about the shooting, I was sorry that lives were lost but grateful the shooter didn't take his guns to the square, to the lighting ceremony, to the celebration. I was sad and a little afraid and I also was unsurprised.

When the news began to report the new coronavirus in China, South Korea, Italy, and then in America, I was sorry for all of us. I was also sad and a little afraid and unsurprised that this other contagion is bringing out the worst in many of us—the xenophobic, the racist.

This March morning, my mother's birthday, she and my daughter both report to me the news of a man in Midland, Texas, who attacked an Asian American family with a knife. He blamed them for the coronavirus and responded while shopping at a Sam's Club with the least sensical sort of violence—by lunging close to a family he seemed to believe carried contagion, by stabbing the adults and the children, ages two and six years old.

"What is wrong with people?" my daughter asks, and I have no answer.

I tell my mother I'm glad the man didn't have a gun.

That sits for a while, our conversation settling, until she remembers to tell me about the celebration. At five P.M. her friends in town and across the country all are going to raise a glass to her, and she's telling me to feel free to join in. I ask about the various technologies—Zoom, Skype, FaceTime—and she says not everyone has the technology or knows how to use it. She's been on the phone already most of the day, talking to friends and texting them, reading her cards and opening a few presents, celebrating.

I have so few answers for my daughter's question—What's wrong with people?

This is America now and arguably always has been. The

contagion has been here from the beginning, and it's growing and we seem unwilling to stop it.

What's right with people, though, of course, sits alongside what's wrong. What's right is found in the simple ways we work despite contagion toward connection. It can be found today in my mother's opening of cards, in all of us at five P.M. raising a glass in small but vital celebration.

SIXTEEN

Ghost Logic

I.

In recent days, my father worries over the people he spots on his property. They're in the driveway, by the barn, crouched low beneath the second-story deck too close to the petunias. He likes to sit out on the deck to watch birds—the cardinals and blue jays who fight over birdseed, the nuthatches and titmice, who peck and sing, respectively.

Sometimes the people down by the barn do things, too, he says, like take the long curve of the gravel drive, making their way toward the barn. The barn houses the dogs, barkers both. My father reports there is no barking. My father reports his perplexity over the dogs' failure to bark.

"Sons a bitches must be getting old," he says.

"Yes," I say. "The sons a bitches."

I long have patterned like this when talking with my father. I agree, repeat a phrase; agree again, repeat a phrase—this back-and-forth forming a regular rhythm. In earlier days, the patterning helped to avoid conflict. I could listen to twenty minutes about the glories of the NRA and say, "Yes, the NRA really is something." Or "The NRA is not dull."

In the last few years, now that he has Lewy body dementia, his mind so often rests in the past. I can listen to him talk about the intricacies of the pearl inlay on his favorite pistol, how it was handcrafted in 1894. How it is a work of art. I can agree, "They really don't make things like they used to." I can pattern my way past sense or meaning but toward love, perhaps, toward a sort of listening that approximates love or mimics it, to a moment or thing that smells like one of those old Xerox sheets—fresh and stale, chemicals and crisp air, shiny and tainted in the way of everyday things that no longer exist in our everyday.

My father reports that sometimes the people crouch next to the bushes he planted underneath the carport's overhang. His house sits atop a lovely hill and is built into its side. The acreage is ringed with CRP land, Conservation Reserve Program land, which means the government pays landowners not to over-farm small parts of their land. My father's CRP land features tall, waving grass like the original prairies.

He doesn't know them, these people, who hide down by the barn with the CRP grass waving and waving in between. He doesn't understand why they're there, why they're not coming up to the house to ask him a question. He reports the people to my stepmother who reports these details to my brother who reports it to me.

"He's seeing things," my brother says.

"He's seeing people," I say. But what I think is, *He's seeing ghosts.*

II.

When I'm seventeen, for a time I live at my boyfriend's house with him, his parents, and their ghost. My boyfriend and his parents are kind, gentle people. My own house sometimes features our town's one police car parked out front, the lumbering body of our one policeman lingering, embarrassed, on our back porch.

My boyfriend's family gathers for dinner and television, and mine gathers for court testimonies and witness statements. We have a ghost, too, of the basement-pipe-rattling, attic-walking variety. Not notable. An ordinary ghost with a paucity of ghost game.

At my boyfriend's house, without human assistance, magazine pages flip and fan on the coffee table before settling themselves. The living room curtains are made of thick polyester that looks like velvet but is not, no matter how many times I touch their edges, expecting them to have grown soft. At night while we occupy our recliners and sofa corners, the ghost sets the curtain bottoms to sway. There's no heat register, no open window. Only the ghost with the accelerated ghost game, the winning game, the game I grow to anticipate.

I should say here, perhaps, for the skeptical, that I have not been raised to fear ghosts or to think them notable or to think about them, really, in any depth. They are as regular and unpredictable as the living. It's better for them if they move along, but if not, then they live with us. We're to be considerate of them just like we're to use coasters when setting down a glass on certain pieces of furniture. I had always thought of ghosts as everyday. My grandmother each day placed a clean, dry dishcloth over drying dishes to keep the ghosts from rattling them.

My parents are regular rural American parents in most other respects. We're a regular American family. My father has two or three or maybe four guns in the house. My parents don't get along, and when they fight, they turn their fists on each other or at least their open hands. My father is bigger. My father always wins, at least until the estrangement, until the inevitable, long-overdue divorce. I suppose there are other ways their marriage could have ended. But in any of those other ways, probably not all of us get to live.

Webster's defines this word, *estrange*, first as "to arouse especially mutual enmity or indifference in (someone) where there had formerly been love, affection, or friendliness." Eventually, in the case of my parents, the secondary definition will come to apply equally: "to remove from customary environment or associations." First my mother will ask my father to leave. She will change the locks.

After, my father will break into the house through the kitchen window, will evict my mother and a friend by force. There will be little to no remaining friendliness for the sake of the children; there will be no indifference, only removal and court testimonies and more and more enmity.

My friends, in the before, when they slept over at my house, which was built in the early 1900s, all were afraid. They thought the bumps and creaks of my childhood home were ghosts. I never saw a ghost in that house, at least not of the spectral kind, but there were unexplained noises, especially from the basement.

Their fear in those moments amuses me until I see in their faces, for a few of them, it is not the sort of screamy sleepover faux fear but is genuine. At their houses, I think, they must not have real things to fear, like fathers. At my house, ghosts are not extraordinary, and neither is violence.

My grandmother saw ghosts, as did her grandmother before her, as have I, as does my daughter. I named my daughter after this great-grandmother, who in the early 1900s divorced the man she married, more than once. She moved her family back and forth to and from Canada, several times.

I don't know a better way to explain home and later home-coming than this.

III.

At my boyfriend's house, I sleep with him in his bed, and other than the living room, his bedroom is the house's only ghost space. If I stay the night on a Tuesday, I wake Wednesday morning at first light with a pressure on my chest, a weight, a heaviness, an inability to lift my arms, to rise from the bed, to speak. The sensation surprises and startles. I feel, not fear exactly, but instead, curiosity and perhaps something close to wonder.

The ghost at my boyfriend's is a jealous ghost, I think, and jealousy, of course, is a sort of violence. This is, however, the first sort of violence I've experienced from a ghost. But ghosts, after all, are everyday, and already, at seventeen, I know violence to be everyday, to be regular.

Once my parents began what would become the long, ugly divorce process, for a time I lived in my childhood home with my father, who had physically removed my mother from the house by throwing her down the back stairs.

One night, a few months into living with my father, I come home from my waitressing job, and the locks have been changed, and I no longer possess the correct key. I come home in my short-sleeved waitress dress, smelling of grease, and I know at first only that the door is locked.

It's dark, fall. I'm not wearing my jacket, and goose bumps rise on my arms in the night chill. I've worked the late shift, so it's after eleven P.M. My father's truck is not in the backyard. I want out of the smell of this dress so badly I have the urge to strip and leave it here on this back porch, under the stars. Upon my father's eventual return, the dress would greet him, would, perhaps, provide a thing about which he would have to think.

It's cool that night, and I stand on the back porch, my arms prickling in the night air. It's late, but my father clearly is out. No amount of knocking brings him to the door. This happens in the pre-cellphone era, so I get back into my car, where I am trapped with my uniform's grease smell.

Sometimes because of cheerleading practice or shooting hoops at the grade school or going out drinking, I have an extra set of clothes in my car. This is not one of those times. I drive the twenty minutes to my boyfriend's with the windows rolled down.

He lives with his parents, who are some of the most loving, most decent people I have encountered or will ever. He lives also with his manic depression, his borderline schizophrenic tendencies, the rise and fall when he decides to forgo his medications.

It is not the first time I've stayed here with the boyfriend and the family and the ghost. But usually I arrive with him, not on my own. It's not usually this late. Usually, I have my things.

That night I am welcomed and made comfortable. His father is still up, and I say, "Ugh, this dress smells," and he smiles and says, "You're fine," and he says it like he means it.

I put my contact lenses into water in juice glasses that once were jelly jars, the kind with the intricate patterns carved into the glass on their sides. My boyfriend gives me two different glasses with two different patterns so I can know by feel which one is the right contact and which one the left. This is what I mean by decency. This is what I mean by care. This is what I know of love.

Once my contacts are out, everything is tactile. I'm so myopic that even though I know this house, I feel along the banister, along the walls from the bathroom to his bedroom.

We fall into sleep, our limbs tied together, and no one thinks to call to check that I'm there, so we are not interrupted by the phone. We sleep the sleep of people who are loved and safe.

I awake in the early morning hours, with the feeling like there's a weight on top of me, and my arms are not cold like the night before but also are not mobile.

I wait. Once my arms begin to loosen, to be again regular arms, I shake awake my boyfriend.

"Oh, yeah," he says. "She's like that."

"Like what?" I say.

"Jealous."

The whole thing is made more strange by how I can't see, not really. Still, the ghost has left me once my boyfriend awakens. Still, I remember which jelly jar is for left and which one for right. Downstairs, his parents are up, and we all eat breakfast together, and everyone at the table is quiet and regular, laughing together and reading the paper, making jokes that are not at anyone's expense.

I think this is how people are supposed to act at the breakfast table, and I start to plan for a life where all days will start like this.

IV.

Before the jealous ghost, there was a jealous ex-girlfriend who worked as a lifeguard at the local swimming pool. After my boyfriend and I first met, after we fell for each other fast and hard, one afternoon he delivered to me his complex diagnoses. We sat in his pickup truck, which shuddered and rumbled, the vents hissing out what passed for cold air.

I'd been to the swimming pool, my hair still damp, still holding in the smell of the chlorine. This man had painted the outside of his truck in pink-and-black zebra stripes. He wrote songs and played electric guitar. We were in the years when heavy metal and hair ballads reigned, and locally, he was, if not king, then minor king or demigod.

The interior of the truck held equal parts comfort and disappointment in its regularity. Its bench seat was not, for example, zebra- or otherwise striped. With his arm around me, my boyfriend said the phrases *manic depressive* and *borderline schizophrenic.*

My hair stuck to the back of my neck and tops of my shoulders, pool-damp. The pool today also included his former girlfriend. All afternoon, every touch of my toes into the water was accompanied by her whistle, blown in a staccato rhythm to a tune maybe only she could hear.

I swam lap after lap to the accompaniment of this music. Stroke, bleat, stroke, bleat, like we were making our own sort of song, until a laughing friend took away her whistle and steered her considerable shoulders toward the concrete building where the lifeguards took their breaks.

She was Amazonian, this ex-girlfriend, and I was small. I was glad all she did was blow a whistle. It was just hot air to go along with the hot air of the day, the sky the cornflower blue of Midwestern summers, the air retaining every ounce of humidity.

I was in charge of watching my younger brother, who the previous year I almost let drown at a lake that held no exgirlfriend Amazonian lifeguard.

To be clear, I meant no disrespect when I noted her broad shoulders and long, strong legs. She was entirely beautiful, with those legs and spectacular breasts. Somehow I'd grown up thinking of women's bodies as their own, each individual, none a reflection on mine, and mine not a reflection on anyone else's. I didn't envy her those breasts. I didn't covet the legs. She was equal parts voluptuous and strong, but I didn't feel superior or inferior in my smallness.

It's a violence when women make those sorts of moves against each other. Or at least it's the start of violence. I felt then and now lucky to have grown up mostly without that sort of mindset. It's one of the ghosts many women have holding them down.

"What?" my boyfriend said. "Do you have like a book in there?"

He had his arm around my waist, his hand near my front jeans pocket.

"What?" I said, feeling in the pocket for a moment. It was entirely possible I had a book in my pocket, but there was nothing. Not even the usual Kleenex, ChapStick, folded dollar bill.

"Nothing," I said.

"That," he said. And his hand tickled me.

"That's my hip bone."

This boyfriend had what I think of as health issues, both manic depression and borderline schizophrenic tendencies. I know that in the narrative of the larger world we call these mental health issues. But why do we distinguish between the brain and, let's say, the heart? Do we ever tell a man having a heart attack he's having a physical health issue? Who is served by this separation, this carving?

This too is the lineage of violence, the passing down, the cycle. We hold in our bodies the stories of others' pain. We hold their bodies, and we are held, and this too is a part of the cycle of violence. It's a part that is not often named.

This boyfriend was a year ahead of me in school and so went off to the University of South Dakota without me in the fall. This was the year my family fell all the way apart. This was the year he fell apart, too—not for the first time, not for the last, and also, most important, not permanently.

But that day in the truck, he teased me about the book in my pocket, and I teased him about how he'd go off to college not knowing the difference between a book and a hip bone. We were both acutely aware in each moment that we were counting down.

V.

After the locking out, after how long it took for my father to remember to give me a key, I realized we were not where I thought we were, we were not in that in-between place I thought of as a better place. My father had done worse, of course, than locking me out. How this locking out was notable, then, how I will remember it so clearly all these years later, was because I was caught by surprise.

This is how women stay with abusive men—whether the men are husbands or boyfriends or fathers. The estrangement times are literally strange times, awkward and unsure. When the abuser goes back to form, the kick of the surprise from the moment is sharp. But it's also swift. It's not lasting, we think. But, of course, it is. I remember how cold my arms were that night on the back porch. The grease smell, the cold arms—they stayed with me. I found waitressing jobs that held other smells. To this day, I almost never forget my sweater. All of which is to say, I still hold those feelings, this memory in my body—I carry it with me in an everyday, regular sort of way, but I do carry it.

It's the same with the night he tries to throw me out the window. It, too, becomes an everyday part of my body.

That night, I'm fourteen and have been grounded by my mother for staying out late, for breaking curfew. I only have a few days left of the grounding, of the forcible confinement to our house. There's a baseball game, and I'm supposed to meet up with friends and with one of the boys on the team from a neighboring town.

This is right before I begin staying out late regularly, before I begin drinking. That night, I'm thinking only of going to a baseball game, of getting out of the stifle of our house. My parents have been raging at each other even more than usual—my grandmother passing away that winter, my father going to the bar more and more as spring turned to summer, my father coming home later and later.

Some nights my mother insists on waiting for him before we can eat dinner. The meal is on the table, and we sit around it, and we watch it grow cold, and we watch my mother grow angrier and angrier.

This is one of those nights. We're having spaghetti, and the grease from the hamburger and the sauce are beginning to congeal, to harden on the top of the bowl, and the ladle just sits there, as we do, waiting.

I am not to this day overly fond of spaghetti. I strongly prefer my food to be hot or cold but not lukewarm. By the time my father arrives, the noodles are difficult to separate, one from the next and the next.

Across town, at the ballpark, the game already will have

started. My parents are not yet estranged though their behaviors to me seem so strange, verging on the bizarre. They're not yet estranged, but they are at war with each other.

I know all this, which is to say, I know better than to bring up the baseball game. My mother earlier had indicated she would consider letting me go. But of course now her mood is ruined. She slams dishes around in the kitchen, ostensibly looking for something she's forgotten to put on the table, but the table already is complete.

My father begins putting spaghetti on his plate and declares it good. He has arrived home in a mood not easily read. Drinking brings out in him either joviality or anger. Tonight he's exhibiting neither of these traits—is not slurring and shoving food around the plate, is not smiling and trying to make jokes.

My mother says, "It's just spaghetti," and then we all begin to eat.

It's quiet enough that I decide to bring up the baseball game. All I say, at first, is "Can I go?"

My mother opens her mouth to speak, but my father interrupts her.

"You're still grounded," he says.

"But Mom said I could maybe go," I say.

"Well," says my father, putting down his fork, "I say you're still grounded."

He had not been the one to ground me. Our mother both worked full-time and set all the household rules. Our mother took care of the house, all of the day-to-day, and our mother enforced the routines and the punishments while our father worked a little and drank a lot.

My mother's face registers the same surprise I feel. I'm

angry then for myself but also for her. Who is this man to think he is the one to decide? What sort of new game are we playing at?

So this is what I ask.

"Oh," I say, "so you're wanting to play parent now?"

Before I finish the sentence, he's out of his chair and has taken me up from mine. He picks me up by my arms near the biceps, and I kick out a little, but there's really not much I can do. He is almost six feet tall and weighs more than twice what I do. I'm just over five feet tall and don't yet weigh even a hundred pounds. He carries me easily though not comfortably by my arms and shoulders.

There is commotion and general yelling. I imagine it's coming from my mother because my sister in those moments usually is all retreat. My brother is only four or five years old.

I think that my father will shake me like that a little and then probably hit me. This is what I'm prepared for. Instead, he shakes and shakes me and then shoves me roughly through the door from the dining room into my bedroom. He throws me over my bed, my body aiming for the window. It's an old house. The windows all have sharp-cornered wood frames. The left side of my rib cage in the back meets the sharp point of the window frame, my head meets the window glass but does not crack it, and I land, hard, on the heat register near the floor. My father closes the door.

It takes me a full minute to get up off the floor. The heat register's cold metal has left an imprint, I think at first, and my back feels cold and strange on the left side. Another minute passes and the numbness begins to fade. The spot in between my bottom ribs in the back is sore to the touch, so I stop touching it. My arms and shoulders are sore anyway, and I stand in my room in front of the window, and I'm shaking, and the bed's right there but the two steps to it seem far. I stand like that a long time before getting into the bed and pulling up the covers. No one bothers me, or put another way, no one checks on me. I fall asleep like that, the lights still on, my dinner still congealing on its plate on the table.

The next day, for the first time, I have discernible, visible marks on my shoulders and forearms in a season other than winter. There's no covering this up, and I'm not going to, anyway. I hurt in many places. My head throbs. The spot on my back is sore and also feels strange. My body feels like a different body.

I don't know yet that it will always thereafter be at least somewhat sore and feel strange in that spot on my rib cage. I don't yet know that the ribs and surrounding cartilage have been damaged in a way that is complicated to correct, that would have required immediate attention including most likely a surgery. There is no surgery; there is no attention, immediate or otherwise. No one asks me how I'm feeling. No one asks if I'm hurt. And this lack is both an additional hurt and a liberation.

There is a phone in my room and therefore a phone book— the old-fashioned kind that includes all the small neighboring towns, its pages yellow and thin.

I don't really know what I'm looking for, but eventually I find it. I write the set of numbers down in pencil twice on two small pieces of paper. One I put in my underwear drawer, tucking it with care between the cups of a bra.

The other piece of paper I hand to my father the next morning as he reads the newspaper. I hand it to him across the distance of the table and then I back away toward the living room.

"What's this?" he says.

"It's Child Protective Services," I say. "If you ever touch me again, I'm going to call."

I don't turn around when I say it. The house is small enough I don't need to in order to be heard. It's still early morning, but I'm dressed in a T-shirt, shorts, and tennis shoes already. I turn around only after I say it, like I'm going to sit down on the couch and watch television, like what's transpired is regular, is everyday. I keep my face straight, my voice neutral and steady.

No one in our house ever uses the front door, so I'm sure the look of complete surprise, complete perplexity that overtakes my father's face has as much to do with logistics as it does with my next action. He thinks I'm going to sit down in front of the television. He thinks he has plenty of time to set down his coffee cup and yell at me or worse.

To get out the back door, after handing over the paper, I would have had to go around him—his chair sits directly in front of the doorway to the kitchen, which leads to the back door, to the regular escape.

His face is weighing a response, his fingers holding the paper scrap like he's worried it might catch fire. And then instead of sitting down on the couch, I open the door to the enclosed front porch, and I pull it shut behind me.

My mother uses this space mostly to store things we don't use very often—old furniture she may one day refinish, oversized sporting equipment like racquets and bats and roller skates. It takes a long minute to get to the front door, another long minute to get the front door open. It's stuck shut from humidity and lack of use.

But it opens. I walk out of the house and turn left. I keep walking and then I run. I wind up the hill past the cemetery, and my legs are shaky, as are my arms, shaky and stiff, and my back is sore along with my head, but the shakiness eases out sooner than I would have guessed, and I begin to forget about my back, my head, my ribs, or to learn the process that will become lifelong—the ignoring, the lessening. That day, though, my legs moving me up the hill, I begin to feel something close to good.

My father is not sitting at the table when I return. He's not in the house. His truck is not in the driveway. When he returns, later that day, we don't talk about the morning or the night before. We never do talk about that morning, and he never puts his hands on me like that again.

If this were fiction, here is the place where I would do something narratively to help the readers to suspend their disbelief. I'd have the father chase the daughter, or he'd start a conversation later, or the parents would fight about what happened. It's nonfiction, though, and the moment to me also still feels improbable. I have no idea why any of this works. My father and I never talk about it, not really. There is no ready or easy explanation.

Many years later, more than a decade, he does apologize for the night at the dinner table. Then, a few years after, when I'm home visiting, he will rescind that apology by getting drunk and telling the story of that night in front of many people, by making it a joke. My mother is there for this joking, for this retelling. She doesn't entirely join in, but she does nod along.

The official narrative on which they seem to agree is that I was a difficult teenager, that I was really a lot of trouble. They seem to agree my lot-of-trouble-ness is an innate quality that both deserved and needed handling. They're not wrong that as a teenager, I will go on both to cause and to get into a fair amount of trouble. But they are wrong about the timing. They are wrong about the cause and effect, about innate versus made. That night, sitting at the dinner table, I wasn't yet really any trouble at all.

Years later, when I work as a reporter, when I interview criminals and trafficked women or when I bartend and break up fight after fight after fight, people will ask me how I do that, how I take risks and seem unbothered. But they are asking the wrong question. It's not in the how but in the *why*, in the *when*.

Why I take the risks can be traced back to this house, this night and the ones leading to it. Being good, not taking any risks in this house, did me no good. If I was to be labeled trouble, in my later life, then I would learn to make it. I would learn to disregard notions of safety as notions only. When you're going to be called trouble anyway, your life then becomes your own. There's liberation and loneliness both in this shift. You become estranged from the part of yourself that was before. There's no way back, after, only forward.

VI.

It's 1:45 in the morning, and a woman is leaving the parking lot of her apartment complex in Sioux Falls, South Dakota, with her husband. Her husband holds a gun, a pistol, to himself, to her, on repeat. They have been married less than a year. She is in the process of leaving him. They have been living for many months in that liminal state we call estranged. In the papers, after, this is how she's most often described, as "his estranged wife."

Even its present tense, *estrange*, seems, well, strange. The present participle, *estranging*, is stranger still. But in my life it's also been more common. The feeling that someone I love is becoming a stranger is always a moving state. It's not static. Because once the feeling becomes static, then it's set. It's a state, an infinitive, a verb that moves quickly from the present to the past—*estranged*. Once it's set, the person and relationship become past-tense bodies.

It is not, in this our America, considered strange that this woman's husband arrives at the apartment with a gun, that he takes her by this particular sort of force. It is considered strange elsewhere, but in America, we're all very used to this sort of problem.

It is not considered strange that there has been, as we say, "a history of domestic violence." This husband was married before. In that marriage also there was a history of this violence we call domestic. The husband—we'll call him Frank—is in the liminal space of a man about to be an ex-husband. At twenty-four, he's been in this space one other time already.

In the first marriage, they, too, spent months estranged, violent months before the divorce. Wife A had warned Wife B to expect violence, to expect an escalation.

But this night, this early morning, as the car leaves the lot, Frank introduces something new to this familiar domestic narrative. Frank has insisted they leave behind in the parking lot their daughter, who is one year old.

After the parking lot, Frank and his wife drive north in the early morning hours through South Dakota and on into North Dakota. We are pre-Internet, we're pre-cellphone, pre-GPS, so as they drive, she has no way of knowing a neighbor saw the taking, saw the baby left in the parking lot. It becomes clear, though, that someone has called the police, because the police begin a pursuit.

Their last moments as husband and wife, then, take place at gunpoint, accompanied by the soundtrack of police sirens. They take place on narrow North Dakota back roads the police later describe as pockmarked.

The policemen report following at speeds greater than seventy miles per hour on those rough roads in the dark. They report barely being able to keep the car in sight.

The chase comes to its end near the Canadian border, just outside a North Dakota town called Langdon. The Langdon high school mascot is the cardinal, a bird John James Audubon sketched and painted more than almost any other bird.

In the rural North Dakota farmyard, Frank and the police both have parked their cars. There is a brief standoff, which Frank ends by saying, "Fuck you. I'm going to die," before fatally shooting himself with his pistol.

The woman flees the car and collapses, sobbing, in the farmyard, in the dark.

VII.

How I get to leave my hometown and my father's house for good is because my boyfriend is going to the University of South Dakota, and so it is on my radar, and so I apply despite knowing no one else there, despite the place being almost completely unknown to me or anyone else I know.

I apply while my boyfriend is still there, in his first semester. He studies music, and sometimes he takes his medication, and sometimes he doesn't.

He calls me late some nights, and it's cold there, but everything's fine. Classes are good. He eats dinner sometimes with the RA from his dorm, a young woman named Jennifer. I'm calling her Jennifer—because all this happens pre-Internet, because bad things happen to her—and there is no reason to name her, no reason to bring curiosity seekers to her so many years later. Back then, she is my boyfriend's resident assistant or RA in his dormitory, and I can say without a doubt that she saves his life. She talks him through the transition from our very small-town experiences, our small-town schools, to the university town, to life there.

He calls me late some nights to say someone is trying to break into his room. There are at least four of them, all armed, and maybe they flew there—he's not sure—but he wishes for a gun or a baseball bat, and do I know where he can find one— a bat or gun?

Sometimes he takes his medication, and sometimes he does not.

"Call Jennifer," I say. "She's just across the hall," I say. "Hang up right now and go over there or call."

And he does. She talks to him in her very calm voice, and though he doesn't last the year at college, he doesn't hurt anyone that year, including himself.

He's already home and is already mostly lost to me by the time I get my news—a full scholarship. All I have to do to maintain it is to keep decent grades and to write stories for the school newspaper.

Years later, my last official contribution to that newspaper, the *Volante,* my last story filed, is the one about the abduction at 1:45 in the morning. None of the other people on the news staff, for various reasons, can take the story, can do the interview with the victim, who they tell me is a former student. I don't recognize the name, and so I agree.

When she arrives at the newspaper office that day, when she sees me, her knees buckle a little and so do mine. I didn't recognize her name, of course, because she got married. But there's no doubt that the woman in my story is Jennifer. I reach out to catch her, and I steady her by the shoulders, and we walk together down the hall like that.

Jennifer is only twenty-three that day, and I'm twenty-two. She is dear to me because she saved the life of the first man I loved. But for any of us to care about this story, we shouldn't need her to be dear. We shouldn't need her to have saved a man. We shouldn't need her to have a baby.

I don't know much about the story she'll tell me over the next hour, except for how it ends. She doesn't know much about my life the past few years, including how the relationship with my boyfriend has ended.

My first year at college, my boyfriend and I try to stay together, but he takes his medication less and less. He calls most nights late, and one night, the phone wakes me from thick sleep, his voice saying, "There are men outside with guns. I don't know why they're after me. I don't." His voice is like someone being strangled from the inside out, like the warning squeal of a rabbit on the run.

This is the moment when I decide to leave him. Once he's a little better, I break up with him, but we do still stay in contact. The last time I see him, he's arrived at school unannounced, is in the parking lot outside my dorm. This time, his voice on the phone sounds less strange, is saying more regular things: "I'm downstairs. Please come down."

So I do. I cross the icy parking lot and sit with him in his Chevy Impala, and the heater isn't working, not really, and he has driven the three hours from home to here without much heat. I know all is not okay. His voice does not sound strangled, but he's speaking flatly and very, very fast.

He's been to Chicago, he says, and he thinks maybe he killed a man. He thinks, maybe, someone has paid him to do it.

"Do you know what it sounds like when you shoot someone?" he asks. "Not even as loud as a bass drum."

His voice is calm as he says it, his hands steady on the wheel of the running car. Our breath fogs patches on the inside of the car's windows like the fake snow people decorate with at Christmastime. It is hard to see out. I sit next to him on the bench seat, though closer to the door than to him. I sit in that car and think of Christmas decorations, of my biology exam the next morning, and his hands beat a rat-a-tat-tat on the wheel.

We stay in the car, not moving, for over an hour. He does most of the talking.

"I just wanted you to know," he says, and my hand finally awakens and reaches for the door handle's cold metal.

He pulls from the glove box a newspaper clipping, which rests under a handgun. The *Chicago Tribune*. What a good paper, I think. I fixate on that detail. I focus. Not the *Sun-Times*—the *Trib*. The clipping has been folded a dozen times.

"I just wanted you to know," he says again, and then I cross the parking lot and put the clipping into a folder in my dorm room, where I sink onto the floor's cool tile, where I rest awhile, the biology exam forgotten, where I wait for the world to stop spinning, where I wait for everything to right itself.

That day in the newspaper office, when Jennifer asks after him, I tell her he's at home with his parents. I tell her they are looking after him. This is not the day for telling any of the rest.

I don't remember too many of the details of what she tells me that day, either. But I remember the last question I ask. Her parents, once they learned the news—that she'd been taken and how—charter a helicopter. As soon as the police call, the parents are in the helicopter on the way to her. So I ask her about this, about the helicopter ride, but I don't recall her answer. It's the part of the story that sticks with me, though, because it's the only part I can't imagine—what it must have felt like when the helicopter arrived, when her parents swooped in and picked her up, all the pieces of her, what it must have felt like when they came for her, when they came to carry her home.

VIII.

I'm talking to my father, and he reports to me the propane man is there. He's got his truck turned sideways, and now my father can't see him anymore, this propane man. He'd better get his shoes on and go check. He'll call me right back.

I have grown used to this narrative thread, the story ending with "I'll call you right back," the waiting for the call that doesn't come. I no longer wait or have any expectation. This day is no different. He does not call right back. He may or may not remember we've spoken. There may or may not have been a propane truck, a propane man.

He has begun a course of treatment, a medication regimen for his Lewy body dementia, and reportedly it's working. When I ask him about it, in person, he says, "At least I'm not seeing people who aren't there anymore. Or if I am, I don't remember." And then he grins his most winning grin.

I'm glad for this moment though the progress feels tenuous, feels like the same sort of moment as the phone call—"I'll call you right back"—and then I wait.

We are now, of course, so many of us in America, experiencing this sort of waiting. Though we are beginning to have a national dialogue about mental illness and guns, we are not quite yet beginning to have a national dialogue about dementia and guns. Part of my waiting, then, is worrying.

If it is delicate or tricky to take away an elder's car keys, it is delicate times a thousand to take away the guns of a man like my father.

In the lucid moments, as with car keys, the person will understand but most likely will not like what is happening. In the less lucid moments, as with car keys, the person will search for the missing guns, will ask after them, will wonder what you've done with them, and what is wrong with you? Don't you know he bought those guns? Don't you know they're his?

My stepmother says, when I ask about the guns, "Oh, yes. We did that long ago," but not all the gun cabinets are empty. So the cabinets, then, tell a different story. I don't know what to make of the contradiction.

I wait for the day my father will call and report the missing guns like he reports the end-of-the-driveway ghosts. He is missing something. What is it? He is missing something, and can I help him, please? Won't I help him look? Won't I?

I am waiting with no answers. I am waiting with no idea how or what I'll reply.

IX.

It's a bright summer day, and we sit on my father's deck, the sky the color of cornflowers, the birds busy at their feeders. I have that fall been to North Dakota, to Standing Rock, where I stayed a little while at the water protector camps, helping sort donations and helping manage and wrangle children.

Someone has told my father about my trip, or, he wonders, did he imagine that.

I tell him he is not imagining things and say only a very little about my time there. It's my last day in Iowa, and I am looking forward to returning home.

My stepmother says, "You were there?" and her eyes grow large. "Oh," she says, "what was that like?"

"I met a lot of nice people," I say, which is true if limited.

My father says "North Dakota," and nods. He and my brother used to visit a friend there sometimes in the fall. "Good pheasant hunting in North Dakota," he says, "but you probably didn't shoot a pheasant."

"I did not," I say, and then we laugh a little.

I think of the men on Magpie Road, the ones I'd first mistaken for bird hunters, but I put them out of my mind. I think instead of the hawk that flew overhead when I walked the children from the camp to school the first day with Tiffany, who was in charge of some of the camp's day-to-day. But I don't say anything about her, nothing further about the camp or birds. My father's face looks like his mind is moving on to other topics, anyway, or is reaching for something, and I am ready to make my exit.

On the drive home, though, I replay that first morning at camp. After Magpie Road, the men with the gun who I mistook for bird hunters, I do this sometimes—replay the days before, the ones that are good days.

The first morning in camp, a hawk circles over the river. It moves in a way people often mistake for laziness, on a high wind, a thermal, but it really is working toward an economy of motion.

The morning comes, and the children need to be walked to school. The night before, I had arrived into sunset, the exact right time—dinner almost ready in the camp kitchen and ten minutes of light left in which to put up my tent in a good spot near the river.

The river, the Missouri, is why we're there, all of us, or is part of why. The other part includes the pipeline that threatens the river and that brings the men, who bring violence, who work to make the women disappear, despite their sovereign right, of course, to exist on their own land.

It rained hard the day before, and so walking the children to school involves a dirt or mud road through a field next to the river, involves waiting for the farmer's cattle to make up their minds. Of the three of them—red-and-white Herefords, a cow and two calves—the cow is the problem. She places her body between the threat and her calves, stamps her hooves in the dirt and shakes her head as if there is a fly. There is no fly, just her worry, just the seven of us as perceived threat.

"Mothers are like that," I say to Tiffany, who is walking the children to school with me, who is showing me the path, so I can pick them up by myself later in the afternoons.

"Yeah," Tiffany says. "Except when they aren't."

We have already instructed the five children to shush and hold still. By all indications, the cow would like to charge. By all indications, she is making up her mind.

The road is all mud after yesterday's rain, and one of the children is wearing cowboy boots that now are hard to recognize as what they are.

I nod to Tiffany, and in this moment, I wonder over the boy's mother. Who sends a boy to camp in cowboy boots? And who are the mothers who get in between their children and danger? And who are the other ones, the "except when they don't" mothers? And what kind of mother am I to be here instead of at home with my own daughter?

I am well prepared, then, for the conversation we have by ourselves on the return—after the cow decides we aren't a real, true worry, after we cross the bridge and into the main camp and curve along the path to the school.

I already know these children well enough from the half-hour walk to instruct two of them to behave for their teachers. That I will be getting a report. That I will be delivering a report to their father, who is on the front lines, and are you listening, boys? I will see your father. I will deliver a report. Already they straighten their postures and stop trying to trip each other. Their sisters give me shy smiles before entering the school's tent. They were quiet on the walk over, but then, their brothers were loud.

On our return, Tiffany and I do talk about our childhoods, about mothers, about men. We talk about her perspective on the violence of the days before I arrived at camp, the private security people who used dogs and bear spray on those at the front line, on men, yes, but also on women and children.

I ask about that, about children on the front line, and she says, when the security arrived, some of the men stayed and some ran. She says, the women ran toward the security detail, toward the dogs, and the children ran after their mothers.

I have no way to verify whether this is fair or true, but it is the news she reports.

"We need more women," she says.

"Always," I say. And we walk on.

On the drive home to Arkansas from my father's house, I replay my conversations with Tiffany and listen to music and replay the conversation some more.

I count nine hawks of varying types and sizes, a good but not an exceptional amount for this mostly rural drive. The last one dives and swoops high over a field, keeping pace a long while with the car, a long enough while that it begins to spook me, to make me question what it is I'm seeing. The hawk is red-brown and large, with long, full tail feathers, and it's the same size as the one who flew above us in North Dakota that day.

It is just a bird, I tell myself. It's not a ghost bird. It's not a ghost of any sort. There's nothing strange about it. The sky is still blue and mostly cloudless.

If I drive fast enough toward home, I will outrun this bird. If I drive fast enough toward home, I will see my daughter, who waits with her own stories, who waits to tell me all her stories. If I drive fast enough toward home, if I stop counting birds, I will surely outrun all the other ghosts, too. If I drive fast enough, I will surely find my way home.

Acknowledgments

I would like to thank the editors and writers who first published some of these essays in journals, magazines, and anthologies: Beth Staples, Anna Lena Phillips Bell, Michael Ramos, Emily Smith, Cinelle Barnes, Billy Stratton, Elissa Washuta, Theresa Warburton, Hannah Ensor, Natalie Diaz, Nick Almeida, Marie-Helene Bertino, Yuka Igarashi, Clint Crockett Peters, Phong Nguyen, Diana Owen, Layli Long Soldier.

This book was formed in part through the generous gifts of financial support and/or time from the following organizations: Fulbright College at the University of Arkansas, the UCross Foundation, Hedgebrook, the Lannan Foundation, the National Endowment for the Arts, and the Sustainable Arts Foundation.

I hold a world of debt and gratitude to and want to thank writers at the following publications whose work I used as source or inspiration. The writers' names and the publications are cited directly in the essays, but I also salute these publications who employ them: the *Pittsburgh Post-Gazette, Granta,* the Sioux Falls *Argus Leader,* the University of South Dakota *Volante,* the Henderson *Gleaner, The Washington Post, The New York Times,* the *Star Tribune,* and the *Orlando Sentinel.*

To my friends, colleagues, first readers, and general support-ers, I owe a world of gratitude. Naming you here does not seem sufficient, but I will offer up your names, anyway: Geffrey Davis, Davis McCombs, Rodney Wilhite, Mary Angelino, Raina Lyons, Jane Blunschi, Allison Hammond, Lisa Corrigan, Katy Henrik-sen, Kelly Hammond, Ana Krahmer, Gail Folkins, Ito Romo, Aaron Rudolph, Dennis Covington, Jill Patterson, Stephen Gra-ham Jones, and all my colleagues and students at all my workplaces—the University of Arkansas and the Institute of American Indian Arts and at *Waxwing*. All of you inspire me. A good many of these essays were first read at the Institute of American Indian Arts summer and winter residencies, so I also thank those audiences for being such good first listeners. Every-thing the students write and read there pushes me to be better, as a writer, as a person.

I could not have written this book without the unflagging support of agent extraordinaire Julia Kardon and the equally extraordinary editorial work of Elana Seplow-Jolley and every-one at Ballantine. Special thanks go to Emily Mahon for the beautiful cover design.

Last, I'd like to thank my family, past, present, future, but in particular—Eva and Matt and Bella the dog.

About the Author

TONI JENSEN teaches in the MFA programs at the University of Arkansas and the Institute of American Indian Arts. She is a 2020 recipient of a Creative Writing Fellowship from the National Endowment for the Arts, and her work has been published in *Orion*, *Catapult*, and *Ecotone*. She is Métis.

tonijensen.com
Twitter: @ToniJens